SOLUTIONS IN
SPORT PSYCHOLOGY

SOLUTIONS IN SPORT PSYCHOLOGY

Edited by

IAN COCKERILL

THOMSON
™

Australia • Canada • Mexico • Singapore • Spain • United Kingdom • United States

Solutions in Sport Psychology

For more information, contact Thomson, Berkshire House, 168–173 High Holborn, London, WC1V 7AA or visit us on the World Wide Web at:
http://www.thomsonlearning.co.uk

British Library Cataloguing-in-Publication Data
A catalogue record for this book is available from the British Library

ISBN 1–86152–773–X

First Edition 2002

Typeset by Saxon Graphics Ltd, Derby

Printed in Great Britain by TJ International, Padstow, Cornwall

Contents

List of figures and tables

List of contributors

Stuart Biddle, Department of Physical Education, Sports Science and Recreation Management, Loughborough University

Peter Clough, Department of Psychology, University of Hull

Ian Cockerill, School of Medicine, University of Birmingham

David Collins, Scottish Centre for Physical Education, Sport and Leisure Studies, University of Edinburgh

Richard L. Cox, Scottish Centre for Physical Education, Sport & Leisure Studies, University of Edinburgh

Joan Duda, School of Sport and Exercise Sciences, University of Birmingham

Keith Earle, Department of Sport Science, University of Hull

Jim Golby, School of Social Sciences, University of Teesside

Chris Harwood, Department of Physical Education, Sports, Science and Recreation Management, Loughborough University

Paul Holmes, Department of Exercise and Sport Science, Manchester Metropolitan University

John Kremer, School of Psychology, The Queen's University, Belfast

Sophia Jowett, School of Health, Staffordshire University

David Lavallee, Scottish School of Sport Studies, University of Strathclyde

Ruth Lavallee, School of Leisure and Sports Studies, Leeds Metropolitan University

Hugh Mantle, School of Education and Social Sciences, Liverpool John Moores University

Anne Marte Pensgaard, School of Sport and Exercise Sciences, University of Birmingham

Deidre Scully, School of Psychology, The Queen's University, Belfast

David Sewell, Department of Psychology, University of Hull

David Shaw, Department of Psychology, University of Central Lancashire

Rachel Tribe, Department of Psychology, University of East London

Sandy Wolfson, Division of Psychology, University of Northumbria

Biographies

Stuart Biddle is Professor of Exercise & Sport Psychology, and Head of the Department of Physical Education, Sports Science & Recreation Management at Loughborough University. He is also associated with the University's Institute of Youth Sport and the British Heart Foundation National Centre for Physical Activity and Health. Stuart is a graduate of Loughborough University and the Pennsylvania State University. In 1988, he was awarded a PhD in psychology from Keele University, UK. He is a Chartered Health Psychologist and in 1999 completed eight years as President of the European Federation of Sport Psychology. In 1998 he was the Distinguished International Scholar of the Association for the Advancement of Applied Sport Psychology, USA. He is Editor-in-Chief of the journal *Psychology of Sport & Exercise* and his main research interests focus on motivational influences on health-related physical activity and on emotion and other psychological outcomes of physical activity. He has published nine edited books on sport, exercise and psychology and in 2001 co-authored *The psychology of physical activity: determinants, well-being and interventions*. Stuart is an 'active commuter' and regularly cycles the 10 miles round trip to work.

Peter Clough is a Chartered Psychologist and an Accredited Sport Psychologist. He is a Senior Lecture in Sport Psychology at the University of Hull and his PhD from the University of Aberdeen investigated the reasons why people run marathons and the benefits and costs associated with that activity. He is particularly interested in the psychology of performance, especially the link between sport and business. Peter has worked with several professional rugby league clubs and this physically intense and emotionally charged sport provided the impetus for his current research into mental toughness.

Ian Cockerill is a Chartered Psychologist, an Associate Fellow of the British Psychological Society and an Accredited Sport Psychologist for both research and athlete support. He is also a member of the British Olympic Association Psychology Advisory Group. He has an MEd from the University of Newcastle-upon-Tyne and a PhD from the University of Leeds. After working for more than 20 years in the School of Sport and Exercise Sciences at the University of Birmingham, he recently left to devote more time to his private psychology practice. He has published research in both motor learning and control and in applied sport psychology and his many publications include five edited books, while conference presentations have taken him to North America and to Russia, as well as to several European countries. Ian has worked with professional and international athletes in athletics, cricket, tennis, golf, swimming, ice skating, Grand Prix motor cycling and cyclo-cross. He is the psychologist with the Badminton Association of England World-Class Performance Programme. He has worked in professional football for more than 10 years with clubs from the English Premier League to non-league and has been with his present First Division club for four years. Ian is Chair of The British Psychological Society's Sport and Exercise Psychology Section and after leaving The University of Birmingham in 2001, the University conferred on him the title of Honorary Senior Research Fellow in the School of Medicine. His other interests include keeping fit and playing jazz, but not necessarily simultaneously.

Dave Collins is Professor of Physical Education and Sport Performance at the University of Edinburgh. He is an Accredited Sport Psychologist, a British Olympic Association Registered Sport Psychologist, has worked with elite athletes across a wide range of sports and is a psychologist with UK Athletics. His research interests are broad, but focus principally on the mechanisms of psychological impact on performance. In his free time Dave enjoys fitness training, curry consumption and the cinema.

Richard Cox was for many years a Lecturer in Sport Psychology at the University of Edinburgh. He is a Chartered Psychologist and an Accredited Sport Psychologist. He gained a PhD in the Department of Psychology, University of Newcastle upon Tyne. Richard was sport psychologist with the British Swimming Team at the Barcelona Olympic Games in 1992 and was one of two sport psychologists appointed by the British Olympic Association to work with the British Olympic Team at its training camp in Tallahassee, Florida, in 1995. Over the past 10 years he has worked with many teams as a consulting sport psychologist, including Scottish Premier League football teams, the Scottish Rugby Team and the Scottish Women's Bowling Team. His other athletes have included a British Open golf champion and a PGA champion, together with a silver medal winner and a finalist at the Sydney Olympic Games, 2000.

Joan Duda is Professor of Sport Psychology in the School of Sport and Exercise Sciences at the University of Birmingham, UK, and an Adjunct Professor in the Department of Psychological Sciences at Purdue University, USA. She obtained a BA in psychology at Rutgers University, an MS at Purdue University and a PhD at the University of Illinois, USA. Joan is currently President of the Association for the Advancement of Applied Sport Psychology, USA, and has been a member of the executive boards of the North American Society for the Psychology of Sport and Physical Activity, the Sport Psychology Academy, and the International Society for Sport Psychology. She has been Editor of the *Journal of Applied Sport Psychology* and is on the Editorial Board of the *Journal of Sport and Exercise Psychology*, the *International Journal of Sport Psychology* and the *Psychology of Sport and Exercise* journal. She has produced more than 130 scientific publications and book chapters on motivation in sport. She is the editor of *Advances in Sport and Exercise Psychology Measurement*, has been an invited speaker in 16 countries and, in 1997, was named the Visiting International Scholar by the Australian Sport Psychology Society. Joan has worked with athletes at all levels over many years, is certified as a Consultant by the Association for the Advancement of Applied Sport Psychology and is listed on the US Olympic Registry. For four years she was the sport psychology consultant to the USA Gymnastics Women's Artistic Program, the National Team and the Women's US Olympic team that won the gold medal in Atlanta. Her hobbies include music, playing tennis and travelling.

Keith Earle is a Sport Psychologist in the Sport Science Department at the University of Hull. He is presently completing a PhD that is investigating the concept of mental toughness and its effect on performance in sport. Keith has assisted professional athletes and international teams over the past six years and he is especially interested in the psychology of team working.

Jim Golby is Head of Sport and Exercise at the University of Teesside, UK. He is a Chartered Psychologist with extensive teaching and consulting experience and has published widely on a variety of sport psychology topics. In addition to his main emphasis on rugby, his research and consulting work has been across a range of sports, including weightlifting, netball, soccer and cricket.

Chris Harwood is a Lecturer in Sport Psychology and the Director of Tennis at Loughborough University and his research interests are in achievement motivation and mental skills in competitive youth sport. His applied research earned him the prestigious PhD dissertation of the year award from the Association for the Advancement of Applied Sport Psychology, USA, in 1998. Chris is an Accredited Sport Psychologist and a BOA Registered Sport Psychologist and he thrives on delivering theory-to-practice education to coaches, parents and performers. As a former professional tennis coach and national standard player, his consulting work has extended beyond racket sports to swimming, athletics, football, hockey, rowing and triathlon. He currently works as the sport psychologist for the LTA's Regional Training Centre at Loughborough and for the Youth Sport Trust.

Paul Holmes is a Senior Lecturer in Sport Psychology in the Department of Exercise and Sport Science at Manchester Metropolitan University and has 14 years experience working with elite athletes. His specialisms are imagery, psychophysiology and attention. He completed his doctoral work in applied cognitive neuroscience while working with the Great Britain Shooting Squad. Paul is an Accredited Sport Psychologist and is a member of the British Olympic Association Psychology Advisory Group. He has travelled extensively with national teams and was a member of England's Commonwealth Games Team in Malaysia, 1998. He currently works with European tour golfers and is the Senior Sport Psychologist for the England Ladies Golf Association. Paul has been a high performing athlete and cricketer and he is now working on reducing his golf handicap.

Sophia Jowett is a Lecturer in the School of Health at Staffordshire University. After completing a degree at the University of Athens she obtained an MSc from Loughborough University and a PhD from The University of Exeter. In 2000 she received the Young Investigator's Award at an International Conference in Sweden and in 2001 was presented with an award by the Greek Society of Physical Educators and Sport Scientists. Sophia has been a competitive athlete and is a qualified athletics coach. She works with athletes from a variety of sports and is actively involved in the work of several professional bodies in sport psychology.

John Kremer is a Reader in Psychology, now part-time, at the Queen's University of Belfast. He was awarded a PhD for his research into group dynamics and leadership at Loughborough University and now combines academic duties with consulting. Over the years he has worked as an applied sport psychologist with a large number of teams and individuals in rugby, golf, soccer, tennis, bowls, hockey, swimming, athletics, sailing and cricket. John's published books include *Psychology in Sport* and *Young People's Involvement in Sport*.

David Lavallee is a Reader in Exercise and Sport Psychology in the Scottish School of Sports Studies at the University of Strathclyde, Scotland. He obtained his academic qualifications in the USA, his home country, and subsequently worked in Perth, Australia, before coming to the UK. David is a Chartered Psychologist, an Associate Fellow of the British Psychological Society and an Accredited Sport Psychologist for research, with more than 60 academic and professional publications. He is Secretary of the British Psychological Society's Sport and Exercise Psychology Section.

Ruth Lavallee is a Senior Lecturer at Leeds Metropolitan University where she has been Director of Undergraduate Sport and Exercise Science for three years. She was awarded a master's degree in Medical Science by the University of Sheffield and has since carried out research into psychophysiological aspects of sport and exercise.

Hugh Mantle is a Senior Lecturer in Sport Psychology at Liverpool John Moores University and was awarded an MBE for his application of science to elite-level sport, particularly canoeing. He is a Chartered Psychologist, an Accredited Sport Psychologist and a British Olympic Association Registered Sport Psychologist. Hugh has coached Olympic canoeists for 16 years and has attended Olympic, European and World Championships. His PhD studies examined the psychological preparation of elite performers for the Olympic Games. Hugh has also been the recipient of the Coach of the Year award. He is presently involved as a consultant to many professional performers in golf, Formula One motor racing, snooker and motor rallying.

Anne Marte Pensgaard is a Research Fellow in the School of Sport and Exercise Sciences at the University of Birmingham. She was born in Norway and received a PhD in Sport Psychology from the Norwegian University of Sport and Physical Education,

Oslo. She subsequently investigated the role of integration into ordinary sport and the development of empowerment among athletes with physical disabilities. Her main research interests are in coping with stress and its relationship with motivation and also in understanding the meaning of the activity among participants in strenuous expeditions. She has published in the *Journal of Sport Sciences*, the *Adapted Physical Activity Quarterly* and the *Scandinavian Journal of Medicine and Science in Sports* and has written two books on mental skills training. Anne Marte has worked as a sport psychology consultant to Olympic athletes since 1995 and was sport psychologist for the Norwegian Women's Soccer Team, gold-medal winners at the Sydney Olympic Games, 2000. Anne Marte is an experienced adventurer and has taken part in expeditions to many regions, including Greenland and Spitsbergen.

Deirdre Scully is a Senior Lecturer in the School of Psychology at the Queen's University of Belfast. Her first degree was in physical education and she gained an MSc and PhD in sport psychology at the University of Illinois. Deirdre is an Accredited Sport Psychologist and she has considerable experience of working with athletes from many sports, including athletics, basketball, golf and swimming.

David Sewell is Dean of the Faculty of Science at The University of Hull and was previously Head of the Department of Psychology in that university. He was responsible for the development of the sport psychology team at Hull and his research has focused on the nature of pre-event cognitions and performance. David has worked with water-polo players, master swimmers and a variety of teams from other sports.

Dave Shaw is a Senior Lecturer in Psychology at the University of Central Lancashire and has published sport-related articles on imagery, confidence and anxiety. He is a member of the British Association of Sport and Exercise Sciences and the Sport and Exercise Psychology Section of the British Psychological Society. He recently established the country's first undergraduate sport psychology degree offering the Graduate Basis for Registration of the British Psychological Society. He has carried out consultancy work in industry and commerce for many years and is now combining these experiences with his knowledge of applied sport psychology to provide support services for athletes, especially golfers. Dave has coached basketball from club to European Cup standard and has played at under-21 level for Scotland.

Rachel Tribe is a Senior Lecturer at the University of East London. She is a Chartered Counselling and Organisational Psychologist and has worked with individuals, families, teams, communities and organisations. Rachel is an active consulting psychologist and experienced in working with refugees and displaced people in both the UK and overseas. She has undertaken projects with the British Foreign and Commonwealth Office, Médecin san Frontières and the Red Cross, together with a variety of national and international governmental and non -governmental agencies. Rachel has several sporting interests and, in particular, she is an enthusiastic swimmer.

Sandy Wolfson is a Chartered Psychologist and an Accredited Sport Psychologist for both research and athlete support. She was born in the USA but has spent the past 25 years in the North East of England after falling in love with the region's scenery, people and sport. She has a degree in Psychology from Ohio State University, a PhD in Psychology from Durham University and is Head of the Psychology Division at the University of Northumbria. Her research interests are in social cognition, especially counterfactual thinking, unrealistic optimism and false consensus as applied to sport, gambling and drug taking. Sandy is an experienced psychology consultant in several sports, focusing more recently on working with elite footballers. She is especially interested in performance variability and players' understanding and analysis of it. Married with two children, she is a fanatical Newcastle United supporter.

Foreword by Bobby Gould

In 1991 I was manager of West Bromwich Albion Football Club, which had just been relegated to what was then the Third Division. One morning my mail included a letter from a sport psychologist. That was all I needed and I quickly had a clear mental picture of the likely media headlines! Three years earlier I had won the F.A. Cup as manager of Wimbledon (nicknamed 'The Crazy Gang') in defeating Liverpool ('The Culture Club') 1–0 at Wembley. I was now being afforded the opportunity of allowing a stranger to explain to me the psyche of the professional footballer!

Some 10 years on and Ian Cockerill and I remain the best of friends and we continue to learn not only about professional footballers, but also about each other's approach to working with players, and about life generally. Over that decade many of the barriers that Ian and I confronted have been removed, although some still remain; the principal one being the need to employ a sport psychologist in the first place. When I moved to Coventry City Football Club in the first season of the Premier League, taking Ian with me as a member of my staff, I had a conversation that went something like this: the Chairman said, 'This fellow who is working with the players' minds, isn't he a bit expensive?', to which my reply was, 'Chairman, it is the discussions and debates I have with him that are keeping me focused.' The matter was never raised again.

As a manager you are expected to have all the answers to all the questions, but what do you do as the manager of Wales when you are beaten 6–4 away to Turkey? My answer was to 'phone a friend'. I telephoned Ian and he suggested that I should ask the players who they thought had played well and, more importantly, which players they believed had helped them most during the game. This simple, but effective, strategy resulted in a very open team meeting, with the next game ending 0–0.

To be a successful athlete in any sport there are probably four key attributes that must be developed, namely technical skill, fitness, tactical awareness and mental strength. It is interesting that two are mainly associated with the body and two with the brain, and, while certain individuals inherit these attributes, each of them can be developed with application and hard work. Sport today places considerable demands on performers and requires the support of specialists to facilitate the integration of mind and body, especially to achieve success as a professional. There are limits to the extent to which a parent, or other family member, teacher, coach or manager is able to contribute to the fulfilment of an individual's potential. Having been involved in professional football for almost 40 years I recognize that during that time there were many occasions when I needed help, but did not know who to turn to. Today, the sports stars of tomorrow have sport psychology available to them if they only choose to accept what it may have to offer them. They must be encouraged to open all doors in order to seek that advice and support.

It was just before the Welsh players went through the door of a meeting room in their hotel following a presentation by Ian that he said to them, 'Whatever you do in the next two days ask yourself, "Can I do better"?' Some 48 hours later when the door closed on our game against Denmark in Copenhagen, the dressing room was euphoric! Wales had won 2–1. Thank you, Ian, for writing that letter from a sport psychologist.

Preface

Psychological factors are recognized as having an important part to play in the attainment of success in sport. Over the past 10 years the number of sport science degree programmes that incorporate sport psychology has increased markedly, while well-qualified and experienced practitioners are being sought by clubs and coaches to work with their athletes. Given that a sound technique and sport-specific fitness are prerequisites for performance success, it has become accepted that these factors alone are often insufficient to produce a winning performance. However, although a specialist doctor and physiotherapist are deemed essential support for those competing regularly, and especially at a high level, the inclusion of a sport psychologist is not universally perceived as an integral part of the support team. There may be several reasons for this, but in recognizing that sub-standard performances are often attributable to psychological factors, together with mounting evidence that a sport psychologist can help to make the difference between winning and losing, the demand for psychological services in sport is increasing.

The purpose of this book is to extend the boundaries of the various excellent textbooks that have been published for students of sport psychology. Each has been useful in outlining fundamental concepts and providing an insight into the range of issues that fall within the discipline. There is now an extensive body of research covering a wide range of psychological factors that are relevant to sport. What has been lacking is a book that draws upon that research to produce a solution to a specific problem that might arise for an athlete, or within a team. To do this, I invited a group of psychologists, all experienced teachers, researchers and practitioners, to address specific problems in sport that have a psychological basis. Each is currently working in the United Kingdom and the case studies that are described are drawn from their work with athletes and coaches at various levels of performance and across a broad age range. The format for each chapter is to identify a frequently occurring problem, describe the underlying psychological theory, review the relevant research and, finally, recommend a solution to the problem. In acknowledging that all athletes are different – and hence their problems are different – the various chapters address typical presenting situations that reflect the concerns of those seeking to attain excellence in their chosen sport.

The chapters have been grouped into four discrete parts, each with a common theme. Part I – 'Sport psychology in practice' – has a wide-ranging title that in this instance focuses mainly upon relationships in sport. Kremer and Scully (Chapter 1) discuss the important concept of team cohesion, known variously as team spirit and 'togetherness'. Seeking the most skilful players for a team does not guarantee a winning side; a well-known fact, but one that is frequently overlooked. Here, some key constructs of team cohesion are identified and a rugby team is used to exemplify some of the problems that a coach faces when the team does not gell. Jowett and Cockerill (Chapter 2) concentrate on the one-to-one relationship that exists between athlete and coach in individual sports. Jowett's triangular model refers to 'Closeness, Co-orientation and Complementarity' as essential components of the relationship and these are analyzed using data generated from the Coach–Athlete Questionnaire. Several case studies are used to illustrate some of the problems that a close working relationship can highlight. They include the long-term coaching relationship that may have become stale, the familial coaching relationship and the marital coaching relationship. Clough, Earle and Sewell (Chapter 3) examine a crucial characteristic of a successful athlete, namely mental toughness. Whenever underperformance occurs, mental toughness is often identified as the missing ingredient and these authors describe their research using the Mental Toughness Questionnaire. The importance of developing a strong association between research by practitioners and practice by researchers is emphasized in this chapter and it is a theme that is repeated throughout the book.

Part II – 'Goals, motivation and commitment' – examines the highly popular area of the 'hows' and the 'whys' of motivation in sport. Duda and Pensgaard (Chapter 4) concentrate on the climate that needs to exist for optimal motivation to take place. They use football to show how a coach who sets task goals is likely to produce a motivational climate where individual players are valued for their contribution to team performance, especially when the team is not playing well. It is proposed that coaches should adopt a five-point strategy for success. First, they should develop individual skills within the team; secondly, provide individual feedback to players; thirdly, acknowledge that players will make mistakes and that mistakes are part of the learning process; fourthly, recognize that every team member is important; and finally, allow players to be part of the decision-making process in respect of team philosophy and team goals. Harwood and Biddle (Chapter 5) continue the theme of motivation by using achievement goals to suggest a way forward for an underachieving young tennis player whose behaviour on court is unacceptable. 'Competitive performance mentality' is used as a vehicle for resolving the player's difficulties and it consists of separating a tennis match into self-challenge (the development of personal skills) and game-challenge (using self-challenge to beat one's opponent). The overenthusiastic parent is discussed in detail and the importance of educating parents and coach in the psychological demands of competitive tennis is emphasized. A good working relationship between player, parent and coach is also stressed, with good communication and the use of feedback deemed essential. Cockerill (Chapter 6) adopts a somewhat different approach in his examination of perfectionism in sport. Perfectionists are described as being dissatisfied with whatever they do, and nothing is good enough. While acute concerns about making mistakes can be extremely debilitating, there are also positive features attributable to perfectionists, namely that they set high standards for themselves and seek to achieve them. The psychopathology of perfectionism tends to be emphasized in the literature and, in general, it is negative aspects that predominate. Various measures of perfectionism are described, while the attitudes and behaviour of an international badminton player are used to show how the condition manifests itself and how negative perfectionism might be eliminated.

Part III – 'Cognitions and confidence' – shows how negative thought processes can have a deleterious effect on the performance of an athlete. Wolfson (Chapter 7) uses research into social cognition to explore attributions, counterfactual thinking and cognitive style. Although each of these concepts could prove difficult for those unfamiliar with them, the author provides a liberal dose of anecdotes, mainly from football, to show how irrational thinking can be limiting for an athlete. Shaw (Chapter 8) describes the case of a golfer who is underachieving owing to a loss of confidence in his skills and poor concentration. An intervention procedure is described in detail and it consists mainly of breaking down the player's pre-shot routine into segments that allow the player sufficient time to consider each phase of the shot. It is often stated that golf is mainly a mental rather than a physical game and Shaw argues that possessing a well-established pre-shot routine can serve to eliminate irrational thinking in golf. Holmes and Collins (Chapter 9) offer a critique of some methods of the approaches to imagery that athletes use. They argue that many interventions fail to address theoretical issues sufficiently and they present a seven-factor model that emphasizes the need for an ecologically valid, or functionally equivalent, approach to the use of imagery in sport. They rely mainly on their work with shooters and gymnasts to show how the seven elements exist within the model and that it is necessary to utilize each one to make imagery effective in sport. Mantle (Chapter 10) uses his extensive experience as a canoe coach to produce an integrated approach to two case studies. As in some other chapters, he adopts both qualitative and quantitative methods to draw up performance profiles for two canoeists whose lack of mental preparation had led to their poor results in international competition. Consistent self-confidence is shown to be crucial for elite performers and keeping a clearly structured training diary that records feelings and emotions as well as quantifying training procedures is also efficacious.

Part IV – 'Injury, counselling and social support' – is the concluding part and it comprises three chapters that deal with situations that may have severe consequences for some athletes. Cox (Chapter 11) presents an interesting insight into specific difficulties faced by an injured rugby player. The intervention that led from the player's early psychological rehabilitation to the stage where he felt able to play at his previous level was a carefully monitored and gradual process. Perhaps the most interesting aspect is the player's own account of working with the psychologist and how he relied upon the support that was provided, but did not become dependent upon it. A very different story is told by Tribe (Chapter 12) that is the reverse of conventional psychological interventions in sport. She presents an absorbing story that tells how sport, in this case football, may be used as therapy to rehabilitate a group of severely disturbed refugees. One particular individual is discussed in detail and his gradual process of recovery from physical and psychological violation is described in a sensitive way. The chapter shows that social support, team building and the development of personal control can not only improve sporting performance, but that the reverse is also true. Being part of a successful football team became a powerful therapeutic medium for the rehabilitation of the players. Chapter 13, by Lavallee, Golby and Lavallee, is located at the end for obvious reasons, and is concerned with coping with retirement from professional sport. It reveals that the transition from professional or elite-level amateur sport can present severe psychological problems for some athletes. At this stage, they are only half way through their working life and there are few that make sufficient money to retire completely. A recently developed questionnaire is used to generate data from a professional rugby team and they are used to show how adjustment to life after sport can be problematic for some players.

A few of the chapters in the book are on familiar themes, but adopt a new approach, while others address issues that may be less well known to students, although athletes and coaches will be very aware of their existence. In every instance, the emphasis is upon showing how an underlying problem in sport can be addressed by examining appropriate theory and using research to produce a solution. Although those individuals mentioned in this book have given their permission to be included, personal details have been changed to ensure that confidentiality is protected.

When I first approached each of the authors to write a chapter there was an unequivocal positive response from each and I wish to thank them for their contributions. Although I spent a large part of 2001 writing, editing and rewriting, the exercise was extremely worthwhile and I trust that I have been able to do justice to each chapter, with relatively few changes to the original versions. I am grateful to Anna Faherty and Melody Woollard of Thomson who were unrelenting in their pursuit of the finished manuscript, which meant that the book was published on schedule.

Finally, I was delighted that Bobby Gould agreed to write the foreword. I have worked with his players from youth academy to international level over more than 10 years and he and I enjoy our discussions about the role of psychology in football and how it can be used effectively. It is always a pleasure and a privilege to be associated with his teams.

Ian Cockerill

part (one)

Sport psychology in practice

chapter one

'The team just hasn't gelled'

JOHN KREMER AND DEIDRE SCULLY

Introduction

It has often been said of a team that it is less than the sum of its parts, and that the combined talents of individual players fall short of the expectations of the team members themselves, of management or of supporters. This starting point, the gap between individual talents and collective endeavours, will be used to explore what sport psychology has to contribute to our understanding of team dynamics, with a particular focus on cohesion, group development, conflict within teams and identity. In particular, the links between cohesion and performance will be highlighted in terms of what makes an effective team in a range of individual, interacting and co-acting sports. The chapter will end by outlining practical solutions to team problems, based on a case study derived from the sport of rugby union football.

The problem

The director of coaching with a leading rugby club has been in touch with you about concerns he has with the collective efforts of his first team squad. He was appointed to the post 12 months ago and feels that although the technical and physical aspects of play are well orchestrated, there is something amiss with the team as a whole.

To outline the background to the current problem, the club has been going through a period of rapid change. Previously it had been a relatively small but 'homely' club, recruiting players locally and with no serious aspirations at a national level. However, with the support of a wealthy local sponsor (an ex-player who is very keen to see the club do well) the club's coffers have swollen and it has been possible to cast the recruitment net widely, thus bringing together a well-paid team of high quality international players.

On paper, the squad has the necessary attributes to be able to compete with, and beat, any team in the league. However, by the start of the season performances have fallen short of the high expectations of the sponsor, the local community and the newly composed coaching staff. Results from the first few games have been disappointing, with the side not showing the capacity to hold on to a lead through to the final whistle. The director feels that not only are individuals underperforming, but that the team as a whole is failing to realize its potential. In his own words, he maintains that, collectively, the squad is characterized by a lack of team spirit. By way of example, he mentions the fact that when the players were away together at a pre-season training camp it was noticeable that although they trained conscientiously there was little evidence of them spending any spare time together or seeking out each other's company.

Only seven of the current squad of 25 players have had previous links with the club or the local area and, again, the director believes this may have a bearing on the lack of team spirit and what he perceives as an inability to identify with the club. A number of the players are ex-internationals and while they are well paid, the coach maintains that many appear to have 'lost their edge'.

The issues

A number of issues are potentially salient to this problem, operating at different levels of analysis; some individual, some team, some organizational or club. Through your initial meeting, it is clear that the director of coaching has already formulated his own ideas as to why the team is underperforming. While he may be on the right track, you feel it would be important to engage in a more systematic evaluation of all potential influences. In particular, the literature dealing with team cohesion, team identity and team performance would seem to be relevant.

TEAM COHESION

Since the 1960s the sport psychology literature has continued to reflect an interest in team cohesion, although some of this research is not always notable for its scientific rigour (Widmeyer, Brawley and Carron 1992). Equally, the number of active 'team' researchers within sport psychology remains relatively small, with the Canadian sport psychologist Albert Carron probably still regarded as the most influential researcher in the area.

Psychology, and likewise sport psychology, can often stand accused of merely confirming common sense, but this is one area where the research findings do not always flow with the tide of accepted wisdom. A prime example is the commonly held belief among coaches (and including the rugby coach in our example) that a tight, cohesive sports team will be a successful team (Sewell 1996), that the team that drinks together will be the team that wins together. Unfortunately, while there is some evidence to suggest that there may indeed be a causal relationship in certain sports, equally the research points to the complexity and ill-defined nature of that relationship, mirroring the wider literature on group performance and cohesion in social psychology (Forsyth

1990). Bearing these caveats in mind, it would not be sensible to follow blindly the lead of many practising sport psychologists in advocating the need to engender a good team spirit at any cost. Instead it may be more prudent to reflect on the accumulated evidence and thus begin to unravel the complexities of the relationship between team cohesion and performance.

What general conclusions can be drawn? First, that many factors interact to determine when group cohesion may influence performance, including in particular the type of sport (interactive versus co-active versus individual). Secondly, that cohesion per se may not always predict team success but that success may be more likely to predict cohesion and hence the relationship is not causal. Thirdly, that the concept of cohesion itself is multifaceted and, finally, that the measurement of dimensions of team cohesion itself is no simple task.

To begin, what is team or group cohesion? Festinger, Schachter and Back (1950) originally defined group cohesion as 'the total field of forces causing members to remain in a group'. While this definition was adopted in early sport psychology texts, later writers felt that it may place too strong an emphasis on the forces of attraction binding members together. Hence, this focus has to be tempered by a complementary concern with the team's goals and objectives. With this in mind, Carron (1982) went on to define team cohesion as 'a dynamic process which is reflected in the tendency to stick together and remain united in the pursuit of goals and objectives'. This definition, which explicitly conceptualizes cohesion as a multidimensional dynamic process, has stood the test of time and formed the core of the model of group cohesion developed by Widmeyer, Brawley and Carron (1985).

This model divides cohesion into two primary categories, (i) Group Integration and (ii) Individual Attractions to the Group. Both categories are subdivided into either task concerns (performance, achievement, productivity) or social concerns (friendships, unity, closeness), thereby yielding four dimensions to group cohesion:

- Group Integration – Task (GI Task)

- Group Integration – Social (GI Social)

- Individual Attractions to the Group – Task (ATG Task)

- Individual Attractions to the Group – Social (ATG Social).

Group Integration (GI) refers to a team member's view of the team as a whole while Individual Attractions to the Group (ATG) represents each member's personal attractions to the team. It is these four scales that are thought to account for most of the variability in cohesion among sports teams.

In a further elaboration of this model, Cota *et al.* (1995) draw a distinction between primary and secondary dimensions of cohesion. Primary dimensions are used to describe levels of cohesion in most groups, while secondary dimensions are only salient to specific types of groups. Primary dimensions, or components, include the task/social and individual/group considerations as proposed by Carron, Windmeyer and Brawley

(1985), along with normative views among group members (Yukelson, Weinberg and Jackson 1984) and the group's resistance to disruption. Secondary dimensions may include particular features of a group that predispose it towards certain states. For example, Cota *et al.* (1995) suggest that the dimension identified as 'valued roles' by Yukelson, Weinberg and Jackson (1984) may be relevant, particularly where roles are strongly defined and not easily interchangeable, including team positions in certain sports.

Measuring team cohesion

The first attempt to quantify team cohesion came with the introduction of the Sports Cohesiveness Questionnaire in the early 1970s (SCQ; Martens, Landers and Loy 1972). The SCQ remained popular for some time, despite never being subjected to a formal validation process. In the early 1980s, a number of alternative questionnaires became available, including the Team Cohesion Questionnaire (Gruber and Gray 1982) and the Multidimensional Sport Cohesion Instrument (Yukelson, Weinberg and Jackson 1984), devices which paid due acknowledgement to the multifaceted nature of cohesion. For example, the Multidimensional Sport Cohesion Instrument measures four factors: attraction to the group, unity of purpose, quality of teamwork and valued roles. However, it was the Group Environment Questionnaire (GEQ), devised by Carron, Widmeyer and Brawley (1985), which rapidly rose to prominence in the mid-1980s and still remains the most popular questionnaire for measuring team cohesion in sport. The GEQ is an 18-item questionnaire that measures the four components of cohesiveness as previously outlined:

1. *ATG Social:* group members' perceptions about personal involvement, acceptance and social interaction.

2. *ATG Task:* group members' perceptions about personal involvement with group tasks, productivity and goals and objectives.

3. *GI Social:* group members' perceptions about similarity, closeness and bonding within the whole group as regards social aspects.

4. *GI Task:* group members' perceptions about similarity, closeness and bonding within the whole group as regards its tasks.

In contrast with earlier scales, the GEQ has been psychometrically validated (Schutz, Eom, Smoll and Smith 1994), most recently by way of a confirmatory factor analysis that confirmed the underlying four-factor structure (Li and Harmer 1996).

Antecedents of team cohesion

According to Carron (1982), there are four primary factors that contribute to the development of a highly cohesive team. These are:

● situational factors (e.g. size, organizational orientation, geographical variables, contractual responsibilities, normative pressures, intergroup conflict)

- personal factors (gender, maturity, personal attributes, shared perceptions, individual satisfaction, similarity)

- leadership factors (coach and captaincy behaviour and styles, communication, coach–athlete relationship, decision-making style)

- team factors (relationships, task characteristics, ability, achievement orientation, homogeneity, intragroup cooperation, experience, norms, stability and team maturity).

Although research in this area is not extensive, there is limited support for the role that some of the elements contained in each of this set of factors may play. By way of example, Widmeyer, Brawley and Carron (1990) demonstrated that squad size was related (normally inversely) to productivity, enjoyment and cohesiveness among basketball players (a situational factor). Yaffé (1975) concluded that passing and ball distribution were related to sociometric friendship ties among soccer players (a personal factor). Carron and Chelladurai (1981) stated that a democratic leadership style was most likely to enhance cohesion in team sports (a leadership factor). Also, Partington and Shangi (1992) proposed that certain psychosocial elements are important determinants of team cohesion, including player talent and attitude, team identity and style of play (team factors).

Consequences of team cohesion

When considering the effects of cohesion, there has been a tendency to focus on only one issue, namely team success (Williams and Widmeyer 1991). Unfortunately, this focus may detract from a more fine-grained analysis of how cohesion may impact on each team member and the group dynamic, both short and long term. To achieve this degree of sophistication it is necessary to disaggregate outcomes into either team or individual. Team outcomes can include performance, success rate, team stability, interactions and communication, synergy and collective efficacy. Individual outcomes can include personal satisfaction along with improved personal states (self-esteem, self-efficacy, trust, reduced anxiety, increased role clarity, role acceptance and role performance). At the very least it would seem appropriate to consider not only performance but also satisfaction when evaluating the effects of team cohesion but, to date, research has tended to place greater emphasis on the former and it is towards this relationship in particular that we now turn.

The performance–cohesion relationship

This relationship has attracted considerable attention over the past 30 years, and especially until the early 1990s. Widmeyer, Brawley and Carron (1993) argued that of the numerous studies that had directly examined the relationship between performance and cohesion, at least four out of five (83 per cent) had found a positive correlation between team success and cohesion, while only a small number of studies reported a negative relationship and only one study had found no relationship. It is revealing that only certain types of sport characterize studies where a relationship has been demonstrated.

In particular, those that have revealed a positive relationship include basketball, hockey, volleyball, American football, ice hockey and golf (predominantly interactive sports), while those showing a negative relationship include rifle-shooting, rowing and bowling (co-acting sports).

Group and team cohesion in general was subject to a comprehensive meta-analysis by Mullen and Cooper (1994), which included reference to over 200 studies. This analysis concluded that a cohesion–effectiveness relationship does exist and that it is often at its strongest in sports teams. Indeed the differences between sports teams and other non-sport real-life groups were so noticeable that the authors cautioned attempts at generalizing from one set of studies to the other. They also confirmed that the effect derives most significantly from task commitment/cohesion, and not from social or interpersonal cohesion. A final conclusion derived from a select sample of longitudinal studies, and one which is important in the context of this discussion, is that 'the stronger direction of effect seems to be from performance to cohesiveness, and not from cohesiveness to performance'. This is not to argue that cohesion cannot influence performance, but that the performance-to-cohesion link is the stronger.

Reflecting this conclusion, both Iso-Ahola and Hatfield (1987) and Slater and Sewell (1994) have suggested a circular or reciprocal relationship between team cohesion and performance, although noting that performance has a stronger influence on cohesion than vice versa.

TEAM MATURITY

A closely related literature concerns the maturity of teams and includes the influence of group development on team performance. Within social psychology, stage models of group development now enjoy widespread acceptance, with Tuckman's stage model (Tuckman and Jensen 1977) still very much to the fore as a framework within which various group processes are identified. Tuckman described group development in terms of four basic stages. First, the group comes together and works through the somewhat formal orientation stage (forming). Next, there may well be heightened tension associated with role differentiation and competiton for status and influence (storming), before norms, rules and standards of behaviour begin to stabilize (norming). Finally, the group will have matured to a stage where it is able to work together as a unit (performing). Clearly this all takes time, and when personnel change any group or team has to work through the process of role differentiation afresh, and performance will invariably suffer in this period of readjustment.

Despite the obvious relevance of such formulations for team sports, and the significance of group development in general for understanding performance in sports involving a high degree of interdependence, there has been a dearth of sport-related research since the 1970s dealing with group development and performance. During that decade a number of significant archival studies set the scene by identifying the relationship between team maturity and success. Research using data derived from sports such as soccer, baseball, basketball and gymnastics demonstrated that turnover rates and performance were negatively related, also revealing large differences between sports in terms of the time taken to reach maturity and then the period for which good teams stayed at the top. For example, Loy, McPherson and Kenyon (1978) cited a breakdown of results of American football teams in the National Football League between 1955 and 1959, by length of member tenure within the team. Those with mature teams (2.25 years or more average playing experience per player) had a winning record some 17 per cent higher than those with young teams (less than 2.25 years). According to the authors, the effective 'half-life' of successful teams was likely to depend on many factors, including the age of players, the type of sport and various facets of group dynamics, including cohesiveness and role differentiation. However, these issues remain largely unexplored and there must be tremendous scope, from both a practical and a theoretical viewpoint, to develop longitudinal research programmes in this area.

TEAM IDENTITY

The concept of team identity has rarely attracted much attention in the sport psychology literature and yet within social psychology, from the 1970s onwards, work on identity, whether social or personal, features significantly in the discourse around intergroup relations (see Ellemers, Spears and Doosje 1999). According to social identity theory (Tajfel 1982), the more closely an individual identifies with a group and is defined in terms of group membership, then the more that person will be inclined to maximize differences between the in-group and the out-group, and this is likely to reflect in competitiveness. Accordingly, 'both in sports teams and in work groups, it is commonly acknowledged that the success of the group in competition largely depends on the extent to which its members are prepared to exert themselves in order to achieve common group goals' (Ouwerkerk, Ellemers and de Gilder 1999, p. 185). While this statement may appear obvious, it highlights the need to consider the extent to which players identify with the club or the team.

Equally, team identity or allegiance has been shown to play a very significant role in ameliorating the effects of social loafing; the more that individuals identify with a group then the less likely it is that they will be prone to social loafing (Williams, Karau and Bourgeois 1993). In a sport such as rugby it is relatively easy to 'hide' and, hence, social loafing may play a significant role in performance. The solution will lie in monitoring individual performance and associated feedback.

Conclusions

Looking at the literature as a whole, three factors emerge as vital to any discussion of cohesion. First, the type of sport or the type of task obviously mediates any effects. The more that the sport requires that team members must rely on each other and are interdependent ('interactive sports') then the more significant cohesion is likely to be (Carron 1988). In other sports, where athletes may represent the same team but individual performance does not depend on teamwork ('co-acting sport'), then team cohesion may be less important in determining outcome. With an awareness of the importance of sporting context, attempts have been made over recent years to classify sports according to where they fall along some notional continuum between being predominantly a co-acting sport, or being an interacting sport (Cratty 1983). The implicit assumption is that the two constructs, co-action and interaction, occupy extreme ends of a continuum and, thus, are inversely related. Perhaps this implicit model needs to be subjected to closer scrutiny, for these two dimensions may not be related at all but, indeed, may be independent. Accordingly, some sports may be both highly interactive and co-active (for example rowing, tug-of-war), whereas some may be highly interactive, but involve less identifiable co-action (for example volleyball). Others may be low on both dimensions (for example fell running, chess) and yet others may be co-active but not interactive (for example archery, bowls). The more that players are interdependent on each other, the more the team's performance becomes a reflection of the synergy, or coordinated action, of the team. Accordingly, the more salient cohesion will be, and in order to be able to apply research to sport itself the issue of how to categorize sports must remain high on sport psychology's agenda.

In reviewing this material, a second point to bear in mind from social psychology is the downside, or the negative effects, of high team cohesion. Group research of various kinds, from traditional conformity experiments through to the varied literature dealing with group decision making (Forsyth 1990), has revealed that the tighter or more cohesive the group, the less likely it is that people will be motivated to express their individuality. In team sports, one consequence is that players may perform to a similar standard and thereby minimize intragroup competition. On the one hand this may encourage high levels of cooperation among players. On the other hand the self-determined norm may not always be of the highest standard. This work also suggests that the more pressure a team is under, for example following a string of defeats, the more team members will be inclined to turn inwards and rate their behaviour in comparison with their teammates (Festinger 1954).

The final point concerns how to proceed given a recognition that cohesion is multifaceted and that early research consistently neglected to appreciate that fact (Mudrack 1989).

Interventions

Having considered relevant literature the task is now to put theory into practice, to see how this material can help inform the advice that can be offered to the rugby coach and his squad of underachievers. From a practical point of view, initially it will be vital to develop a good working relationship with the coach, for without that rapport and understanding it is highly unlikely that any advice will be heeded. The model of intervention must be underpinned by an acknowledgement of the centrality of the coach, the support role that the sport psychologist is able to provide for that person and an understanding of, and sensitivity to, the dynamic which exists between coach and players (Terry 1997; Kremer and Scully 1998). The coach brings his own 'theories' to this situation and the task of the sport psychologist will be to work with, and then perhaps beyond, these constructions, always recognizing that many good coaches are also intuitively good human-resource managers.

Initially it would be useful to empower the coach by making him aware of the issues already described above and, in particular, the complexities of the relationship that exists between team cohesion and performance. In building on that knowledge it may be useful to discuss appropriate skills for handling 'team' issues when and if they arise. For example, Syer (1991) argued that in order to foster 'togetherness' within a squad of players, a coach must constantly monitor the development of cliques and potential sources of conflict. This will lead to dealing effectively with potential problems, while being mindful that certain levels of conflict can sometimes be highly functional and motivating. During team meetings Syer (1991) recommends that the coach should acquaint each player with his or her responsibilities, establish team goals, create open communication channels and monitor the psychological well-being of both fit and injured team members. Additionally, Yukelson (1998) suggests that the coach must be in tune with the interpersonal grapevine within the group, most usefully by maintaining a dialogue with both informal and formal leaders within the team.

All of this practical advice is sound, irrespective of the particular problems facing the team at this time. As for the players, Huang and Lynch (1994) suggest that by constantly offering positive affirmation statements, each team member can offer support and positive encouragement, thus helping the team to focus on its objectives and at the same time developing a sense of togetherness among players.

With due acknowledgement of the coach's thoughts on the matter, it is also important to carry out a systematic assessment of the problem at hand. This should include gathering further information on aspects of team and individual performance from alternative, and preferably objective, sources to ensure that the analysis with which you have been presented is, in fact, accurate. Assuming that 'team' issues still feature as a significant area of concern, a second stage of data gathering would typically involve individual interviews with members of the squad. The use of questionnaires in such interviews has long been debated (Gould and Pick 1995) and almost certainly will depend on context or circumstance, along with the personal preference of the sport psychologist. While some find the use of such measures overly formal, constraining and distracting, others welcome the opportunity to quantify data in a systematic way.

For those inclined towards quantification, the GEQ would seem well suited to this situation, perhaps along with a measure of motivational orientation because it would be important to consider the motivational profile of each player. For example, it could be that the coach has failed to accommodate individual differences when trying to motivate his squad, or has made assumptions that do not square with reality. The interview should endeavour to determine what makes each player in the squad 'tick', perhaps most usefully working to a dynamic process model of motivation that can consider the relationship between effort, performance, reward and satisfaction across the career of an athlete (Kremer and Busby 1998). This process will establish whether there is a general motivational problem applicable to the entire squad, or whether interventions should continue to operate at an individual level. As the substantial literature on participation motivation makes clear, across an athlete's career many factors, both intrinsic and extrinsic, are likely to ebb and flow in terms of their significance, and it would be important to identify the individual profile for each player. It is highly likely that this process of investigation will suggest a combination of individual and collective interventions, the former focusing on whatever issues are of special concern to the player, the latter dealing with group processes.

Focusing attention on the latter, data gathered from interviews should be able to pinpoint which issues are most important, whether in terms of team cohesion, maturity or identity. Looking briefly at each, if cohesion is a problem then it may be appropriate to turn to team-building techniques (Syer 1991), at the very least to help players become better acquainted with each other. According to Syer and Connolly (1984), the benefits of team building are three-fold:

1. From a coaching perspective togetherness helps to satisfy players' needs, enhances loyalty to the team and coach and harnesses support among team members.

2. In times of stress it helps provide buffers and facilitates the provision of clear feedback on personal performance.

3. It enables a team to have the edge over a less together, but technically superior, team.

This work should proceed with an awareness that the objective is not to create a team that is necessarily comfortable or conflict-free, but one where the team atmosphere is conducive to repeatable good performances. As to the process itself, Lovell and Collins (1996) have suggested a staged approach, which would involve, for example, brainstorming and negotiation in order to enhance a feeling of ownership over the process. As a part of this process, Cripps and Cann (1996) emphasize the importance of work on team goal setting for the squad and for the club as a whole, often encompassing cultural issues and including playing, social and financial matters. For more experienced players, a focus on goal setting may help to address any motivational problems associated with performing at a level below that which they were once capable.

In terms of maturity, it may be that the team has had insufficient time to work through natural stages of development (in Tuckman's terms, forming, storming, norming and performing). Thus, it may be appropriate to consider a series of sessions designed specifically to help the group develop as a unit. The identification of significant and influential group members will play a vital part in this process.

Finally, in relation to social identity, it may well be that the squad has not developed a true sense of 'who they are' and have been asked to borrow the identity the club once had, but to which they may feel no sense of allegiance. Time could usefully be spent with the players as a whole, asking them to define 'who they are' through an appraisal of their weaknesses and strengths (in that order!).

For each of these interventions it would be essential to ensure that the coach plays a pivotal role in proceedings and that the players are made aware of what the objectives of the exercise are. As to the content of the sessions, they have to be guided by constant monitoring of the team atmosphere and, indeed, 'monitor and review' should remain the watchwords that guide the intervention as it continues to develop, hopefully along with the team.

References

Carron, A. V. (1982) 'Cohesiveness in sport groups: Interpretations and considerations', *Journal of Sport Psychology* 4:123–128.

Carron, A. V. (1988) *Group Dynamics in Sport*, London, Ontario: Spodym.

Carron, A. V. and Chelladurai, P. (1981) 'The dynamics of group cohesion in sport', *Journal of Sport Psychology* 3:123–139.

Carron, A. V., Widmeyer, W. N. and Brawley, L. R. (1985) 'The development of an instrument to assess cohesion in team sports: The Group Environment Questionnaire, *Journal of Sport Psychology* 7:244–266.

Cota, A. A., Evans, C. R., Dion, K. L., Kilik, L. and Longman, R. S. (1995) 'The structure of group cohesion', *Personality and Social Psychology Bulletin* 21:572–580.

Cratty, B. J. (1983) *Psychology in Contemporary Sport: Guidelines for Coaches and Athletes*, Englewood Cliffs, NJ: Prentice-Hall.

Cripps, B. and Cann, G. (1996) 'Team goal setting in rugby union football: A nominal group technique'. In J. Annett and H. Steinberg (eds.), *How Teams Work in Sport and Exercise Psychology*, pp. 31–39, Leicester: British Psychological Society.

Ellemers, N., Spears, R. and Doosje, B. (eds.) (1999) *Social identity*, Oxford: Blackwell.

Festinger, L. (1954) 'A theory of social comparison processes', *Human Relations* 7:117–140.

Festinger, L., Schachter, S. and Back, K. (1950) *Social Pressures in Informal Groups*, Stanford, CA: Stanford University Press.

Forsyth, D. (1990) *Group Dynamics*, Pacific Grove, CA: Brooks/Cole.

Gould, D. and Pick, S. (1995) 'Sport psychology: The Griffith era, 1920–1940', *The Sport Psychologist* 9:391–405.

Gruber, J. J. and Gray, G. R. (1982) 'Responses to forces influencing cohesion as a function of player status and level of male varsity basketball competition', *Research Quarterly for Exercise and Sport* 53:27–36.

Huang, C. and Lynch, J. (1994) *Thinking Body and Dancing Mind: Tao Sports for Extraordinary Performance in Athletics, Business and Life*, London: Bantam Books.

Iso-Ahola, A. and Hatfield, B. (1987) *Psychology of Sports: A Social Psychological Approach*, Dubuque, IA: William C. Brown.

Kremer, J. and Busby, G. (1998) 'Modelling participation in sport and exercise: An integrative approach', *Irish Journal of Psychology* 19:447–463.

Kremer, J. and Scully, D. (1998) 'What applied sport psychologists often don't do: On empowerment and independence'. In H. Steinberg, I. Cockerill and A. Dewey (eds.), *What Sport Psychologists Do*, pp. 21–27, Leicester: British Psychological Society.

Lenk, H. (1969) 'Top performance despite internal conflict'. In J. W. Loy and G. S. Kenyon (eds.), *Sport, Culture and Society'*, New York: Macmillan.

Li, F. and Harmer, P. (1996) 'Confirmatory factor analysis of the Group Environment Questionnaire with an intercollegiate sample', *Journal of Sport and Exercise Psychology* 18:49–63.

Lovell, G. and Collins, D. (1996) 'Applied interventions for improving team effectiveness'. In J. Annett and H. Steinberg (eds.), *How Teams Work in Sport and Exercise Psychology*, pp. 57–65, Leicester: British Psychological Society.

Loy, J. W., McPherson, B. D. and Kenyon, G. (1978) *Sport and Social Systems: A Guide to the Analysis, Problems and Literature*, Reading MA: Addison-Wesley.

Martens, R., Landers, D. and Loy, J. (1972) *Sports Cohesiveness Questionnaire*, Washington DC: AAHPERD Publications.

Martens, R. and Peterson, J. A. (1971) 'Group cohesiveness as a determinant of success and member satisfaction in team performance', *International Review of Sport Sociology* 6:49–61.

Mudrack, P. E. (1989) 'Defining group cohesiveness: A legacy of confusion', *Small Group Behavior* 20:37–49.

Mullen, B. and Cooper, C. (1994) 'The relation between group cohesion and performance: An integration', *Psychological Bulletin* 115:210–227.

Ouwerkerk, J. W., Ellemers, N. and de Gilder, D. (1999) 'Group commitment and individual effort in experimental and organizational settings'. In N. Ellemers, R. Spears and B. Doosje (eds.), *Social Identity: Context, Commitment, Content*, pp. 184–204, Oxford: Blackwell.

Partington, J. T. and Shangi, G. M. (1992) 'Developing and understanding of team psychology', *International Journal of Sport Psychology* 23:28–47.

Ruder, M. K. and Gill, D. L. (1982) 'Immediate effects of win loss on perceptions of cohesion in intramural and intercollegiate volleyball teams', *Journal of Sport Psychology* 4:227–234.

Schutz, R. W., Eom, H. J., Smoll, F. L. and Smith, R. E. (1994) 'Examination of the factorial validity of the Group Environment Questionnaire', *Research Quarterly for Exercise and Sport* 65:226–236.

Sewell, D. (1996) 'Chicken or egg? In search of the elusive cohesion–performance relationship'. In J. Annett and H. Steinberg (eds.), *How Teams Work in Sport and Exercise Psychology*, pp. 11–18, Leicester: British Psychological Society.

Slater, M. R. and Sewell, D. F. (1994) 'An examination of the cohesion–performance relationship in university hockey teams', *Journal of Sports Sciences* 12:423–431.

Syer, J. (1991) 'Team building: The development of team spirit'. In S. J. Bull (ed.), *Sport Psychology: A Self-help Guide'*, Marlborough, Wilts: Crowood Press.

Tajfel, H. (ed.) (1982) *Social Identity and Intergroup Relations',* Cambridge: Cambridge University Press.

Terry, P. (1997) 'The application of mood profiling with elite sports performers'. In R. J. Butler (ed.), *Sports Psychology in Performance,* Oxford: Butterworth-Heinemann.

Tuckman, B. W. and Jensen, M. A. (1977) 'Stages of small group development revisited', *Group and Organizational Studies* 2:419–427.

Widmeyer, W. N., Brawley, L. R. and Carron, A. V. (1985) *The Measurement of Cohesion in Sport Teams: The Group Environment Questionnaire,* London, Ontario: Sports Dynamics.

Widmeyer, W. N., Brawley, L. R. and Carron, A. V. (1993) 'Group cohesion in sport and exercise'. In R. N. Singer, M. Murphey and L. K. Tennant (eds.), *Handbook of Research on Sport Psychology,* pp. 672–694, New York: Macmillan.

Widmeyer, W. N., Brawley, L. R. and Carron, A. V. (1990) 'The effects of group size in sport', *Journal of Sport and Exercise Psychology* 12:177–190.

Widmeyer, W. N., Brawley, L. R. and Carron, A. V. (1992) 'Group dynamics in sport'. In T. S. Horn (ed.), *Advances in Sport Psychology.* pp. 163–180, Champaign, IL: Human Kinetics.

Williams, J. M. and Widmeyer, W. N. (1991) 'The cohesion–performance outcome relationship in a co-acting sport', *Journal of Sport and Exercise Psychology* 13:364–371.

Williams, K. D., Karau, S. J. and Bourgeois, M. (1993) 'Working on collective tasks: Social loafing and social compensation'. In M. A. Hogg and D. Abrams (eds.), *Group Motivation: Social Psychological Perspectives,* pp. 130–148, London: Harvester Wheatsheaf.

Yaffé, M. (1975) 'Techniques of mental training: Case studies in professional football'. In G. J. K. Anderson and D. A. Tydesley (eds.), *British Proceedings of Sport Psychology,* London: British Society of Sport Psychology.

Yukelson, D. (1998) 'Communicating effectively'. In J. M. Williams (ed.), *Applied Sport Psychology,* third edition, pp. 142–157, Mountain View, CA: Mayfield.

Yukelson, D., Weinberg, R. and Jackson, A. (1984) 'A multidimensional group cohesion instrument for intercollegiate basketball teams', *Journal of Sport Psychology* 6:103–117.

chapter two

Incompatibility in the coach–athlete relationship

SOPHIA JOWETT AND IAN COCKERILL

The coach–athlete relationship serves as a platform from which the coach and the athlete interact in unique ways in order to bring about performance accomplishments, success and satisfaction. In other words, the coach–athlete relationship becomes the principal process vehicle from which needs are expressed and fulfilled. The effectiveness of coaches' tasks of providing technical, tactical and strategical instruction, as well as other tasks of planning, organizing, evaluating, directing and supporting depend upon the relationship between coach and athlete. However, McCready (1984) has argued that coaches often spend much of their time and energy on the technical and administrative elements of coaching because of their better-defined and more controllable nature. Forming an athletic relationship where both the coach and the athlete feel comfortable and confident is often perceived as a formidable task because of the attitudes, feelings and motivations involved that are less controllable. However, coaches who neglect the influential nature of the coach–athlete relationship in the process of coaching are risking the successful development of an athlete's potential (Lyle 1999).

Coe (1996) has explained that when the athlete and the coach are in perfect harmony great things can be achieved. Indeed, in track and field athletics as in many other sports, effective coach–athlete relationships have been associated with top-level sport performance. Real-life examples from the sport of athletics illustrate this important point: Ron Rodden and Linford Christie (100m Olympic gold medallist), Frank Dick and Daley Thompson (decathlon Olympic gold medallist), Peter Coe and Sebastian Coe (1500m Olympic gold medallist), Bruce Longden and Sally Gunnell (400m hurdles Olympic gold medallist), Charles van Commonee and Denise Lewis (heptathlon Olympic gold medallist), and Alex Stanton and Paula Radcliffe (World cross-country champion).

Not all coach–athlete relationships are effective and successful. Coaches' negative approaches to coaching often influence the development of inadequate relationships with their athletes (Martens 1987; Smoll and Smith 1989). There may be coaches who subject athletes to strict, regimented and militaristic drills to fulfil their own ambitions through their athletes, and who do not care if they are injured, burned out or depressed.

Such coaches believe that winning at all cost is the only thing worth striving for and they may reject many talented athletes in order to develop one who will be successful. They design training programmes around the athlete with the most talent, a form of behaviour that can be described as negative coaching. According to Ryan (1996), negative coaching approaches are arrogant, ignorant and ultimately betray the trust that is implicit within the coach–athlete relationship.

This chapter seeks to provide a framework for understanding the nature of the coach–athlete relationship, and the means for identifying, eliminating and preventing potential relational barriers and interpersonal conflict are discussed. Initially, case studies are presented to illustrate frequently occurring, yet distinct, coach–athlete relationships, each of which describes difficulties in the athletic partnerships. The problems are such that the athlete's performance and general well-being are affected. In the first case study, John and Lynne's athletic relationship reached its peak at a major athletic event, after which a steady decline in their interactions have led Lynne to believe that John is not interested in her training. Specifically, Lynne has started to feel that her coach's instructions and support lack structure and direction. The second case study refers to a familial coach–athlete relationship, where the coach is the parent of the athlete. Mary, the coach, and Andy, the 14-year-old athlete and son, have been working together since Andy was eight years old. Over the past 12 months Andy has experienced a need for greater independence and feels that he does not want to be continually under his mother's wing. Mary recognizes the tensions that exist and the need to act upon them before Andy's performance is affected. In the third and final case study, coach Peter and athlete Sarah have been married for almost a year; their dual relationship as husband and wife, as well as coach and athlete has started to show signs of strain. Sarah feels uncertain whether their coach–athlete relationship can survive and be effective for much longer.

Case study

The case of John and Lynne

Lynne has been training seriously for badminton for more than 10 years and John has coached her for almost half that time. During this period all their preparation has been geared towards the Olympic Games which resulted in a gold medal. Lynne believes that their coach–athlete relationship before and during the Olympic Games was based fundamentally upon a long-term friendship that that was reinforced by trust and honesty, a continuous give and take, and a sense of stability. After the Olympics, Lynne started to blame John for pushing her too hard and not recognizing that she was in a slump, for not setting clear goals and for not allowing her time and space to reorganize her life. She also referred to criticisms and negative remarks that John has started to make during training, especially when she does not play well. John, on the other hand, feels that Lynne's lifestyle has changed completely, and that has prevented her from concentrating on her training with the same zeal as she did before the Games. John has explained that Lynne's rejection of his instructions and opposition to his advice following the Olympics have led to difficulties in coaching

Lynne as he did previously. Both agree that their relationship and ability to cooperate on court have become distant and impersonal. They wish to rebuild their committed, close and cooperative athletic partnership similar to the one they had previously.

The case of Mary and Andy

Mary feels that the relationship established with Andy over the course of their athletic partnership has been very successful. The success is readily reflected in Andy's gradual improvement over the years. Currently, Andy is ranked number two in his age group. Both Mary and Andy feel that their close coach–athlete relationship has been the result of their family attachment. However, over the past two years Andy has become sensitive to his mother's intensity in training and competitions. He describes his mother as a very supportive and influential figure, but her continuous presence is overpowering and sometimes even embarrassing. Mary agrees that Andy has been unhappy during training and it sometimes appears that he is no longer interested in athletics. However, Mary has learned from a recent conversation with him that he wants to remain in the sport and that he is committed. It is in competition that Andy's determination and devotion to the sport are most evident. Mary recognizes that adolescence can be a difficult period for developing athletic talent, because athletes become less dependent upon and compliant with coaches' instructions and training. Mary feels that by being patient Andy will eventually understand that his mother, as his coach, is there to help him achieve his performance goals. Meanwhile, she wants to know how to alleviate the tensions evident during training and at home and how to restructure their relationship so that Andy will feel confident and comfortable.

The case of Peter and Sarah

Peter is a former athlete, a sport science graduate and a full-time national coach. He coaches a squad of six talented track and field athletes, including his wife. Peter and Sarah started to work together as coach and athlete a year ago, at about the time that they were married. Both agree that they have implicit trust in each other's abilities and a desire to work hard to achieve their mutual goals. Their principal goal is to make the Olympic team, but conflicts have begun to emerge, mainly due to their dual-role relationship of wife/athlete and husband/coach. Sarah is concerned that issues from training impinge constantly upon their personal lives; training dominates everything they do, even when they attempt to escape from it for a while. Peter recognizes that his dual role as coach and husband are difficult as one frequently contradicts the other. At home, he tries hard to be the husband that Sarah wants him to be, as well as the coach that she needs at the track. However, he believes that a coach can have a positive influence on issues such as resting and dietary patterns and mental preparation, all of which can be pursued effectively at home. The fact that Peter plays the role of coach at home makes Sarah tense, angry and generally upset. Negative feelings affect both their marriage and their athletic relationship and while Peter wants to help Sarah to realize her ambitions, he does not understand why his behaviour is upsetting her.

The research

The coach–athlete relationship has been examined mainly from a leadership perspective. Both the Multidimensional Model of Leadership in Sport (Chelladurai 1993) and the Mediational Model of Coach–Player Relationships (Smoll and Smith 1989) have been used extensively to study the dynamics involved between coach and athlete. Despite both models' interpersonal character and the valuable information that they have generated about how coaches coach, or should coach, in order to have a positive impact on athletes' psychosocial and physical development, their scope is limited. They focus on behavioural aspects of coaching (Lyle 1999; Kuklinski 1990; Douge and Hastie 1993), but given that the coach–athlete relationship involves aspects other than coach behaviour, an alternative conceptual framework has been developed (Jowett 2001a; 2001b). It was designed to examine the dynamics involved between the coach and the athlete from what is termed a relationship perspective, which asserts that coaches and athletes' behaviours need to be considered alongside their emotions and cognitions.

Kelley *et al.* (1983) have defined a dyadic relationship as one in which two people's behaviours, emotions and thoughts are mutually and causally interconnected. Accordingly, Jowett and her colleagues (Jowett 2001a; 2001b; Jowett and Cockerill 2001; Jowett and Meek 2000a; 2000b) described the coach–athlete relationship as a situation in which the coach's and athlete's emotions, thoughts and behaviours are interdependent. In order to operationalize the nature of the coach–athlete relationship, a careful examination of the interpersonal relationship and behaviour literature has pointed to the interpersonal constructs of Closeness (Berscheid, Snyder and Omoto 1989), Co-orientation (Newcomb 1953) and Complementarity (Kiesler 1997). The three constructs mirror the constituents of the coach's and the athlete's emotions, thoughts and behaviours respectively.

- *Closeness* concerns the emotional tone of the coach–athlete relationship and it reflects the extent to which coaches and athletes are connected, or the depth of their attachments. For example, coaches' and athletes' expressions of like, trust and respect, as opposed to dislike and distrust, indicate a positive interpersonal affective state.

- *Co-orientation* refers to similar views and opinions, or the common ground that coaches and athletes establish in the course of their athletic partnership. Effective communication is important in enabling coaches and athletes to share each other's experience, knowledge, thoughts, values and concerns.

- *Complementarity* is defined as the type of interaction that the coach and the athlete perceive as cooperative and effective. Cooperation is a principal complementary act that aims to either aid the performance of the athlete, or contribute to the ease with which both coach and athlete coordinate their efforts during training and competition. Thus, complementarity is evident according to the extent of cooperation within the coach–athlete relationship.

The interpersonal constructs of Closeness, Co-orientation and Complementarity have been used extensively, albeit independently, to study various types of interpersonal relationships (e.g. friendships, marital and romantic relationships). However, they have never been used conjointly in the study of coaches and athletes. Thus, the first phase of the work was to identify the nature and the usefulness of these constructs in a sporting context. A series of qualitative case studies were conducted to examine the nature of typical and atypical coach–athlete relationships in two distinct cultural settings, British and Greek. The typical coach–athlete relationship refers to the coach and athlete who are not related in any way other than their relationship as a coach and athlete, whereas the atypical relationship is a dual-role relationship in which the coach and athlete are also related through familial, marital or educational ties (see Jowett 2001a; 2001b). Two atypical coach–athlete relationship cases were examined initially; a Greek marital coach–athlete relationship (Jowett and Meek 2000a), and a British familial coach–athlete relationship (Jowett and Meek 2000b), with the athletes competing at international and national level, respectively. In addition, two instances of a typical coach–athlete relationship were studied, one athlete being an English county-level swimmer (Jowett and Pearce 2001) and the other a Greek international track and field athlete. Finally, typical coach–athlete relationships from the perspective of 12 Olympic medallists were examined retrospectively (Jowett and Cockerill 2001). These former elite athletes competed in a variety of individual sports and represented several different nations. By utilizing the interpersonal constructs of Closeness, Co-orientation and Complementarity, interviews were conducted and revealed that the constructs are salient components of the coach–athlete relationship.

The most significant findings from the case studies are presented here. The athletic relationship of all participants examined was characterized by feelings of closeness, co-oriented views and complementary acts of interaction. Feelings of closeness, such as being cared for, committed, respected, trusted, liked and valued were important in fostering coaches' and athletes' intrapersonal feelings (e.g. self-confidence, motivation) and interpersonal feelings (e.g. stability, harmony). This observation is consistent with research in interpersonal relationships that purports that trust, love and liking are critical components of positive personal and relational outcomes (Hinde 1997). More specifically, sport psychology research suggests that the need to be close to and part of the other is the only dimension that differentiates compatible from incompatible coach–athlete dyads (Carron and Bennett 1977). Furthermore, Hellstedt (1990; 1995) has emphasized that athletes require assistance from both parents and coaches who value, help, support and care about them. Thus, it is likely that coaches who are able to assume the role of mentor are more likely to show genuine concern and respect for their athletes and develop athletic relationships with their athletes that are both committed and trusting (Bloom, Durand-Bush, Schinke and Salmela 1998).

Negative emotional expressions (e.g. frustration, anger, jealousy, distrust) were also present in various degrees and forms in the cases examined. For example, the marital coach–athlete relationship was unique in that no major problems, difficulties or complications surfaced in their athletic relationship. However, when they were asked to discuss marital and more personal issues, negative features began to emerge within the relationship. One issue that was associated with negative feelings, particularly with anger and frustration, was that of the dual role of husband as coach. Athletes felt that their husbands continued to behave as coaches by exercising unreasonable authority and control in the home. However, athletes' feelings of anger and frustration were moderated by high levels of perceived co-orientation – that is, having shared knowledge and a mutual understanding of one another. They tended to rationalize their husbands' behaviour as helping acts that were geared towards achieving common goals.

On the other hand, the athlete within the familial relationship reported experiencing negative feelings about her father/coach at the age of about 14. At that age the athlete explained that she needed to feel more responsible for her actions, to be more independent and feel capable of undertaking tasks that she wished to complete without overt support and guidance. Ryan and Deci (2000) have shown that for optimal functioning athletes should experience competence, autonomy and relatedness in their social lives. Competence and relatedness were evidently satisfied by the performance accomplishments achieved in the familial relationship examined and close attachments experienced, although autonomy was thwarted. Jowett and Meek (2000b) found that one athlete did not feel independent, self-directed, intrinsically motivated, committed and subsequently satisfied with the athletic relationship established with her father/coach. In hindsight he admitted that, 'I was accused of doing too much for [athlete]', suggesting that the athlete's initiative and independence were not enforced by her father/coach. By contrast, an athlete within a typical athletic relationship reported feelings of being distant and detached from her coach and referred to an emotional void that prevented her from relating to him (Jowett and Meek 1999). Within this dyad, autonomy and competence met, although relatedness appeared to be an underlying cause of the athlete's dissatisfaction.

Several studies have shown that coaches' ability to adapt their coaching to the needs of the athlete by creating an environment that fulfils those needs, is a contributing factor in the actualization of talent (Csikszentimihalyi, Rathunde and Whalen 1993; Kalinowski 1985). Moreover, Ryan and Deci (2000) have recently suggested that athletes' needs for autonomy, relatedness and competence are likely to vary according to their stage of emotional development. Thus, it is important to pay attention to what athletes need as they pursue their sport and to be clear about how they are able to meet those needs when they interact and relate with their coaches.

MORE EFFECTIVE INTERACTIONS

Open channels of communication enabled the majority of the coach–athlete relationships examined to establish co-oriented views as shared knowledge and understanding. All athletes and coaches participating in the interviews referred to the importance of this kind of compatibility. Specifically, interviews with the majority of coaches and athletes indicated that as knowledge of the other increases, so does the capacity to understand the other's perspective. Subsequently, understanding each other's position leads to effective interactions in both training and competition. This view is consistent with the literature, with several authors (Martens 1987; Yukelson 1992; Anshel 1994; Yambor 1995) suggesting that coaches are in a strong position to support their athletes' development if they know them well. It was proposed that the perceived co-orientation of dyads, or dyad members, reveals whether specific needs are expressed and fulfilled in the relationship (Jowett and Cockerill 2001; Jowett and Meek 2000b).

As expected, the marital and the familial coach–athlete relationship, owing to their closer relationships as husband and wife, or as father and daughter, revealed a higher rate of exchange of information than a typical coach–athlete relationship. For example, the case of typical coach–athlete dyads in swimming referred to open channels of communication, information exchange, self-disclosure and active involvement in the goal-setting process, although the intensity and frequency of these interactions were limited. It was speculated that the intensity and frequency of communication were less pronounced owing to the typical nature of the coach–athlete relationship and the non-elite standard of the coaches and athletes, namely county (Jowett and Pearce 2001). At this level, coaches are expected to work with a larger number of athletes, making it difficult to maintain a high level of communication with each. Interestingly, an absence of communication was also evident in a typical coach–athlete relationship operating at the elite level in track and field (Jowett and Meek 1999). In this instance, lack of communication and, in turn, Co-orientation were due to communication barriers induced by the dyad, such as constant disagreement, blaming and negative authority, such as criticism and ignorance. The dyad not only disagreed with and misunderstood each other on a regular basis, but both individuals failed to recognize their misunderstandings. Gould *et al.* (1999) have shown that ineffective coach–athlete communication, for example disagreements and misunderstandings, are associated with incompatible roles and responsibilities. Misunderstandings of this kind were particularly evident in the typical coach–athlete dyad referred to here.

According to interpersonal theory, Complementarity occurs on the basis of (a) reciprocity of the control dimension (dominance pulls submission and vice versa), and (b) correspondence of the affiliation dimension (friendliness pulls friendliness and hostility pulls hostility) (Kiesler 1983). Our case studies (Jowett and Cockerill 2001; Jowett and Meek 2000a; 2000b) have shown that all coaches and athletes described their behaviours as being complementary, whereby the coach leads and the athlete executes, indicating a reciprocal pattern of behavioural interaction. These data showed that the coaches' and athletes' perceptions of their roles and tasks on the track, in the pool and on the playing field represented the perceived demands of their sports. Therefore, it was suggested that Complementarity, in terms of reciprocity, is inherent within coaches' and athletes' required athletic roles and tasks (Jowett 2001a). Furthermore, the majority of the coaches and athletes stated in their interviews that they viewed each other as friends, highlighting the correspondence dimension. Specifically, athletes viewed their coach as someone who was always ready to provide the support and training they needed. In terms of correspondence, it was proposed that Complementarity is dependent upon personal characteristics, such as anxiety, esteem, confidence and motivation (Jowett 2001a). That is to say, within a coach–athlete relationship how friendly one is depends upon individual differences, whereas how controlling one is depends upon the roles and tasks performed by both participants.

An absence of Complementarity in terms of correspondence was evident in two single cases, namely the typical, which operated at elite-level sport (Jowett and Meek 1999), and, to a lesser extent, the familial relationship (Jowett and Meek 2000b). An absence of Complementarity in the athletic relationship was associated with antagonism and conflict and low Co-orientation. More specifically, the inability or absence of desire among the dyads to update their common ground regularly through the exchange of information by clarifying goals, motives and needs, caused confusion about rules, roles and responsibilities. Good (1991) has proposed that 'increasing the amount of communication increases the amount of cooperation' and 'for successful communication, a high level of mutual knowledge is required. Anything that contributes to this will enhance our belief that we are clear about what the other intends' (p. 233). Thus, if the dyads' channels of *effective* communication had been open, then acceptance and understanding might have been established, leading to a complementary set of transactions in training and competition.

The second research phase followed the descriptive data generated from the qualitative case studies and sought to construct a valid and reliable self-report instrument to examine coach–athlete relationships (Jowett and Ntoumanis 2001). The validation of the Coach–Athlete Relationship Questionnaire (CART-Q) involved a principal component analysis (PCA) and a confirmatory factor analysis (CFA). The PCA revealed that the constructs of Closeness and Complementarity were easily discernible components in the solution, whereas the tenability of Co-orientation was not sustained and a different construct emerged. A careful examination of the new component, its constellation of items and the literature, indicated that this component reflected the interpersonal construct of Commitment (Rosenblatt 1977). In operational terms, Commitment may be described as the intention of athletes and coaches to remain in their dyadic athletic relationship. Consequently, Commitment represents the cognitive relational aspect, Closeness represents the emotional aspect and Complementarity represents the behavioural-relational aspect of the coach–athlete relationship. The three-dimensional nature of the coach–athlete relationship was subsequently substantiated in the CFA.

The elimination of Co-orientation was not anticipated and was of particular interest because the case studies supported its existence as a salient component in the coach–athlete relationship. As stated previously, Co-orientation is defined as open channels of communication from which a common ground is developed between coaches and athletes. (Jowett and Ntoumanis 2001) has suggested that the failure to obtain the construct of Co-orientation during the validation of the CART-Q was attributable to the method used to measure congruence and mutuality in the coach–athlete relationship.

Subsequently, Laing *et al.*'s (1966) interpersonal method was used to examine dyadic relationships, to revive the construct of Co-orientation and to examine its role within the relationship (Jowett 2001c). Laing *et al.* (1966) have claimed that the interpersonal perception method enables the evaluation of aspects of the construct of Co-orientation. For example, Table 2.1 shows the relationship between Co-orientation and Laing *et al.*'s (1966) interpersonal method.

Table 2.1 Comparisons of models of Co-orientation and interpersonal perception

Point of comparison	Co-orientation construct	Interpersonal perception method
1. C's direct – A's direct perspective	Agreement	Agreement/Disagreement
2. C's direct perspective – A's meta-perspective A's direct perspective – C's meta-perspective	Accuracy	Understanding/ Misunderstanding

Key: C = Coach; A = Athlete

Source: Laing et al. (1966) *Interpersonal Perception: A Theory and a Method of Research*. Copyright © 1966 Springer Publishing Company, Inc., New York 10012. Used by permission.

As shown in Table 2.1, each dyad member has two perspectives for evaluation, a direct perspective and a meta-perspective. The direct perspective reflects a coach's/athlete's view of object X (e.g. I trust my athlete/coach), and the meta-perspective reflects a coach's/athlete's view of the other's view of object X (e.g. My athlete/coach trusts me). Laing *et al.* (1966) argued that comparisons between direct perspectives and meta-perspectives are helpful in understanding dyads. For example, a comparison between a coach's direct perspective and an athlete's direct perspective on the same issue yields either agreement or disagreement. Moreover, a comparison between a coach's meta-perspective and an athlete's direct perspective of the same issue yields either understanding or misunderstanding. Figure 2.1 illustrates possible comparisons between the differing perspectives of coach and athlete.

In accordance with Laing *et al.*'s (1966) method, the CART-Q measures athletes' and coaches' Closeness, Commitment and Complementarity from a direct perspective. In other words, CART-Q can be used to measure coaches' and athletes' views for the other member in the relationship (e.g. I feel responsive to my athlete's/coach's efforts). As Figure 2.1 illustrates, a comparison between coaches' and athletes' direct perspectives provides an indication of the dyad's level of Co-orientation in terms of agreement on the issues of Closeness, Commitment and Complementarity. The CART-Q was subsequently modified to reflect coaches' and athletes' meta-perspectives (e.g. My coach/athlete is responsive to my efforts), where its construct validity and reliability were found to be sound (Jowett 2001c). Thus, athletes' and coaches' levels of Co-orientation, in terms of understanding within the issues of Closeness, Commitment and Complementarity, may

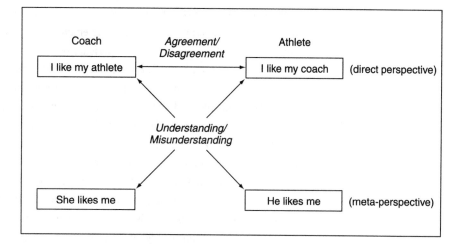

FIGURE 2.1   *Degrees of agreement and understanding with the interpersonal perception method*

be examined by asking dyad members to complete both versions of the CART-Q (CART-Q/D: direct perspective and CART-Q/M: meta-perspective).

This application of the interpersonal method proposed by Laing *et al.* (1966) enables the measurement of Co-orientation in the coach–athlete relationship relative to Closeness, Commitment and Complementarity. It is proposed that Co-orientation will moderate the impact of Closeness, Commitment and Complementarity on important variables such as social support, satisfaction, motivation and group cohesion. The significance of Co-orientation is illustrated in an example of a coach and an athlete who may disagree about their levels of Closeness: for example, the coach feels very close to the athlete, whereas the athlete feels only fairly close to the coach. Disagreement on the issue of Closeness may be a reflection of how social support is provided by the coach and received by the athlete. The coach supplies social support, both emotional and informational, to the athlete, but the latter does not openly accept the offer owing to perceived low levels of Closeness or negative feelings. Incompatibility may subsequently impact on both the coach's and the athlete's well-being, motivation and performance accomplishments.

Identifying and eliminating incompatibility in the coach–athlete relationship

Potential for conflict exists in every relationship. Conflict is defined as the experience of some incompatibility between people (Deutsch 1973). However, it is interesting to speculate about how conflict is manifested within a coach–athlete relationship. The way that the relationship has been conceptualized and operationalized indicates that characteristics such as Closeness, Commitment and Complementarity affect how conflicts are created, construed and managed. Thus, when Closeness is underlined by negative feelings of dislike, distrust and disrespect, when Commitment is characterized by distancing and isolation, and when Complementarity is subjected to antagonism and contradictions, then conflict, or the experience of incompatibility, is eminently possible between coach and athlete. The Laing *et al.* (1966) method is useful for identifying incompatibility and for locating its position in a relationship, and once the information is available, effective and appropriate relationship-enhancement programmes can be developed to combat areas of incompatibility in a relationship.

Laing *et al.*'s (1966) method was applied to illustrate Mary and Andy's situation. They completed both versions of the coach–athlete Relationship Questionnaire to assess direct and meta-perspectives relative to Closeness (feelings), Commitment (thoughts) and Complementarity (behaviours). A comparison of Mary and Andy's direct perspectives (how the coach/athlete feels, thinks and behaves in relation to the athlete/coach), revealed that Mary reported higher levels of Commitment and Complementarity in relation to Andy. Figure 2.2, known as a Dyad Map, illustrates an area of agreement between Mary and Andy located in the dimension of Closeness. By contrast, Commitment and Complementarity are areas of disagreement and possible incompatibility.

Mary's direct perspective (how the coach feels, thinks and behaves in relation to the athlete) was compared with Andy's meta-perspective (how the athlete perceives the coach's feelings, thoughts and behaviours in relation to the athlete). The comparison indicates levels of understanding and/or misunderstanding from the athlete's point of view. As Figure 2.3 shows, Andy's perceptions matched his mother's/coach's views for Closeness and Commitment. The discrepancy for Complementarity indicates that Mary's behaviour during training does not correspond with Andy's perception of how she interacts with him during training. In effect, Andy perceives that his mother/coach is close and committed, but not as complementary as Mary believes she is.

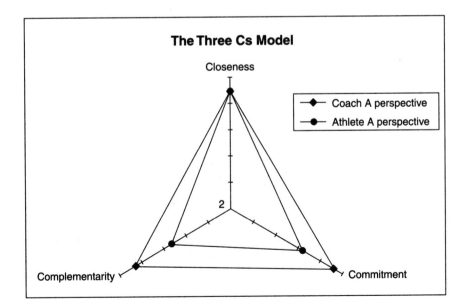

FIGURE 2.2 *Coach's view of athlete and athlete's view of coach*

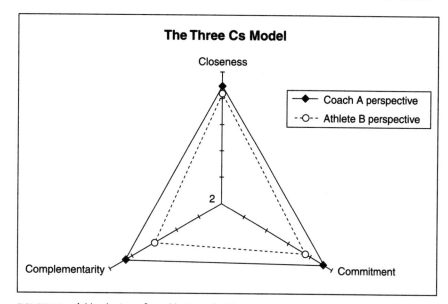

FIGURE 2.3   *Athlete's view of coach's view of athlete and coach's view of athlete*

Andy's direct perspective (how the athlete feels, thinks and behaves in relation to his coach) was compared with Mary's meta-perspective (how the coach perceives the athlete's feelings, thoughts and behaviour in relation to the coach). The comparison illustrates levels of understanding and/or misunderstanding from the coach's perspective. Figure 2.4 shows that Mary's perceptions match those of her son/athlete for all three components. This observation illustrates an accurate understanding of the dyadic relationship by the coach. More specifically, Mary recognizes that Andy is close to her as his coach, but he lacks both Commitment in their athletic relationship and Complementary acts of interaction for training and instruction owing to the low incidence of intensity reported.

It may be concluded that Mary and Andy, although emotionally close as coach and athlete, have difficulties in their athletic relationship in respect of Commitment and Complementarity. The application of developmental theories (Selman 1980), and cognitive or social exchange theories (Kelley 1979; Kelley and Thibaut 1978) are relevant to understanding the nature of conflict and subsequently eradicating it. While a lengthy discussion of such theoretical frameworks is beyond the scope of this chapter, it is appropriate to attempt an explanation of Mary's and Andy's interpersonal conflict and to suggest a possible solution for alleviating their incompatibility. In terms of Rawlings' (1994) dialectical approach, people strive to maintain homeostasis between simultaneous pulls in opposite directions, such as the freedom to be dependent or independent. According to Rawlings, failure to maintain a balance between the poles will produce conflict. Hence, if Mary and Andy wish to improve the quality of their athletic relationship, they need to work at maintaining balance.

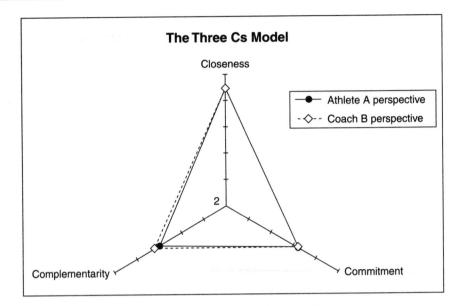

FIGURE 2.4   *Coach's view of athlete's view of coach and athlete's view of coach*

Balance in their relationship can be maintained through effective communication, which has been viewed in both popular and academic literature as a social skill (Kidd 1975; Parks 1981), with skill used as a metaphor for communication when people refer to effective communication as a set of techniques to be acquired. Specific techniques for communicating competently and effectively have been discussed extensively in the sport psychology literature (Martens 1987; Yukelson 1992; Lee 1993; Anshel 1994; Yambor 1995). In terms of interpersonal conflict, communication can be used to resolve potential incompatibilities and to maintain a harmonious coach–athlete relationship. When a source of conflict is identified and mutually understood, communication is likely to play a straightforward, positive role in conflict resolution. For example, Andy acknowledges the existence of low levels of Commitment and Complementarity and, in turn, Mary perceives Andy similarly. Thus, if both were to discuss their needs, goals and motives in a clear, consistent, direct, supportive, focused and reciprocal way, an improvement in Complementary transactions in training and increased Commitment could occur. A likely outcome is that both coach and athlete will be satisfied and the quality of their athletic relationship will be preserved.

Finally, it is appropriate to consider the relevance of Performance Profiling (PP), based upon Kelly's (1955) Personal Construct Theory. It has been used as a technique to ensure that coach and athlete are 'on the same page' (Dale and Wrisberg 1996). PP seeks to encourage coach and athlete to air their views, thoughts and opinions about a particular problem. In doing so, both coach and athlete can gain an insight into a problem from which a joint plan of action is subsequently drawn up to eliminate obvious weaknesses. The technique is recommended for the resolution of conflict between coach and athlete, especially when the conflict is difficult to specify. Often, interpersonal conflicts do not have a clear structure and are difficult to isolate and define. When coach and athlete do not share similar perceptions of a critical issue, as is the case with Mary and Andy, PP may assist in identifying, clarifying and defining the problem areas.

Concluding remark

To date, little has been written in applied sport psychology about the ways in which a compatible and successful coach–athlete relationship may be developed in order to identify and eliminate the problems that tend to occur within an ineffective partnership. This chapter has suggested a way forward by incorporating empirical research within hypothetical, but typical, cases in order to examine the important relationship that exists between athlete and coach. It is believed that the quantitative procedure described in this chapter provides a means whereby that relationship can be first investigated and then strengthened.

References

Anshel, M. H. (1994) *Sport Psychology From Theory to Practice* (second edn), pp. 203–240, Arizona: Gorsuch Scarisbruck.

Berscheid, E., Snyder, M. and Omoto, A. M. (1989) 'Issues in studying close relationships: Conceptualising and measuring closeness'. In C. Hendric (ed.), *Close Relationships*, pp. 63–91, Newbury Park, CA: Sage.

Bloom, G. A., Durand-Bush, N., Schinke, R. J. and Salmela, J. H. (1998) 'The importance of mentoring in the development of coaches and athletes', *International Journal of Sport Psychology* 29:267–281.

Carron, A. V. and Bennett, B. B. (1977) 'Compatibility in the coach–athlete dyad', *The Research Quarterly* 48:670–679.

Chelladurai, P. (1993) 'Leadership'. In R. N. Singer, M. Murphey, and L. K. Tennant (eds.), *Handbook on Research on Sport Psychology*, pp. 647–671, New York: Macmillan.

Coe, S. (1996) *The Olympians: A Century of Gold*, London: Pavilion.

Csikszentmihalyi, M., Rathunde, K. and Whalen, S. (1993) *Talented Teenagers: The Roots of Success and Failure*, New York: Cambridge Press.

Dale, G. A. and Wrisberg, C. A. (1996) 'The use of a performance profiling technique in a team setting: Getting the athletes and coach on the "same page"', *The Sport Psychologist* 10:261–277.

Deutsch, M. (1973) *The Resolution of Conflict: Constructive and Destructive Processes*, New Haven, CT: Yale University Press.

Douge, B. and Hastie, P. (1993) 'Coach effectiveness', *Sports Science Review* 2:14–29.

Good, D. A. (1991) 'Cooperation in a microcosm: Lessons from laboratory games'. In R. A. Hinde and N. Groebel (eds.), *Co-operation and Pro-social Behavior*, pp. 224–237, New York: Cambridge University Press.

Gould, D., Guinan, D., Greenleaf, C., Medbery, R. and Peterson, K. (1999) 'Factors affecting Olympic performance: Perceptions of athletes and coaches from more and less successful teams', *The Sport Psychologist* 13:371–394.

Hellstedt, J. C. (1990) 'Early adolescent perceptions of parental pressure in the sport environment', *Journal of Sport Behaviour* 13:135–144.

Hellstedt, J. C. (1995) 'Invisible players: A family systems model'. In S. M. Murphy (ed.), *Sport Psychology Interventions*, pp. 117–146, Champaign, IL: Human Kinetics.

Hinde, R. A. (1997) *Relationships: A dialectical perspective*, Hove, UK: Psychology Press.

Jowett, S. (2001a) *The coach–athlete relationship examined: Conceptual and methodological frameworks*. Submitted for publication

Jowett, S. (2001b) *The psychology of interpersonal relationships in sport: The coach–athlete relationship*. Unpublished doctoral dissertation, University of Exeter: United Kingdom.

Jowett, S. (2001c) *Relationships between satisfaction and different perspectives of the coach–athlete relationship*. Poster presentation: Annual Conference of the British Association of Sport and Exercise Sciences, Newport, South Wales, September.

Jowett, S. and Cockerill, I. M. (2001) 'The coach–athlete relationship: An Olympic perspective'. In A. Papaioannu, Y. Theodorakis and M. Goudas (eds.), *Proceedings of the Tenth World Congress of Sport Psychology*, Vol. 3, pp. 235–237, Skiathos, Greece.

Jowett, S. and Meek, G. A. (1999) 'A coach–athlete dyad in crisis', *Journal of Sports Sciences* 18:51–52.

Jowett, S. and Meek, G. A. (2000a) 'Coach–athlete relationship in married couples: An exploratory content analysis', *The Sport Psychologist* 14:157–175.

Jowett, S. and Meek, G. A. (2000b) *Outgrowing the family coach–athlete relationship: A case study*. Paper presented at the First International Conference of Sport Psychology, New Millennium, Halmstad, Sweden.

Jowett, S. and Ntoumanis, N. (2001) *The Coach–Athlete Questionnaire (CART-Q): Development and initial validation*. Submitted for publication.

Jowett, S. and Pearce, J. (2001, May/June) 'An exploration into the nature of the coach–athlete relationship in swimming'. In A. Papaioannou, Y. Theodorakis and M. Goudas (eds.), *Proceedings of the Tenth World Congress of Sport Psychology*, Vol. 3, pp. 227–229, Skiathos, Greece.

Kalinowski, A. G. (1985) 'The development of Olympic swimmers'. In B. S. Bloom (ed.), *Developing Talent in Young People*, pp. 139–192, New York: Ballantine.

Kelley, H. H. (1979). *Personal Relationships*, Hillsdale, NJ: Lawrence Erlbaum.

Kelley, H. H., Berscheid, E., Christensen, A., Harvey, H. H., Huston, T. L., Levinger, G., McClintock, E., Peplau, L. A. and Peterson, D. R. (1983) *Close Relationships*, New York: Freeman.

Kelley, H. H. and Thibaut, J. W. (1978) *Interpersonal Relations*, New York: Wiley.

Kelly, G. A. (1955) *The Psychology of Personal Constructs: Vols. I and II*, New York: Norton.

Kidd, V. (1975) 'Happily ever after and other relationship styles: Advice on interpersonal relations in popular magazines', 1951–1973, *Quarterly Journal of Speech* 61:31–39.

Kiesler, D. J. (1983) 'The 1982 interpersonal circle: A taxonomy for complementarity in human transactions', *Psychological Review* 90:185–214.

Kiesler, D. J. (1997) *Contemporary Interpersonal Theory Research and Personality, Psychopathology and Psychotherapy*, New York: Wiley.

Kuklinski, B. (1990) 'Sport leadership: An overview', *New Zealand Journal of Health, Physical Education and Recreation* 23:15–18.

Laing, R. D., Phillipson, H. and Lee, A. R. (1966) *Interpersonal Perception: A Theory and a Method of Research*, New York: Springer.

Lee, M. (1993) *Coaching Children in Sport: Principles and Practice*, London: E and F. N. Spon.

Lyle, J. (1999) 'Coaching philosophy and coaching behaviour'. In N. Cross and J. Lyle (eds.), *The Coaching Process: Principles and Practice for Sport*, pp. 25–46, Oxford: Butterworth-Heineman.

Martens, R. (1987) *Coaches Guide to Sport Psychology*, Champaign, IL: Human Kinetics.

McCready, G. (1984) 'The coach as a developer of human resources', *Sports* 3:1–6.

Newcomb, T. M. (1953) 'An approach to the study of communicative acts', *Psychological Review* 60:393–404.

Parks, M. R. (1981) 'Ideology in interpersonal communication: Off the couch and into the world'. In M. Burgoon (ed.), *Communication Yearbook*, Vol. 5, pp. 79–107, New Brunswick, NJ: Transaction Books.

Rawlings, W. K. (1994) 'Being there and growing apart: Sustaining friendships during adulthood'. In D. J. Canary and L. Stafford (eds.), *Communication and Relational Maintenance*, pp. 233–254, San Diego, LA: Academic Press.

Rosenblatt, P. C. (1977) 'Needed research on commitment in marriage'. In G. Levinger and H. L. Rausch (eds.), *Close Relationships: Perspectives on the Meaning of Intimacy*, Amhurst, MA: University of Massachusetts Press.

Ryan, J. (1996) *Little Girls in Pretty Boxes: The Making and Breaking of Elite Gymnasts and Figure Skaters*, London: The Women's Press.

Ryan, R. M. and Deci, E. L. (2000) 'Self-determination theory and the facilitation of intrinsic motivation, social development and well-being', *American Psychologist* 55:68–78.

Selman, R. L. (1980) *The Growth of Interpersonal Understanding*, New York: Academic Press.

Smoll, F. L. and Smith, R. E. (1989) 'Leadership behaviours in sport: A theoretical model and research paradigm', *Journal of Applied Social Psychology* 19:1522–1551.

Yambor, J. (1995) 'Effective communication'. In K. P. Henschen (ed.), *Sport Psychology: An Analysis of Athlete Behaviour*, pp. 383–391, Longmeadow, MA: Mouvement.

Yukelson, D. P. (1992) 'Communicating effectively'. In J. Williams (ed.), *Sport Psychology: Peak Performance to Personal Growth*, pp. 142–157, Palo Alto, CA: Mayfield.

chapter three

Mental toughness: the concept and its measurement

PETER CLOUGH, KEITH EARLE AND DAVID SEWELL

British striker Jane Sixsmith bowed out of the international game today – but not before blaming her country's miserable performance at the 27th Olympics on the players' lack of mental toughness. (Hull Daily Mail, October 2000.)

Being asked to solve a problem that is ill-conceived, ill-defined and ill-considered is the lifeblood of sport psychology. Coaches and athletes are more prone than most to using clichés, abbreviations, or shorthand words or phrases. The latter are often picked up from, and by, the media and an informal iterative process begins until a particular term becomes *de rigueur*. This chapter examines one media-hyped term, namely mental toughness, and it is explored in detail from definition to its objective measurement.

The aims of a consultation

When meeting a coach or player for the first time, the principal focus is directed towards a clear definition of the issues for consideration, and one way to facilitate the process is to utilize what is referred to as the TOODIR approach. The procedure has been adapted by the sport psychology research team at Hull University from a technique practised widely in management consulting and it involves six main stages:

1. **T**une in

2. **O**btain information

3. **O**perationalize the problem

4. **D**ecide upon a course of action

5. **I**ntervene

6. **R**eview.

Tuning into the 'psychological universe' of players or coaches is arguably the key skill for the practitioner sport psychologist who wishes to tackle a specific issue, rather than utilize a generic and standard intervention procedure. It is important to understand how an athlete sees the world and to demonstrate that their perspective is fully acknowledged. After gaining an understanding of the psychological context, the sport psychologist can begin to gather specific information about the presenting issue. The tuning-in stage places information obtained in a broader context, because it is often not what an athlete says that is important, but how it is said and even what is not said. At the end of an initial but extensive data trawling, the sport psychologist can begin to operationalize the problem by converting it into specific issues to address.

Defining mental toughness

It was during the tuning-in and operationalizing phases of many initial contacts that we identified a recurring and challenging phenomenon. It was apparent that more than 75 per cent of our initial contacts with players and coaches had, at least in part, involved a request for procedures to develop mental toughness. The message is sometimes implicit, but it is more frequently an explicit request. Following the TOODIR mode, a key question to ask a coach or athlete is 'what do *you* mean by mental toughness?'. More often than not the question produces either no response or, at best, a hesitant rearrangement of the words; for example '… you know, being tough mentally'. Over the past few years this type of conversation has become more frequent, perhaps reflecting the media's current preoccupation with mental toughness. The expression is used frequently in interviews, newspaper reports and during match commentaries.

The issue, therefore, is that if we don't fully understand what coaches and players mean by this term, and they find it difficult to articulate their understanding, it is almost impossible to focus accurately upon a problem, which can lead to misunderstandings and frustrations. Thus, it was decided that as a sport psychology team we should try to operationalize the concept of mental toughness.

The definition process involves two separate, but related strands: (a) obtaining the views of practitioners, players and coaches and (b) reviewing academic research findings. Both aspects are closely intertwined, but there remains little crossover and interaction between the two. Many applied sport psychology users appear to have relatively little interest in the research context and pedigree of tools and techniques, preferring to take a far more pragmatic approach. Conversely, their ideas and experience may often fail to enter into and impact upon the academic world. A separation of the two constituents is unfortunate and has probably limited the development of sport psychology. For example, Kimeicik and Blissmer (1998) stated 'the worlds of the researcher and the practitioner are quite different, which makes it very difficult for theory to influence practice or vice versa'. They argued that collaboration and partnership between researchers and practitioners would advance the field by allowing an interaction of ideas, experience and feedback. At Hull University we have created an applied research team that operates within an academic environment, for example seeking to publish in established scientific journals, while being equally at home within the sports stadium. We felt that we were in a strong position to tackle one of the significant questions that still exists in applied sport psychology, namely 'What is mental toughness?'

WHAT DOES MENTAL TOUGHNESS MEAN TO THE ATHLETE AND COACH?

The starting point in our attempt to define the concept was to speak with athletes and to carry out a search of articles and media interviews for comments about mental toughness, some of which are reported here.

- 'The ability to carry on when the world seems to have turned against you, and keep your troubles in proper perspective.' (FA Nationwide League soccer player)

- 'Capacity to face all pressures and deal with them internally, delivering the same level of performance outwardly, regardless of what pressures one feels internally.' (Professional tennis player)

- 'The ability to maintain effective control over the environment by displaying commitment to deliver, confidence in their ability, resilience to negative pressures, ability to see change as a positive opportunity and a recognition of their own limits to handle stress.' (Professional rugby league coach)

- 'Resilient – not easily balked in the face of opposition or adversity.' (Northern Ford Premiership rugby league player)

At an applied level, mental toughness has been described (Brennan 1998, p.3) as:

> the ability to handle situations. It's somebody who doesn't choke, doesn't go into shock, and who can stand up for what he believes. It's what someone has who handles pressures, distractions and people trying to break their concentration. It involves focusing, discipline, self-confidence, patience, persistence, accepting responsibility without whining or excuses, visualizing, tolerating pain and a positive approach.

Accordingly, mental toughness appears to consist of both commonly recognized sport psychology interventions, such as focusing and visualization, alongside specific personality characteristics that include persistence, resilience, confidence and discipline. Loehr (1994) has defined mental toughness as 'the ability to consistently perform toward the upper range of your talent and skill regardless of competitive circumstances'. He expanded his definition by identifying four key emotional markers in respect of toughness:

- *Flexibility:* the ability to remain balanced and avoid becoming defensive when put under unexpected pressure.

- *Responsiveness:* the ability to remain focused under pressure.

- *Strength:* having a powerful fighting spirit.

- *Resiliency:* the ability to bounce back from disappointments, mistakes and missed opportunities.

MENTAL TOUGHNESS AND THE RESEARCHER

A key concept rooted firmly within the health psychology literature in the stress–illness relationship is that of hardiness (Kobasa 1979). There has been a plethora of research investigating the concept and the 'hardy personality' (e.g. Funk 1992). Simply stated, hardiness is an individual trait that acts as a buffer between life stressors and an individual's reaction to them. Kobasa (1979) considered that it is an important determinant of the way that individuals perceive situations and how they decide upon an appropriate set of actions. Decisions can best be made by transforming an event so that it can be perceived as less threatening and helping to avoid illness-provoking biological states such as adaptational exhaustion (Selye 1956) or depressed immunological surveillance (Schwarz 1975; Kobasa, Maddi and Kahn 1982).

Kobasa proposed control, commitment and challenge as three key components of hardiness and they are summarized as follows:

- *Control* is expressed as 'a tendency to feel and act as if one is influential (rather than helpful) in the face of the varied contingencies of life' (Averill 1973; Seligman 1975; Kobasa, Maddi and Kahn 1982). Control provides the cognitive ability to incorporate stressful events into 'an ongoing life plan' (Kobasa 1979) using knowledge, skill and choice, thus influencing how situations are appraised. It allows an individual to choose the most appropriate course of action when faced with a potentially stressful situation and this, in turn, is likely to transform a threatening situation into something more acceptable for that individual.

- *Commitment* is a 'tendency to involve oneself in, rather than experience alienation from whatever one is doing, or encounters' (Maddi, Hoover and Kobasa 1982). It is relevant to cognitive appraisal as it helps to identify and give meaning to new situations in the individual's environment. At the action level it makes the person proactive rather than passively accepting of the situation.

- *Challenge* is expressed as 'the belief that change, rather than stability, is normal in life and that the anticipation of changes are interesting incentives to growth rather than threats to security' (Kobasa, Maddi and Kahn 1982). Seeing potentially stressful occurrences as being challenging has the effect of mitigating the stressfulness of the situation. In relation to coping strategies, the challenge disposition empowers the individual to develop and to grow instead of protecting what the individual already has.

Research into hardiness has shown that possessing this characteristic may be more effective at buffering stressors than either social support or physical exercise (Kobasa *et al.* 1985). Studies by Maddi (1991) and Rhodewalt and Agostsdottir (1984) have found that hardy individuals are more likely to cope with stressors by transforming them mentally into something less threatening. Furthermore, physiological responses have been related to a hardy personality; for example, Contrada *et al.* (1991) found associations with heart rate and blood pressure patterns in both the resting state and in response to stressful situations. However, little research has been carried out into the relationship between hardiness and performance effectiveness in sport. One of the few studies to investigate this relationship was that of Maddi and Hess (1992), who investigated basketball performance using eight specific performance indicators examined over a season. Although it is known that a high positive correlation does not imply a causal relationship, the results showed significant correlations between seven out of the eight performance indicators and a total hardiness score.

Dienstbier (1989; 1991), who investigated the relationship between arousal and physiological toughness, provided an interesting perspective on mental toughness. He examined individual confrontations with stress that evoked both central and peripheral physiological arousal. A stressor was described as a situation in which an individual appraises it as threatening or harmful. This organism–situation interaction can lead to either appraisals of challenge (positive emotion) or to appraisals of stress (negative emotion). Dienstbier summarized the research by concluding that in non-human experiments, subjects were able to be 'toughened up' by exposure to intermittent stressors (Weiss *et al.* 1975). This has obvious parallels with stress inoculation training, which has been shown to be effective with some athletes. In addition, research with humans investigating the arousal–performance relationship has consistently shown positive correlations between better performance and hormonal levels. For example, Johansson, Frankenhaeuser and Magnusson (1973) found that a sample of sixth-grade Swedish boys and girls, whose adrenaline levels increased between watching a movie and taking a maths test, outperformed those with hormonal decreases. The increases also showed stronger resistance to errors, particularly in later phases of the test.

Similar studies were undertaken by Rauste von-Wright *et al.* (1981) who found that adrenaline increased in schoolchildren and correlated with examination performance. Further research with Scandinavian adults found that better performance correlated with adrenaline increases (Johansson and Frankenhaeuser 1973; Ellertsen, Johnson and Ursin 1978). Johansson *et al.* (1973) reported that children who showed increased levels of adrenaline were more satisfied with school life and, according to their teachers, had better social adjustment and emotional stability. Dienstbier (1989) proposed that there are four toughening manipulations that influence physiological mediators, which, in turn, are reflected in performance and temperament characteristics. These are:

- *Early experience:* the ways in which children have faced extreme stress in early life and its relationship to differences in their resilience (Garmezy 1983).

- *Passive toughening:* Weiss *et al.* (1975) highlighted the positive impact of repeated exposure to cold water and electric shocks and an increase in stress tolerance.

- *Active toughening:* by exercising aerobically, self-regulated toughening can occur.

- *Ageing:* all effects for ageing are opposite to those for the three other manipulations.

Dienstbier's (1989) model has important implications for the nature of the techniques that are currently involved with long-term coping. Techniques that include relaxation-type interventions (biofeedback, autogenic training, meditation, tranquillizers) that provide short-term relief, could possibly be removing the very situations that lead to toughening. Dienstbier (1991) further proposed that toughening could be elicited by exposure to physical activity, suggesting that psychological benefits may accrue from successful participation in exercise programmes through feelings of mastery and improved body image. He stated (p. 87):

> *Life in a mechanized world can easily result in insufficient physical demands, so that natural toughening is not fostered, and the neuroendocrine systems associated with arousal are not maintained near the optimum point of their genetic ranges. Strains are therefore likely for related systems. Obvious manifestations of such strain include weight control problems, poor muscle tone, and poor endurance in physical coping. Less obvious manifestations suggested by this model include poor psychological coping endurance (stress tolerance), susceptibility to anxiety and depression, attention and learning deficits, susceptibility to cardiovascular diseases, and reduced immune capacity.*

Mental toughness in practice

At this stage it is appropriate to locate the mental toughness concept within a practical context. Theoretical models within health psychology offer the practitioner insight into the constituents of mental toughness, especially the work associated with psychological hardiness. However, the weakness of those models is that they fail to capture the unique nature of the physical and mental demands of competitive sport. In contrast, ideas generated by solely practical sport psychologists may identify sport-specific elements, but lack theoretical rigour. Accordingly, it was decided that if a model of mental toughness is to be useful it must:

- Have its roots in established and robust psychological theory, rather than simply be a reflection of current practice.

- Have clear links with psychological interventions used by practitioners.

- Relate to the 'common sense', but ecologically valid, views of coaches and athletes.

Such a model must, therefore, be a combination of psychological theory and applied sport psychology. The model developed in this chapter pays a healthy respect in theoretical terms to the 'hardiness' approach utilized within health psychology. However, based on the more applied aspects of sport psychology, both anecdotal and relating to the interventions used in the field, it was decided that confidence is also an important factor relating to sport performance. This factor has not been considered as a distinct element in previous models of hardiness.

Further evidence supporting the ecological validity of the model came from the players themselves. The following were identified as important issues encountered by a Superleague (rugby league) side:

- Control: reaction to mistakes by themselves.

- Control: reaction to fluctuations in performance.

- Control: coping with biased crowds.

- Control: handling indifferent refereeing decisions.

- Control: reaction to being 'yellow-carded'.

- Commitment: attitude towards training.

- Commitment: reaction to heavy defeat.

- Challenge: response to injuries.

- Challenge: 'bad press', being dismissed by the media.

- Confidence: being on the bench.

- Confidence: disagreements with the coach.

At this stage, a preliminary model of mental toughness is proposed. It consists of a combination of four components – namely control, commitment, challenge and confidence – and is referred to as the 4Cs model of mental toughness. By integrating evidence from research, athletes, coaches and sport psychologists, we were able to produce a new and comprehensive definition of mental toughness:

> *Mentally tough individuals tend to be sociable and outgoing; as they are able to remain calm and relaxed, they are competitive in many situations and have lower anxiety levels than others. With a high sense of self-belief and an unshakeable faith that they control their own destiny, these individuals can remain relatively unaffected by competition or adversity.*

The development of a measure of mental toughness

At this juncture it is pertinent to mention that the starting point of this work was to consider a series of requests from coaches for toughening players. Once we had developed a definition of mental toughness that successfully incorporated relevant aspects from both a practical and a theoretical perspective, the next stage was to develop a measure of the concept. Being able to describe mental toughness is of little practical value to a coach or to athletes as their requirements will always emphasize its practical application. At this juncture it is also helpful to refer to Vealey and Garner-Holman (1998), who identified four main objectives of psychological measurement in sport. The first role of measurement is to identify potential problems, or issues. Secondly, the information can be used to increase athletes' self-awareness, thereby allowing them to make better decisions. Thirdly, psychological measurement can then be used to provide a way of predicting sporting performance. Finally, measurement provides a way of evaluating the impact of any interventions by providing pre- and post-measures.

DEVELOPING THE QUESTIONNAIRE

At this stage, the scale development process was ready to commence. The process incorporates the three discrete areas: research literature, opinions of athletes/coaches and opinions of sport psychology practitioners. Items were written to measure each of the four components (challenge, commitment, confidence and control) and they were modified and/or removed after extensive trials with athletes to ascertain item clarity, conciseness and intelligibility. A 48-item mental toughness questionnaire (MT48) was produced that provided an overall score for mental toughness and scores on the four sub-scales. Alongside the MT48, the MT18 (18-item questionnaire) was developed (see the appendix to this chapter for the questionnaire and scoring key) to make it more accessible and usable for the end-user (sports people). The two instruments have a correlation of $r=0.87$, indicating a strong relationship. However, the MT18 only provides an overall score for mental toughness and not a profile of sub-scales, as with the MT48.

The MT48 has been completed by more than 600 athletes from a range of sports and it has been found to be highly reliable, with a reliability coefficient of 0.9. Preliminary work has shown that athletes are willing to complete it (face validity), with an average completion time of less than 15 minutes.

The validity of the instrument has been assessed in a number of ways. For example, the content validity (does it measure all aspects of mental toughness?) has been determined by examining the literature, athletes and interventions. Construct validity (does it relate to other measures?) has also been established, as the MT48 relates to a number of other constructs, including optimism ($r = 0.48, p<0.01$), self-image ($r=0.42, p<0.05$), life satisfaction ($r = 0.56, p<0.01$), self-efficacy ($r = 0.68, p<0.01$) and stability ($r = 0.57, p<0.01$).

For practical purposes the most important type of evidence is that of criterion-related validity (does the questionnaire relate to performance?) and the following studies provide evidence that it does.

Study one

This study investigated the effects of physical workload on mental fatigue and performance on a cognitive task, which can easily equate to what athletes have to cope with during a game. Twenty-three participants were fitness tested (VO2 Max.) and then asked to cycle at various workload levels (30 per cent, 50 per cent and 70 per cent). A number of self-ratings (physical demands, mental demands and effort) were obtained during the experiment at three intervals (after 5, 15, and 25 minutes during a 30-minute exercise period). Figure 3.1 shows the data associated with the amount of perceived physical demand.

For analytical purposes participants were classified as either high or low mental toughness (based on a median split). As illustrated, there was no difference in perceived physical demands when physical workload was low (30 per cent of VO2 Max.). However, as the workload increased (to 50 per cent) there was a discernible trend for the less mentally tough to perceive higher physical demands. When the workload level reached 70 per cent there was a statistically significant difference in the perceived physical demands of the high and low mental toughness groups, illustrating the well-known cliché that 'as the going gets tough, the tough get going'.

Study two

In this study the effect of feedback on performance was investigated. The ability to 'bounce back' or show resilience in the face of adversity is a key feature of any elite-level sports performer. The study consisted of 79 participants who were given either positive or negative feedback after completing a number of motor tasks. They then carried out a cognitive task (planning exercise) as an objective measure of performance. Results

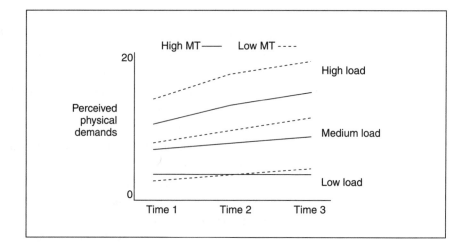

FIGURE 3.1   *Relationship between perceived physical demands and mental toughness*

showed that, overall, the more mentally tough subjects performed better on the planning exercise. However, more interestingly, there was a significant interaction ($F=4.36$; $df=1$, $p<0.05$) between mental toughness and feedback. The performance of the more mentally tough participants remained consistent with positive and negative feedback, whereas the less mentally tough scored less well after negative feedback (see Figure 3.2).

Finally, the MT48 has been investigated for fairness, and although it differentiates between elite, regional and recreational athletes, it does not discriminate across gender. While this is a positive sign, we hope to continue the analysis and also to look at the impact of race and disability.

In summary, the MT48 measure of mental toughness appears to be an accurate, fair and useful way of evaluating this key concept in sport psychology.

Conclusions

This chapter describes a process relating to one of the key skills that a sport psychology practitioner must be able to carry out, namely operationalizing a problem. The use of shorthand terminology, colloquialisms and jargon is common in the discipline and it is relatively easy to fall into the trap of trying to fix something that is not really broken. The desire of coaches and athletes to produce mentally tough players is likely to result in a wide range of psychological interventions, but unless an agreed definition of mental toughness is available, the efficacy of those interventions cannot be assessed.

The model described here is the result of the synthesis of practical sport psychology and research thinking and, as such, provides a useful starting point for discussions with players and coaches. It means that the practitioner does not need to start with what interventions are available, but can determine whether mental toughness is the problem, whether one or more aspects of mental toughness is the problem, or whether the concern is something unrelated to mental toughness. Too often a comprehensive psychological skills training package is used as a universal panacea for any perceived psychological problem. By operationalizing the terms we use more succinctly, we can target our involvement more effectively and ensure that (a) this is what the customer thinks they want and (b) it is appropriate to what they really need.

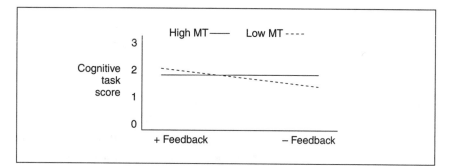

FIGURE 3.2 *Relationship between performance, feedback and mental toughness*

The development of the model allowed the design and development of an instrument to measure a seemingly elusive concept more objectively. Individual players can be assessed and the impact of an intervention analysed appropriately. In addition, we have emphasized the importance of using the right tests in the right way. The way that tests are sometimes used in sport psychology would probably be considered unacceptable in occupational, educational or clinical psychology.

Finally, the work also demonstrates the importance and potential benefits of better integration between researchers and practitioners. Sport psychology is still seen by some as a Cinderella subject, with part of the problem being the lack of acknowledgement of research by practitioners and of practice by researchers. If this schism continues, the development of sport psychology as a discipline in its own right will be limited.

References

Averill, J. R. (1973) Personal control over aversive stimuli and its relationship to stress. *Psychological Bulletin* 80:286–303.

Brennan, S. (1998) 'Mental toughness wins out'. In D. S. Looney, *Christian Science Monitor*, 90, Issue 173.

Contrada, R. J., Dimsdale, J., Levy, L. and Weiss, T. (1991) 'Effects of isoproterenol on T-wave amplitude and heart rate: A dose-response study', *Psychophysiology* 28:458–462.

Dienstbier, R. A. (1989) 'Arousal and physiological toughness: Implications for mental and physical health', *Psychological Review* 96:1, 84–100.

Dienstbier, R. A. (1991) 'Behavioral correlates of sympathoadrenal reactivity: The toughness model', *Medicine and Science in Sports and Exercise* 23, 7:846–852.

Ellertsen, B., Johnsen, T. B. and Ursin, H. (1978) 'Relationship between the hormonal responses to activation and coping'. In H. Ursin, E. Baade and S. Levine (eds.), *Psychobiology of Stress: A Study of Coping Men*, pp. 105–124, New York: Academic Press.

Funk, F. C. (1992) 'Hardiness: A review of theory and research', *Health Psychology* 11:335–345.

Garmezy, N. (1983) 'Stressors of childhood'. In N. Garmezy and M. Rutter (eds.), *Stress, Coping and Development in Children*, pp. 43–84, New York: McGraw-Hill.

Johansson, G. and Frankenhaeuser, J. (1973) 'Temporal factors in sympatho-adrenomedullary activity following acute behavioral activation', *Biological Psychology* 1:63–73.

Johansson, G., Frankenhaeuser, M. and Magnusson, D. (1973) 'Catecholamine output in school children as related to performance and adjustment', *Scandinavian Journal of Psychology* 14:20–28.

Kimeicik, P. and Blissmer, B. (1998) 'Applied exercise psychology: Measurement issues, In J. L. Duda (ed.), *Advances in Sport and Exercise Psychology Measurement*, pp. 447–460, Morgantown, WV: Fitness Information Technology.

Kobasa, S. C. (1979) 'Stressful life events, personality, and health: An inquiry into hardiness', *Journal of Personality and Social Psychology* 37:1–11.

Kobasa, S. C., Maddi, S. R., and Kahn, S. (1982) 'Hardiness and health: A prospective study', *Journal of Personality and Social Psychology* 42:168–177.

Kobasa, S. C., Maddi, S. R., Puccetti, M. C. and Zola, M. A. (1985) 'Effectiveness of hardiness, exercise, and social support as resources against illness', *Journal of Psychosomatic Research* 29:525–533.

Loehr, J. E. (1994) *The New Toughness Training for Sports*, New York: Plume Publishers.

Maddi, S. R. (1991) *The personality construct of hardiness*. Unpublished manuscript. University of California, Irvine.

Maddi, S. R. and Hess, M. J. (1992) 'Personality, hardiness and success in basketball', *International Journal of Sport Psychology* 23:360–368.

Maddi, S. R., Hoover, M. and Kobasa, S. C. (1982) 'Alienation and exploratory behavior', *Journal of Personality and Social Psychology* 42:884–890.

Rauste-von Wright, M., von-Wright, J. and Frankenhaeuser, M. (1981) 'Relationships between sex-related psychological characteristics during adolescence and catecholamine excretion during achievement stress', *Psychophysiology* 18:362–370.

Rhodewalt, F. and Agostsdottir, S. (1984) 'On the relationship of hardiness to the Type-A behavior pattern: Perception of life events versus coping with life events', *Journal of Research in Personality* 18:212–223.

Schwarz, R. S. (1975) 'Another look at immunologic surveillance', *New England Journal of Medicine* 293:181–184.

Seligman, M. E. P. (1975) *Helplessness*, San Francisco: Freeman.

Selye, H. (1956) *The stress of life*, New York: McGraw-Hill.

Vealey, R. S. and Garner-Holman, M. (1998) 'Applied sport psychology: Measurement issues'. In J. L. Duda (ed.), *Advances in Sport and Exercise Psychology Measurement*, pp. 433–446, Morgantown, WV: Fitness Information Technology.

Weiss, J. M., Glazer, H. I., Pohorecky, L. A., Brick, J. and Miller, N. B. (1975) 'Effects of chronic exposure to stressors on avoidance-escape behavior and on brain norepinephrine', *Psychosomatic Medicine* 37:153–160.

Appendix to chapter three

THE 18-ITEM MENTAL TOUGHNESS QUESTIONNAIRE (MT18)

Please indicate your response to the following items by **circling one** of the numbers, which have the following meaning:
1 = strongly disagree; **2** = disagree; **3** = neither agree nor disagree; **4** = agree; **5** = strongly agree.

Please answer these items carefully, thinking about how you are **generally**.

Do not spend too much time on any one item.

1) Even when under considerable pressure I usually remain calm	1	2	3	4	5
2) I tend to worry about things well before they actually happen	1	2	3	4	5
3) I usually find it hard to summon enthusiasm for the tasks I have to do	1	2	3	4	5
4) I generally cope well with any problems that occur	1	2	3	4	5
5) I generally feel that I am a worthwhile person	1	2	3	4	5
6) 'I just don't know where to begin' is a feeling I usually have when presented with several things to do at once	1	2	3	4	5
7) I usually speak my mind when I have something to say	1	2	3	4	5
8) When I make mistakes I usually let it worry me for days after	1	2	3	4	5
9) In discussions, I tend to back-down even when I feel strongly about something	1	2	3	4	5
10) I generally feel in control	1	2	3	4	5
11) I often wish my life was more predictable	1	2	3	4	5
12) When I am feeling tired I find it difficult to get going	1	2	3	4	5
13) I am generally able to react quickly when something unexpected happens	1	2	3	4	5
14) However bad things are, I usually feel they will work out positively in the end	1	2	3	4	5

15) I generally look on the bright side of life	1	2	3	4	5
16) I generally find it hard to relax	1	2	3	4	5
17) I usually find it difficult to make a mental effort when I am tired	1	2	3	4	5
18) If I feel somebody is wrong, I am not afraid to argue with them	1	2	3	4	5

MT18 QUESTIONNAIRE SCORING KEY (R = REVERSED ITEM)

Question number
1
2R
3R
4
5
6R
7
8R
9R
10
11R
12R
13
14
15
16R
17R
18

Goals, motivation and commitment

Enhancing the quantity and quality of motivation: the promotion of task involvement in a junior football team

JOAN DUDA AND ANNE MARTE PENSGAARD

Motivation is the cornerstone of any activity involving voluntary exertion and investment. When athletes are optimally motivated, they work hard in training and give 100 per cent effort when competing. Optimally motivated athletes persist when facing difficulties, whether those challenges revolve around unsuccessful sport outcomes (dealing with an important loss or a losing streak), physical problems (injury) or psychological issues (a loss of confidence). Over the course of their sport involvement, athletes who are optimally motivated have maximized their talent and have performed to their ability and training levels on a more consistent basis. They love their sport and, when their sport career is over, optimally motivated athletes can consider their playing days as a period of their lives when they developed as a person – that is physically, mentally, emotionally, socially and perhaps even morally. Thus, *optimal* motivation is more than high motivation; it is also quality motivation. When the quantity and quality of athletes' motivation are elevated, the stage is set for athletic achievement as well as positive, enriching sport experiences.

Fostering athletes' motivation is an important aim for all coaches. To enhance the motivational striving of athletes – with respect to both the quantity and quality of that motivation – it is necessary to have insight into the thoughts and affective processes that underlie the actions athletes take. We need to understand what sport means to athletes. Why do they participate and how do they interpret their athletic endeavours? When are they feeling a sense of accomplishment and when are they personally disappointed with what transpired in training or competition? When are athletes feeling confident about what they can do, or have just done, and when do they doubt their abilities? In essence, to foster sport motivation it is critical to be aware of how athletes subjectively define success and failure in an athletic context and how they judge their competence. Further, it is important to recognize the role of the coach in promoting different definitions of success and ways of construing competence among her or his athletes. In short, the motivational climate created by coaches can influence the motivational processes of sport participants.

As anyone who has been associated with sport knows, optimal motivation is not always in evidence among athletes. An example of the types of motivational difficulties we might find in sport is presented in the following section. The hypothetical scenario depicts the motivation-related challenges facing a junior level football team that is struggling with its desire to play the game. In this illustration, it is not only that the quantity of motivation is low on this team, but also that the quality of the motivational processes described is questionable.

Motivation problems in sport: a case example

A junior level boys football team ranked nationally has been experiencing an increasing lack of motivation among the players. The start of the season had been very promising and the team was placed third after five matches. However, the last four have resulted in losses and the atmosphere has changed significantly from the optimistic tone a few months earlier.

The coach of the team is a great believer in toughening the players by punishing mistakes. Typically, he pays more attention and provides more positive feedback to the better players on the squad. Less-skilled players tend to receive limited recognition. This coach has an authoritarian coaching style and all decisions regarding tactics and training methods are made by him. Competition between the players within the team is emphasized and the starters are made to feel that they need constantly to 'look over their shoulders' with respect to who on the team might be taking over their position. The coach stresses that great footballers are born that way and believes that possessing high ability is critical to success in the sport. When the players are playing five-a-side during the training session, or involved in other play-related activities, the coach stresses drill outcomes rather than how the players are doing and how hard they are trying. When it comes to matches, the message is clear. In the perspective of the coach, 'winning is the only thing' and he lets the players know that he doesn't care what they have to do to ensure a victory. When interacting with the players, the coach treats them only as footballers and feels that it is better not to get to know them as people.

Motivation within the team had been high during the initial matches, when everything went well. It was when the bad results started to come that the lack of motivation became apparent. After a while, most of the players became afraid of making an error because they knew they would be yelled at and, to avoid the humiliation, they didn't take any chances when playing. Pre-game anxiety was high and players had trouble maintaining concentration in games. Team members started to turn on each other and team cohesion was evaporating rapidly.

Little by little, the players started to miss training sessions. When they did appear, they didn't produce their best effort. They felt that there was actually no use trying hard because it would not be rewarded. The enjoyment of football was not there anymore, and the players grew more and more dissatisfied. In terms of individual players and also the team as a whole, skills were not developing as they should. Before the end of the season several team members had left the team.

Theoretical framework

The type of motivational climate described in the football team scenario is what would be called an ego-involving climate within the achievement goal framework (Nicholls 1989; Ames 1992). Within sport settings, two types of motivational climates have been distinguished, namely an ego-involving climate and a task-involving climate (Newton, Duda and Yin 2000). An ego-involving sport environment is characterized by social comparisons within and between teams, a focus on competitive outcomes and differential treatment of individuals as a function of ability level. In an ego-involving atmosphere, mistakes usually result in punitive action by the leader. A task-involving climate, on the other hand, emphasizes both individual and team-based development. The exertion of effort and collaboration are reinforced in a task-involving sport setting. Errors are regarded as a natural part of the learning process and feedback is provided on a more individual basis.

Achievement goal theory (Nicholls 1989; Ames 1992) assumes that whether achievement situations are more or less task-involving or ego-involving impacts the achievement goals adopted and the state of involvement manifested by individuals. When participating in sport, athletes can be task-involved and/or ego-involved. These states of involvement can fluctuate throughout a training session or during a game, but the motivational atmosphere operating makes it more or less likely that task-involvement or ego-involvement will be evident.

When task-involved, athletes are focused on what they are doing and concentrate upon how to improve their overall skill level. Athletes in a state of task-involvement feel successful when they have mastered the task, experienced personal improvement or learning and have given their best effort. A sense of high competence when task-involved is based on self-referenced criteria. Task-involvement entails a more intrinsic way of processing sport.

If athletes are ego-involved, they are principally concerned with demonstrating superior skill to other competitors. They focus upon establishing competence and skill and, because of this objective, the activity at hand is really a means to an end, rather than an end in itself. Consequently, in contrast with an athlete who is task-involved, an ego-involved athlete is less likely to be 'in the moment'. When in a state of ego-involvement, trying hard can be a risky endeavour. If the ego-involved athlete does exert effort and outstanding ability is not confirmed (losing or playing poorly), he or she can feel even less competent. Thus, when ego goals are the motivating factor, not trying can be a way of avoiding subjective failure and preserving one's credibility.

According to achievement goal theory (Nicholls 1989; Ames 1992; Dweck 1999), individuals are more likely to be optimally motivated when task-involved. In sport, for example, this adaptive pattern is predictable whether the athlete perceives skill level to be high, or realizes that his or her competence is inferior. Why should this be? The answer is that when task-involved, concern is with improving and giving one's all. Regardless of ability level, athletes should try to identify areas in which they can develop. Moreover, when task-involved, athletes judge their level of competence in terms of their own progress and effort. Consequently, an athlete's sense of confidence is more buoyant when task-involved.

Achievement goal theory predicts that ego-involvement can lead to motivational problems. This is especially held to be true when an athlete does not value task goals; that is, low in task orientation (Duda 2001) and lacking confidence. At least in the short term, ego-involvement can be coupled with good performance and high motivation as long as the athlete is strongly confident in his or her level of skill. Over time, difficulties can occur for the athlete who is ego-involved and believes that his or her competence is high (Duda 2001). This is because in the physically, psychologically and competitively demanding arena of sport, it is difficult to maintain a sense of high normative ability. Further, recent research has raised questions about whether quality motivation can actually exist when ego-involvement predominates (Duda 2001).

Supporting research

A growing body of research suggests that the most productive environment as regards satisfaction with one's game, team and coach (Walling, Duda and Chi 1993; Treasure 1997; Balaguer, Duda and Crespo 1999; Balaguer et al. in press), perceptions of improvement (Balaguer et al. in press), intrinsic motivation (Goudas and Biddle 1994) and reported enjoyment (Kavussanu and Roberts 1996) among athletes is a task-involving climate. When a task-involving environment prevails, athletes are more likely to believe in the efficacy of training and high effort as determinants of sport success (Seifriz, Duda and Chi 1992). Players in such situations tend to use more effective coping strategies and feel more able to control the stressors encountered during competition (Kim and Duda in press).

Among sport participants, perceptions of an ego-involving sport climate have been linked to the view that one must have inherently high ability to be successful (Seifriz, Duda and Chi 1992). An ego-involving setting is associated with greater performance worry among athletes (Walling, Duda and Chi 1993). This seems to be the case even at an elite level. For example, a study of Olympic athletes revealed higher reported (negative) stress during the Olympic competition when the climate created by the coach was more ego-involving and less task-involving (Pensgaard and Roberts 2000). When feeling anxious, athletes have been found to be more prone to employ avoidance or emotion-focused coping strategies when the motivational climate is more ego-involving (Kim and Duda in press).

Recent work on high-level tennis and handball players has indicated that when the coach-created environment is deemed more task-involving and less ego-involving, athletes perceive the coach to be providing more instruction (Balaguer, Crespo and Duda 1996). Further, in such a perceived motivational climate, athletes feel that the coach gives more social support and allows them to feel valued as individuals beyond their athletic roles and responsibilities.

Intervention strategies

As it is mainly the coach who creates the climate within any sport group, it becomes essential that the coach is aware of the implications of his or her coaching style. When a team is doing well, the creation of an ego-involving climate may not be detrimental in terms of indices of sport achievement. When a team is winning, an ego-involving coach will be satisfied and so will the players if they are predominantly ego-oriented. But when a team is struggling and winning is no longer the norm, an ego-involving atmosphere is likely to have an unfavourable effect on the motivational processes of the team. When winning is the only criterion of success and losing becomes the status quo, there is little, if anything, to maintain motivation. In a task-involving climate, on the other hand, there are several criteria for success. For example, the team may lose a match, but with several players having improved their performance. Moreover, the very nature of an ego-involving climate makes it more likely that players will be motivated by a fear of failure. In contrast, a task-involving environment should 'set the stage' for athletes and teams to concentrate on what needs to be done to accomplish their goals. This situation is expected to promote a focus on personal and collective task mastery and those definitions of success which are more within the athlete's/team's control.

MODIFYING THE MOTIVATIONAL CLIMATE

If we reconsider the hypothetical scenario set out earlier, there are a number of things the coach can do to try and change the maladaptive pattern being exhibited by the players. When a team has potential to be at the top of their league, winning will always be an important goal towards which the team should aim. However, by emphasizing additional criteria of success, such as individual and team improvement and the exertion of intense effort, the coach increases the probability of achieving success and, thereby, enhances athlete and team motivation.

The underpinnings of a perceived motivational climate, however, are more than the goals that coaches reinforce within the team and the criteria of success that are emphasized. The motivational climate is multidimensional; it is conveyed in coach-to-athlete and coach-to-team interactions in training and competition and in the way in which the training sessions and competitive encounters are structured. Besides standards of success being bolstered, the nature of and bases for their evaluation and recognition will contribute to the motivational atmosphere within a team.

It is important to consider what, in the opinion of a coach, are the specific triggers for success, and also for failure. For example, how are athletes within the team grouped and what types of within-group exchanges are emphasized by the coach? Who 'runs the show' and how much input do players have with respect to their own and the team's activities? In terms of drills and workouts, how are they arranged? Answers to such questions will inform athletes about the team climate a coach is creating.

Based on the work of Ames (1992), guidelines have emerged as regards how training sessions and the competitive context can be designed and implemented in order to foster a more task-involving climate. Such guidelines illustrate the multifaceted characteristics of the motivational climates that are shaped by coaches. In each instance, examples of strategies and actions that can be employed by the coach of the football team referred to earlier are described in the following sub-sections.

Learning and improvement equals success

A key feature of a task-involving climate is a clear focus on the ongoing development of the team's and each player's skills and knowledge about the game. In addition to an overall outcome goal for the team, such as winning the series, the team and the coach should collaborate to develop process goals for the team and for each player. For example, a team goal could be to work on specific defensive and offensive patterns of play. Each player should also have one or two specific personal tasks to work on, such as improving endurance, skill at long passing or the accuracy of dead-ball kicks. If the focus is on learning and improvement, the players and team will always be able to monitor progress regardless of the results of games. However, it is of vital importance that the players take part in any process goal-setting programme and that feedback provided by the coach is commensurate with this emphasis.

Personal feedback

Every player wants recognition and attention from the coach, and in a task-involving climate the coach rewards high levels of effort regardless of outcome. This means that a player should be pleased only when he or she has demonstrated maximum effort; merely winning or beating others is insufficient to warrant an athlete feeling satisfied! When players do work hard to effect improvement, feedback from the coach is best presented with reference to that athlete alone and privately whenever possible. Negative feedback to a player should, of course, always be provided in a one-to-one situation and not in front of the team. This also provides the player with an opportunity to offer an opinion and for constructive dialogue to ensue.

Mistakes are part of learning

Every coach wants the team to be creative, have courage, enjoy challenges and rise to the occasion. A task-involving climate provides the foundation for such behaviours and attributes because players are allowed to fail without being penalized. They are free to work towards their potential. A coach who wishes to create a task-involving climate knows that learning takes time and that patience and trust in both the players and the team philosophy are crucial to success.

When the team or an individual fails to perform as expected or with maximal effort, it is crucial that any negative feedback is informational. The coach should make it clear about what is perceived as a mistake and, rather than punish, provide constructive feedback about how the situation may be improved or overcome. That is, both individual footballers and the team should *know more* rather than be *more afraid* after making a mistake in training or during a game.

Everybody is important

It can be a challenge for a coach to be able to work with and understand all members of the team, rather than focusing principally on star players. However, successful teams are characterized by their ability to perform at a consistently high level, even when key players are injured or have lost form. A coach must recognize that no individual can win a match single-handed and thus trust and respect are necessary for every player in the squad. Even those at the highest level have expressed how important this is if success is to be attained (Pensgaard and Roberts in press).

In any team, players will invariably recognize differences in skill between fellow team members. While this is not a problem, what can be maladaptive is when each footballer fails to understand how they fit into the overall scheme of things; namely, the team's goals and its philosophy. In a task-involving football team, the coach will take time to explain each player's roles and responsibilities.

Player input

If a coach wants players to buy into his or her philosophy of football and to remain loyal to it during less-successful times, they should allow all players to proffer their opinions and beliefs about the ways in which different challenges might be met. By doing this, the coach will produce more motivated players who are more responsible when it is necessary to solve specific tasks, because they feel greater ownership of decisions that are made. A coach can derive valuable input from players and will be able to check whether they understand the overall philosophy that is being espoused.

Conclusion

Achievement goal theory, and the plethora of sport-based studies emanating from this theoretical framework, indicates that the nature of the coach-created climate is important to athletes' motivational processes. The literature also provides evidence regarding the short-term and potential long-term benefits of having coaches build a task-involving team environment. To encourage such an atmosphere, numerous interrelated aspects of that environment need to be manipulated successfully by the coach. It needs to be developed gradually, the aim being to nourish and develop players' task involvement day in and day out. Given that a task-involving climate prevails, it is argued that the achievements of footballers will be maximized, their experiences in the team will be quality experiences and their personal growth will be fostered.

(📖 References)

Ames, C. (1992) 'Achievement goals, motivational climate and motivational process'. In G. C. Roberts (ed.), *Motivation in Sport and Exercise*, pp. 161–176, Champaign IL: Human Kinetics.

Balaguer, I., Crespo, M. and Duda, J. L. (1996) 'The relationship of motivational climate and athletes' goal orientations to perceived/preferred leadership style', *Journal of Sport and Exercise Psychology (Abstract)* 18:S13.

Balaguer, I., Duda, J. L., Atienza, F. L. and Mayo, C. (in press) 'Situational and dispositional goals as predictors of perceptions on individual and team improvement, satisfaction and coach ratings among elite female handball teams', *Psychology of Sport and Exercise.*

Balaguer, I., Duda, J. L. and Crespo, M. (1999) 'Motivational climate and goal orientations as predictors of perceptions of improvement, satisfaction and coach ratings among tennis players', *Scandinavian Journal of Medicine and Science in Sports* 9:381–388.

Duda, J. L. (2001) 'Goal perspectives research in sport: pushing the boundaries and clarifying some misunderstandings'. In G. C. Roberts (ed.), *Advances in Motivation in Sport and Exercise*, pp. 129–182, Champaign, IL: Human Kinetics.

Dweck, C. S. (1999) *Self-theories: Their Role in Motivation, Personality, and Development*, Ann Arbor, MI: Psychological Press.

Goudas, M. and Biddle, S. (1994) 'Perceived motivational climate and intrinsic motivation in school physical education classes', *European Journal of Psychology of Education* 9:241–250.

Kavussanu, M. and Roberts, G. C. (1996) 'Motivation in physical activity contexts: The relationship of motivational climate to intrinsic motivation and self-efficacy', *Journal of Sport and Exercise Psychology* 18:264–280.

Kim, M.-S. and Duda, J. L. (in press) 'Predicting coping responses: An integration of Lazarus' Transactional Theory of Psychological Stress and Coping and Goal Perspective Theory', *Journal of Sport and Exercise Psychology.*

Newton, Duda, J. L. and Yin, Z. (2000) 'Examination of the psychometric properties of the Perceived Motivational Climate in Sport Questionnaire-2 in a sample of female athletes', *Journal of Sport Sciences* 18(4):275–290.

Nicholls, J. G. (1989) *The Competitive Ethos and Democratic Education*, Cambridge, MA: Harvard University Press.

Pensgaard, A. M. and Roberts, G. C. (2000) 'The relationship between motivational climate, perceived ability and sources of distress among elite athletes', *Journal of Sports Sciences* 18:191–200.

Pensgaard, A. M. and Roberts, G. C. (in press) 'Elite athletes' experiences of the motivational climate: The coach matters!', *Scandinavian Journal of Medicine and Science in Sports.*

Seifriez, J., Duda, J. L. and Chi, L. (1992) 'The relationship of motivational climate to intrinsic motivation and beliefs about success in basketball', *Journal of Sport and Exercise Psychology* 14:375–392.

Treasure, D. C. (1997) 'Perceptions of the motivational climate and elementary school children's cognitive and affective response', *Journal of Sport and Exercise Psychology* 19:278–290.

Walling, M. D., Duda, J. L. and Chi, L. (1993) 'The Perceived Motivational Climate in Sport Questionnaire', *Journal of Sport and Exercise Psychology* 15:172–183.

chapter five

The application of achievement goal theory in youth sport

CHRIS HARWOOD AND STUART BIDDLE

Identifying the issue

William is a 13-year-old tennis player who is highly ranked in his age group at county level. His coach is eager for him to be selected for the national scheme that financially supports some of the leading junior players. Selection would mean a much-reduced financial burden on William's parents, more individual coaching, greater attention from national coaches at training camps, international experience abroad, private medical cover and access to sport science support. It would mean that William would receive the benefits of a very extensive performance programme. William's father, Eric, is very keen for this to happen, particularly considering the expenses that he currently incurs. Players are normally selected for the scheme on the basis of results and also potential, but most players in this age group tend to perceive that results are the determining criteria for selection.

William is clearly aware of the national scheme and many of his friends and rivals are supported by it. He desperately wants to be selected because he knows what it would mean to his father and coach, as well as understanding the opportunities that would be available to him. The national coaches know, however, that William has a chequered past in terms of his behaviour on court and his attitude towards competition. It is also common knowledge among the coaches that his father is a 'pressure parent' who some-times exhibits extremely volatile behaviour at court-side. These opinions are based on a number of observations:

1. William has a tendency to start matches extremely nervously and is sometimes unable to consolidate a lead or to close out matches. This is often due to increases in unforced errors and changes in game style, as when aggressive play changes to 'pushing' the ball defensively at critical periods within the match.

2. William shows negative body language (head and shoulders drop), low anger management (likely to throw his racket), and lack of emotional control (self-criticism) on key points within a match.

3. William has a tendency to 'pose' and show off during easy matches where he knows that he is going to win, but which sometimes catches him out. By contrast, he also has a tendency to 'throw in the towel' and 'tank' matches when he is a set down and well down in the second set, for example giving up when 6–3, 4–1 down.

4. His consistent visual attention to his father, to whom he turns after every point as if to seek reinforcement or to check his reaction.

5. Eric will grimace at court-side when his son loses a point, and on one occasion he is reported to have driven home in disgust and left his son alone at the tournament without a lift home.

6. William's lack of coach support at tournaments and the absence of someone qualified to help him to review his performances after winning or losing.

These observations present the selection panel of national coaches with a great deal of information. Although the national coaches believe William to be a technically gifted player with a sound physical fitness profile, his results are inconsistent. He struggles to beat higher-rated players and it is the player that he would expect to beat 'on paper' against whom he behaves badly. While William does not impress the coaches by his results, it is his potential for improving his mental skills that is the main focus of their concern. Our suggestions of possible solutions to William's difficulties are based on achievement motivation and, in particular, achievement goals. The following section describes the basic principles of, and relevant research within, achievement goal theory, followed by a suggested practical solution for William.

Achievement goals: introduction and background

The study of motivation has been a key area of interest to sport psychologists since the early 1990s. Much of the enthusiasm stems from the work of educational psychologists in the late 1970s and early 1980s, who proposed that motivation should be viewed more in terms of personal thoughts and perceptions rather than some innate quality. Specifically, Maehr and Nicholls (1980) argued that 'success and failure are not concrete events. They are psychological states consequent on perception of reaching or not reaching goals' (p. 228). Based on this reasoning, they defined three types of achievement motivation: ability-orientated motivation, task-orientated motivation and social approval-orientated motivation. Ability-orientated motivation is when 'the goal of the behaviour is to maximize the subjective probability of attributing high ability to oneself' (p. 237). This has been modified in sport psychology to refer to an 'ego' goal orientation where success is defined as the demonstration of superiority over others (Duda 1993).

According to Maehr and Nicholls (1980), in task-orientated motivation 'the primary goal is to produce an adequate product or to solve a problem for its own sake rather than to demonstrate ability' (p. 239). This reflects a 'task' goal orientation (Duda 1993). The third goal, social approval-orientated motivation, has been investigated less in sport than the other two. This dimension of achievement motivation was defined by Maehr and Nicholls (1980) as 'conformity to norms or virtuous intent rather than superior talent' (pp. 241–242).

Nicholls (1989) has since argued that the two main goals, task and ego, are based on how people think about, or define, competence. Those who are ego-involved perceive ability as limiting the effects of effort on performance. They are keen to show their high capacity of ability often at the expense of effort. Indeed, having to try hard and exert effort to achieve a certain standard of performance can actually indicate low ability in the thinking of the ego-involved individual. Nicholls refers to those who are ego-involved as holding a 'more differentiated' view of ability in that ability and effort are clearly separate from each other. When a person is ego-involved, they judge their ability relative to others and have to demonstrate superior ability or outperform others to be satisfied. In contrast, those who are task-involved hold a 'less differentiated' conception of ability as they believe that ability equates to effort, and 'the harder you try, the more able you feel'. Those who are highly task-involved use cues such as levels of effort and task completion to assess their competence in an entirely self-reflective manner. A task-involved performer is satisfied if they perform to a level that reflects how they have mastered a task or made personal improvements.

A major tenet of achievement goal theory is that individuals will be *predisposed* to task and ego orientations as a result of socialization experiences in their sport and these orientations will subsequently influence whether an individual will adopt a task or ego goal in a specific situation. In addition, the prevailing motivational climate will also affect the adoption of achievement goals (Ntoumanis and Biddle 1999a). In short, the nature of the goal state (i.e. levels of task and ego-involvement) that is activated in a specific sport situation will be determined by individual preference (goal orientation) and situational cues (motivational climate) (see Figure 5.1). Little research has been conducted on goal states *per se*, while a great deal of literature is now available on goal orientations and motivational climate (Duda and Whitehead 1998; Ntoumanis and Biddle 1999a).

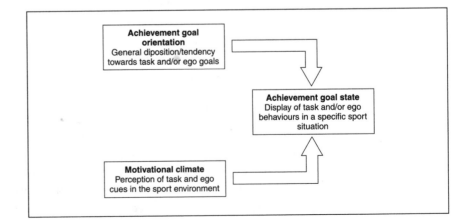

FIGURE 5.1 *Task and ego goal involvement states are created from goal orientations and the motivational climate*

The independence of task and ego goals

Goals and competence perceptions have now been studied in the context of sport and shed light on important motivational processes. Typically, goal orientations are assessed using questionnaires (see Duda and Whitehead 1998) yielding scores on task and ego goals. There is now consistent evidence that the adoption of a task goal in sport can be motivationally adaptive (see Duda 1993). However, ratings of task and ego goal orientations are usually found to be uncorrelated. Hence, we have argued elsewhere that goal profiles should be studied whereby combinations of task and ego are accounted for (Fox *et al.* 1994; Harwood, Hardy and Swain 2000). In other words, some people will be low in both task and ego, some high in task but low in ego, or any other combination. Fox *et al.* (1994) found that high task/high ego and high task/low ego children were similar in their motivational responses when asked about sport in general. A general conclusion is that a high task orientation is positive, either singly or in combination with a high ego orientation.

GOALS AND BELIEFS

The study of the links between goal orientations and beliefs about the causes of success is fundamental to the understanding of motivated achievement behaviour in sport. Research in the classroom, as well as in sport and physical education contexts, has shown that task and ego goal orientations are differentially correlated with beliefs about the causes of success. Typically, a task orientation is strongly correlated with the belief that success in sport is due to motivation/effort, but unrelated to the belief that ability causes success in sport. Conversely, ego orientation is correlated with ability beliefs but correlates rather weakly with motivation/effort (see Duda 1993). Such findings provide an explanation for why a focus on task orientation is beneficial. Effort is controllable, and believing that trying hard will bring some success reflects the 'I can!' feeling so often desired by coaches.

GOALS AND INTRINSIC MOTIVATION

When goal orientations have been studied in respect of their relationships with motivation, one popular index has involved the assessment of intrinsic motivation. For example, Duda *et al.* (1995) showed that a high task and low ego goal orientation was associated with high enjoyment in one sample, and a high task orientation was associated with high perceived effort in another. Both enjoyment and effort are indicators of intrinsic motivation.

GOALS, AFFECT AND NEGATIVE THINKING

Studies of goals in sport have also investigated the emotional, or affective, correlates of achievement goals, although at times it is difficult to separate out measures of intrinsic motivation (for example enjoyment) from affect. A meta-analysis of achievement goals and affect to clarify relationships reported in the literature (Ntoumanis and Biddle 1999b) analysed 36 studies and 39 samples (*N*=7649) and found a strong correlation between task orientation and positive affect (*r*=0.55). The strength of this correlation is indicated by the fact that 139 missing, or yet unknown, studies averaging null correlations would have to exist to bring the correlation down to a coefficient of 0.10, considered weak.

A central topic for the study of affect in sport has been anxiety (Jones 1995). Hall and Kerr (1997), for example, found that in young fencers ego goal orientations were significant predictors of pre-competitive cognitive anxiety. Correlations between ego goal orientation and cognitive anxiety for fencers low in perceived ability were positive and very high two days, one day and 30 minutes prior to competition. Conversely, task orientation scores were negatively associated, showing that a task orientation is associated with reduced cognitive anxiety.

More recently, researchers have shown an interest not just in the anxiety response itself, but also how athletes cope with stress and anxiety (Hardy, Jones and Gould 1996). Ntoumanis, Biddle and Haddock (1999) considered whether the adoption of different coping strategies by student athletes was associated with task and ego goal orientations. They found that task orientation was associated with the use of problem-solving coping strategies, such as trying hard, seeking social support and curtailing competing activities. On the other hand, those with high ego scores were more likely to use the emotion-focused strategy of 'venting emotions'. Items assessing this coping strategy reflect getting upset, losing one's cool and letting out negative feelings, thus preliminary evidence suggests a more positive coping response is likely from task–oriented athletes and it appears highly relevant for our study of William.

It has already been suggested that those adopting a task goal orientation appear more likely to adopt problem-solving coping strategies when faced with adversity. In addition, evidence is emerging that links task orientation with less-negative thinking in sport. For example, in the Sydney Olympic Games, Goode and Archer lost their badminton semi-final after failing to convert a match point, but won the bronze medal match after coming back from match-point down. Thus, the potential for negative thinking at such crucial times and in such important matches is high.

In one study, Hatzigeorgiadis and Biddle (1999) found that 'thoughts of escape' during a competition were less likely to be reported by task-oriented snooker and tennis players, but more likely for ego-oriented players with low perceived competence. Such negative thoughts are similar to those expressed by some players when they say 'let's get it over with!' prior to a match that is most probably important to them. Adopting a task-oriented perspective appears to reduce such thoughts. Given that Hatzigeorgiadis and Biddle (2000) found that measures of cognitive interference are related to measures of concentration disruption, negative thinking and cognitive anxiety, the need to address this issue is clear, and no more so in tennis where the potential for cognitive interference is high.

TASK AND EGO-INVOLVEMENT

The discussion so far has centred on goal orientations or the general predisposition to adopt task and/or ego goals. These predispositions are considered to develop through early socialization experiences, including interactions with parents, teachers and peers. However, less attention has focused on the actual achievement goals that performers adopt in specific situations, namely *goal states* that are referred to as task-involvement and ego-involvement. For example, if a performer is high in task-involvement and low in ego-involvement prior to a tennis match, their achievement goal at the time is probably to perform to the best of their ability. They will seek improvements in their game, with less concern for showing superior skills to their opponent. The opposite of this is the player who is totally focused on winning or upon not losing the match, with little emphasis placed on how the game is played. Understanding and measuring levels of task and ego-involvement is an important objective for sport psychologists, as the momentary thoughts, feelings and behaviours that characterize performers such as William are indicative of their motivational states at the time. This is why most research has investigated those situational factors that actually influence the activation of task and ego-involvement beyond simply player's goal orientations.

Work with elite swimmers and tennis players (Harwood and Swain 1998; Swain and Harwood 1996) has demonstrated how pre-competition levels of task and ego-involvement may be predicted not only by dispositional goal orientation, but also by situational factors. In tennis, they included match-specific perceptions of ability (expectancy of winning the match), the perceived importance and value of the match and players' perceptions of the achievement goal most preferred and recognized by parents, coaches and the national governing body. These findings allow sport psychologists and coaches to understand which contextual factors will make players more task-involved, by comparison with those that make them more ego-involved. In other words, it is important to consider how best to teach a player to attain the right motivational frame of mind.

Motivational climate

It has been argued that achievement goals form an important and powerful influence on motivation in sport. However, some researchers have also emphasized the importance of the achievement environment, or climate. The climate can be created by coaches, parents and anyone who has potential for influencing the group. Two main climates have been identified that reflect the work of Ames in school classrooms (Ames 1992). A 'mastery' (task) climate is perceived by team members when they are directed towards self-improvement, the coach or parent emphasizes learning and personal progress, effort is rewarded, mistakes are seen as part of learning and choice is allowed. On the other hand, a 'performance' (ego) climate is one that encourages inter-individual comparison, where mistakes are punished and high normative ability is rewarded.

From an analysis of 14 studies with a total sample size of almost 4500, it has been shown that the correlation between a mastery climate and positive motivational outcomes such as satisfaction, positive attitudes towards lessons and intrinsic motivation is 0.71, indicating a large effect (Ntoumanis and Biddle 1999a). By contrast, performance climate was correlated in a small-to-moderate way, but in a negative direction with positive outcomes (−0.30). Negative outcomes were also assessed and comprised factors such as worry and the emphasis on normative ability. The effect for mastery climate on negative outcomes was also small-to-moderate and negative (−0.26), and for performance climate on these outcomes it was moderate and positive (0.46). Accordingly, these results indicate the importance of a mastery climate in promoting positive psychological outcomes in sport.

Given these findings, there is a need to assess whether motivational climate can be changed and, if so, how? Ames (1992) developed a number of practical strategies for interventions in school classrooms by adopting the TARGET structures that define a mastery climate (see Table 5.1). These strategies are considered to be important because they provide a comprehensive framework for both researchers and coaches to prescribe a wide range of motivational principles and techniques that are consistent with a mastery climate. There are few intervention studies in this area, but those that do exist support the positive influence of a mastery motivational climate and the negative influence of a performance climate on cognition, affect and behaviour.

Table 5.1 Ways of creating a mastery motivational climate

TARGET	STRATEGIES
Task: Coaching activities	Have variety and individually challenging activities; have the players set process rather than outcome goals
Authority: How the coach operates with the players	Let players have a 'say' in matters such as leadership roles, decisions, practices, etc.
Recognition: What is rewarded?	Recognize personal progress and improvement in players
Grouping: Use of groups	Be flexible over groupings in practice, avoid always having the most or least skilled players together
Evaluation: Use of feedback	Evaluation based on improvement and effort; allow players to evaluate themselves as well as be evaluated by others; avoid public evaluation
Time: Scheduling	Allow time for practice and improvement; help players with time management to encourage practice

Towards a practical solution for William

Knowledge of achievement goal theory and an awareness of the dimensions that comprise a 'motivational climate' are critical starting points for a practical solution to William's situation. It is not simply about developing 'mistake management' techniques, or concentration and relaxation rituals between points. Such strategies may often produce solutions to symptoms, but they do not address the underlying problem or root cause.

Tennis is not only highly ego-involving in that it judges success based on win/loss outcomes, it is also highly non-task-involving in that it does not provide objective personal performance feedback to the player. The outcome of a match does not offer any direct information to the player on how they performed relative to themselves. This is unlike sports such as swimming or track and field, where you receive clear information about your performance, irrespective of the position you finish in the competition. Consequently, the ego-involving nature of tennis has knock-on effects for coaches, parents and peers who will tend to judge a player on outcomes achieved at the expense of taking a close look at the performance itself.

It is important to ensure that young performers develop high levels of task orientation and take this on-court in the form of high task-involvement. They need to be able to feel satisfaction from playing good tennis or mastering a particular shot, regardless of whether they showed superior skills to their opponent. Even if they lose a well-fought point, they still need to keep a positive perspective on how well they played and what they learned from the exchange. At the same time, they need to be competitive and be able to appreciate the fundamental importance of challenging the opposition. The importance given to the demonstration of superior skills is normally facilitated by evidence of ego orientation.

Accordingly, within certain limitations, being ego-involved can provide a player with important psychological tools:

● It can help to focus resources on the opposition and develop an appropriate game plan. Head-to-head competition means that it helps to know something about the other head! Ego-involved players will easily be able to allocate attention to their opponent; it is the amount and quality of that attention that the sport psychologist or coach needs to monitor carefully.

● It provides competitive direction and purpose to each point even if a player is playing well below par. For example, without ego-involvement a player is less likely to care whether they win or lose. With ego-involvement, backed up with a high level of task-involvement, this kind of player will be resourceful to the end of the match. As one coach put it, 'this individual has the personality to win the match with a rusty spanner if his well-equipped tool box happens to have been left at home!'

Thus, any practical solution that incorporates the tenets of achievement goal theory and motivational climate should generally be centred on strategies that ensure high levels of task orientation and positive forms of ego orientation. A solution will invariably involve mental training, but may also require a change in the behaviour of coaches and parents.

ASSESSMENT ISSUES AND FINDINGS

For William, and with this theoretical background in place, several key factors have been established:

1. He has a high ego orientation and his behaviour indicates that he is highly ego-involved in matches, particularly against those players that he is expected to beat.

2. There is little evidence of task-oriented behaviour and no post-match routine in which his performance is reviewed, either by himself or with the aid of a coach or parent.

3. Eric, his father, is also highly ego-oriented and his behaviour and actions reinforce this. Little task-oriented behaviour is evident. The coach is not doing anything to help the situation.

4. The nature of tennis, the national scheme, his rival peers, his coach and father together are probably responsible for developing William's overall 'performance' as opposed to 'mastery' motivational climate.

Psychological and environmental assessment by a sport psychologist in national age group tennis would occur over a number of days or weeks. There is also a range of direct and indirect methods that a sport psychologist should apply for a full assessment of the player. Implicit knowledge of tennis and an awareness of the psychological demands of the game at junior level are highly desirable. Further, assessment would not only involve direct observation of the player and significant others both on and off court, but would also include formal and informal discussions with them using fairly specific and structured questions. This process seeks to establish a comprehensive psychological and motivational skills profile that characterizes not only the player, but also the coach and parents. However, the factors that supersede the effectiveness of any assessment and subsequent work are the honesty, adherence and commitment of the clients.

COMPONENTS OF A PRACTICAL INTERVENTION

A practical solution that has been identified by the first author incorporates a coordinated series of intervention techniques with players, coaches and parents. The objectives of these techniques are:

1. To educate William, his coach and parents about the psychological demands of tennis, the implications/consequences of negative attitudes, and the importance of developing an appropriate motivational focus or attitude to competitive match play.

2. To increase William's use of task-involving cognitive strategies both in training, pre-match, in-match and post-match.

3. To help him understand, restructure and cope with the ego-involving nature of tennis and specific matches.

4. To actively reshape the tennis motivational climate by enhancing the frequency of task-involving behaviour of significant others in key contexts; in training, at home, pre-match and post-match.

5. To develop a 'working relationship' between player, coach and parent based on enhanced communication and feedback about achievements and skill development;

The specific sessions and tasks described in the following sub-sections comprise elements of a programme previously executed by the first author acting as an educator/facilitator. The programme should ideally be conducted over at least a four-month training and competition period before being revised.

Stage 1: Initial education sessions

Ideally, there should be four educational sessions of 60–90 minutes with William, his coach and parents separately. In the first session, the consultant may explore each person's knowledge of the psychological demands of tennis and discuss what makes tennis psychologically tough. This allows the consultant to talk about the nature of tennis and then to present, with exemplar player quotes if possible, the different motivational profiles that players could possess. For example:

- 'Tennis is just about winning … no more, no less … no-one looks at how well you played' (high ego/low task exemplar).

- 'I just go out and play, I don't really care if I win or lose' (high task/low ego exemplar).

- 'It's about performing to the best of your ability, being competitive and hungry, and learning about why you might have won or lost on that particular day' (high task/high ego exemplar).

Each party could then be asked about the merits and limitations of each of these attitudes, not simply within a particular match, but also for long-term participation and persistence. The consultant will need to tailor the approach and presentation of information according to the cognitive level of the client (for example, William or Eric). An effective consultant will use examples from the modern game to elucidate information from both the perspective of a 13-year-old player and also the mature parent. Overall, the main purpose of the session is to help each to understand the motivational skills required to play the game successfully at junior level.

In the second session the consultant may introduce his/her view of what characterizes the ideal motivational approach and the attitude that they want the player, coach and parents to work towards developing in training and competition. The 'Competitive Performance Mentality' (CPM) is a psychological approach to tennis devised by the first author and based on the belief that in any tennis match the player faces two achievement challenges: (a) the *self-challenge*: to maximize, improve and/or maintain current standards of personal skills in each area of tennis; and (b) the *game challenge*: to use the self-challenge to overcome the test/opponent set for them on that day.

Possessing a CPM for matchplay reflects a goal-involvement profile of both high task-involvement and highly functional ego-involvement. There is an important distinction between being ego-involved because you want to impress others with your ability or fear losing due to others' expectations (that is, social approval ego-involvement), and being ego-involved because you understand and appreciate the functional challenge of the game. There are major differences between these two explanations for being ego-involved and it is the authors' belief that the latter is a more positive, natural and adaptive approach to match play. The consultant may then consider:

1. The self-challenge to provide the foundation for personal success.

2. How tennis challenges you to be competitive and that the game challenge is simply a test set by tennis. That winning or losing matches is not something to fear simply because of the impressions that others have of you.

3. How the two challenges exist for every match, whatever the situation or level of opposition.

4. How either, both or neither of the challenges may have been met successfully at the end of the match.

5. How critical it is to review and appraise the self-challenge first (own skills), and to appraise the game challenge by reflecting on the skills of the opponent and aspects that tested your resources in the match.

A meeting of this kind with parents can help them to understand what kind of role-related actions and verbal and visual behaviours constitute 'Competitive Performance Parenting'!

In session three, the player, coach and parents may join as a group if the consultant feels that all are committed to the perspectives that have been introduced. This session acts as a troubleshooting and contingency management session to explore and brainstorm those elements of tennis that can distract players from a CPM and turn them into highly ego-involved pressure players. These factors may include the ranking, rating, age, seeding or current form of the opposition; verbal expectations of the coach or parents pre-match; stage of tournament or importance of match; playing for a team; the presence of national coaches; negative visual reactions by parents or coach based upon the outcome of a point. This exercise helps a player to appreciate how easy it is to lose focus on what is fundamentally their most important goals, namely personal performance and process. Further, it helps both coach and parent to recognize what they should do, but don't, and even more importantly, the actions, reactions and words that they take or say, but shouldn't.

A useful acronym to help players to cope with the ego-involving characteristics of tennis, and to refocus their attention on the importance of self-challenge/game challenge is 'RESISTANCE'. Players, coach and parents can be informed about when, where and how each word can weaken their RESISTANCE and provoke an ego-involved state of mind in the absence of high task-involvement. Each word is followed by a typical cognitive restructuring phrase that might be used by the player, or reinforced by coach or parents. RESISTANCE refers to:

Rating: 'It's not the rating or ranking that produces the performance.'

Esteem: 'Separate the person from the outcome.'

Seeding: 'Matches aren't played on paper, they are played on tennis courts.'

Importance: 'Any match is just as important as any other match.'

Score: 'It's not about the score, it's about your effort, discipline and focus.'

Team: 'Effective team members play like the player who gained selection.'

Audience: 'An audience's main desire is to witness a player trying their best.'

No justice: 'One bad line call or net cord does not win or lose a match.'

Comparison: 'Never base achievements solely on comparisons with others.'

Endorsements: 'High fashion and designer labels never won a tennis match.'

The 10 dimensions typify the competitive tournament climate, with coaches and parents often fanning the flames by talking about seeding, ratings and comparing notes about whom they expect to win the match, or be selected. This type of NON-RESISTANCE behaviour is typical of most coaches and parents at tournaments. Nonetheless, although one might argue that this behaviour is part of the game, never doubt the impact that such behaviours have on developing high ego orientations in players. In sum, one of the key objectives for this session is for the player, parents and coach to consider the quality of their verbal interactions with others. In particular, it is to demonstrate how coaches and parents typically engage in high ego-involving, non-task-involving behaviours and interactions at tournaments.

In the final educational session for each member of the group, the consultant introduces the structure and content of the working programme. While the previous sessions have focused on what is required, and why, the final session represents 'how' it takes place. In order to maintain a cohesive triangular approach to the problem, each member may be identified as the Competitive Performance Player, Competitive Performance Parent and Competitive Performance Coach. The responsibilities of each member might be as detailed in the next section.

Stage 2: Implementation of action tasks

The Competitive Performance Player

William's programme involves a number of tasks designed to develop a greater appreciation and awareness of game-relevant skills. Evaluating himself on the achievement of these personal skills and tasks should condition a higher level of task orientation and shape a more positive ego-oriented side to his attitude. These action tasks include:

1. Development of a pre-match performance routine and checklist for his matches.

2. A match goal-setting sheet (Harwood 1996), which lists up to three specific self-challenge performance goals alongside process goals for his 'thinking' and 'doing' routine in between points.

3. A self-reflective review and rating of these goals and processes at an agreed time post-match, if possible, regardless of outcome. This review should take place following the 'outcome sink in, emotions sink out' period.

4. A more considered report of the self-challenge and game challenge where he is asked to reflect upon the course and flow of the match; the 'on form' skills that satisfied him; his thoughts, feelings and behaviour throughout the match; the opponent's skills and aspects that put him under pressure; areas for improvement and what he learnt from the two challenges.

5. The calculation of a competitive performance score for the match by allocating points for the level of performance overall, achievement of set goals, behaviour throughout the match and the outcome of the match (i.e. points earned for the level of self-challenge and game challenge). This gives the player a personal achievement standard, akin to swimming/athletics, which he can work from and for which he was responsible.

6. In conjunction with the coach, the completion of a daily training review sheet noting down the goals of his training session, and what he felt that he had achieved with respect to technical, tactical, physical and/or mental aspects of his game.

7. Mentally recording any player, coach or parent who makes a 'NON-RESISTANCE' comment to him, then smile, and reinforce RESISTANCE as a Competitive Performance Player.

These tasks form basic, but essential, routines designed to help a player increase resources for personal achievement. The key performance contexts (training, pre-match, in-match and post-match) from which the player is able to draw feelings of success and satisfaction are also covered in these tasks. Constant reference and reinforcement of the self-challenge and game challenge, alongside RESISTANCE restructuring, will gradually foster the activation of positive task and ego-involvement states.

The Competitive Performance Parent

By the final session it should be clear to William's parents that they play a critical role in their son's motivational development. Their role comprises not only the quality of their verbal and visual behaviours, but also how proactive their involvement is in assisting the coach. A skilled consultant may refer to the principles of TARGET and highlight to parents the practical 'dos' and 'don'ts' in each specific category. With the focus on recon-structing Eric's behaviour, in particular, and developing a Competitive Performance motivational climate, both parents should commit and adhere to four core action tasks:

1. Familiarize themselves with the task-oriented approach to apply in key performance contexts, and make statements and ask questions such as 'How did your strokes feel today?', 'You looked fast around the court and recovered well between shots', 'What were your tactics and were they effective?', 'I thought that you could have reacted better after that point, what do you think?'. Each of these points that could be made after the match relates to technical, physical, tactical or mental skill areas. The consultant and Eric could work together towards developing a list of typical compet-itive performance comments or questions to put to William for different situations. Remember, each context is a 'climate' in its own right, so what Eric says before a match in the car is just as important as what he says after William returns from or

leaves for a practice session. His son is about to experience, or has just experienced, an achievement context and Eric must be assertive in facilitating a 'mastery' climate for both situations with the way he interacts with his son.

2. Complete a 'language log book' that Eric will refer to daily on the frequency and nature of competitive performance comments or questions that he makes to his son. Parents have previously found this is a useful exercise for conditioning themselves to behave in a different manner.

3. Learn a simple match analysis and charting system to provide useful performance feedback for the player after the match. Many parents could be more proactive when watching matches. A well-qualified coach should have a number of simple charting systems (such as charting match flow) to teach Eric to keep him focused and to provide William with valuable performance information upon which to reflect.

4. Check the completion of the player's pre- and post-match routines, as well as read through the player's match review and reflections, offering support wherever possible. If a parent watched the match, their match analysis may help the player gain more objective information on the achievement of specific pre-match goals.

The Competitive Performance Coach

The final session with William's parents could be tailored to the coach's needs. All of the action tasks asked of parents would similarly apply to the coach, given that he can contribute to the development of an ideal motivational climate for William. However, there are a few coach-specific tasks that would greatly enhance our coordinated approach. These tasks include the following:

1. Incorporate the TARGET dimensions into coaching sessions (Table 5.1). This will require the coach to check delivery style and the quality of information transmitted to the player. For example, the purpose of specific drills should be clear and relevant to the player. Both performance and process goals should be set where possible; feedback should be performance-related; the player should be encouraged to rate and evaluate success on a drill; recognition should be given for personal improvement and high levels of mental and physical effort. These are the core requirements for a session that seeks to foster the highest quality of motivation from the player.

2. Spend at least 15 minutes at the start of every week discussing and checking the player's training log for the previous week. This is not only helpful in reinforcing to the player the importance of completing a log book, but also in allowing the coach to determine whether messages are being received. If the player has played a tournament, for example, it is the responsibility of the coach to discuss the player's match review/report and agree on the content of future sessions. In this respect, the player recognizes that his areas for personal improvement in matches are valued and are an immediate focus of attention for the coach.

The Competitive Performance Triangle

It should be clear that William, his coach and Eric are not isolated units in the intervention. In fact, the success of the intervention and its effect on readjusting both the attitude and behaviour of father and son rests on the interdependent features of the triangle. Nevertheless, there are two further strategies that could help strengthen links within the triangle:

1. Each individual should be encouraged to develop contingency contracts, which consist of expectations and acceptable behaviours that each one is committed to. Parent, player and coach read through each other's contract, agree with the list of expectations and behaviours, agree to adhere to their own contract and sign each one. These written agreements should be considered essential to the effectiveness of the intervention and monitored closely by all three.

2. The three should be encouraged to meet on a regular basis to discuss achievements and other tennis-related issues, including any breaches of contract. Each member would be asked to present a short personal progress report, with the player chairing the meeting to emphasize their responsibility as a competitive athlete.

Summary

The practical suggestions described here are extensive and detailed yet reflect common sense. They are extensive because it is necessary to modify the cognitions, behaviour and beliefs of a social unit within an environment that does not lend itself well to change. Having carried out the educational role and set up the programme, the consultant should be on hand to review progress and be quick to recognize unacceptable behaviour from anyone. While the professional consulting process requires time and money, both can be well spent if each member of the triangle adheres to their roles and responsibilities.

While reading this case study we hope that it is possible to perceive a natural transfer to other sports and to recognize that achievement goal and climate interventions in youth sport are similar to those in any other sport when faced with a performer processing negative attitudes and behaviour in competition. There may, indeed, be truth in the cliché that 'attitude is everything'!

References

Ames, C. (1992) 'Achievement goals, motivational climate and motivational processes'. In G. C. Roberts (ed.), *Motivation in Sport and Exercise*, pp. 161–176, Champaign, IL: Human Kinetics.

Duda, J. L. (1993) 'Goals: A social cognitive approach to the study of achievement motivation in sport'. In R. N. Singer, M. Murphey and L. K. Tennant (eds.), *Handbook of Research on Sport Psychology*, pp. 421–436, New York: Macmillan.

Duda, J. L., Chi, L., Newton, M. L., Walling M. D. and Catley, D. (1995) 'Task and ego-orientation and intrinsic motivation in sport', *International Journal of Sport Psychology* 26:40–63.

Duda, J. L. and Whitehead, J. (1998) 'Measurement of goal perspectives in the physical domain'. In J. L. Duda (ed.), *Advances in Sport and Exercise Psychology Measurement*, pp. 21–48, Morgantown, WV: Fitness Information Technology.

Fox, K., Goudas, M., Biddle, S., Duda, J. and Armstrong, N. (1994) 'Children's task and ego goal profiles in sport', *British Journal of Educational Psychology* 64:253–261.

Hall, H. K. and Kerr, A. W. (1997) 'Motivational antecedents of pre-competitive anxiety in youth sport', *The Sport Psychologist* 11:24–42.

Hardy, L., Jones, G. and Gould, D. (1996) *Understanding Psychological Preparation for Sport*, Chichester: Wiley.

Harwood, C. G. (1996) 'Maximizing competitive performance through effective goal setting'. In *Coaches and Coaching* 22, Spring:16–20; Lawn Tennis Association.

Harwood, C. G., Hardy, L. and Swain, A. (2000) 'Achievement goals in competitive sport: A critique of conceptual and measurement issues', *Journal of Sport and Exercise Psychology* 22:235–255.

Harwood, C. G. and Swain, A. B. (1998) 'Antecedents of pre-competition achievement goals in elite junior tennis players', *Journal of Sport Sciences* 16:357–371.

Hatzigeorgiadis, A. and Biddle, S. (1999) 'The effects of goal orientation and perceived competence on cognitive interference during tennis and snooker performance', *Journal of Sport Behavior* 22:479–501.

Hatzigeorgiadis, A. and Biddle, S. J. H. (2000) 'Assessing cognitive interference in sport: Development of the Thought Occurrence Questionnaire for Sport', *Anxiety, Stress and Coping* 13:65–86.

Jones, G. (1995) 'More than just a game: Research developments and issues in competitive anxiety in sport', *British Journal of Psychology* 86:449–478.

Maehr, M. L. and Nicholls, J. G. (1980) 'Culture and achievement motivation: A second look'. In N. Warren (ed.), *Studies in Cross-cultural Psychology, Vol. II*, pp. 221–267, New York: Academic Press.

Nicholls, J. G. (1989) *The Competitive Ethos and Democratic Education*, Cambridge, MA: Harvard University Press.

Ntoumanis, N. and Biddle, S. (1999a) 'A review of motivational climate in physical activity', *Journal of Sports Sciences* 17:643–665.

Ntoumanis, N. and Biddle, S. J. H. (1999b) 'Affect and achievement goals in physical activity: A meta-analysis', *Scandinavian Journal of Medicine and Science in Sports* 9:315–332.

Ntoumanis, N., Biddle, S. J. H. and Haddock, G. (1999) 'The mediating role of coping strategies on the relationship between achievement motivation and affect in sport', *Anxiety, Stress and Coping* 12:299–327.

Swain, A. B. and Harwood, C. G. (1996) 'Antecedents of state goals in age-group swimmers: An interactionist perspective', *Journal of Sports Sciences* 14:111–124.

chapter six

In pursuit of the perfect performance

IAN COCKERILL

The use of superlatives is commonplace when describing sporting achievements, but it may be overdone. Describing an athlete or a performance as the best, the fastest or the most skilful is a frequent occurrence among those who talk and write about sport. Given the rewards that are available for whoever is number one in the world in their sport, it is unsurprising that, for some, the attainment of perfection can become an obsession. There are weekly stories of individual athletes who follow a daily disciplined routine that they hope – perhaps even expect – will lead to them being perfect. To have a perfect golf swing, take a perfect penalty or run a perfect race is something that many sportsmen and sportswomen pursue relentlessly in their training.

On the one hand it is laudable to seek excellence in whatever one does, but an irrational drive for perfection can be psychologically damaging and, if taken to extremes, ultimately destructive. The perfectionist athlete will set high performance standards and difficult goals, both of which are necessary in order to attain success. But therein lies the problem, because the perfectionist often has difficulty in defining what that success is. For them, winning does not necessarily imply that they have been successful, particularly if the performance fell below the standard they set.

One of the duties of a sport psychologist is to assist an athlete in fulfilling potential while living a balanced life. This is easy to say, but much more difficult for the athlete to achieve in the present competitive climate, where coming second is often regarded as failure. 'Nobody's perfect' and 'Simply the best' are frequently heard phrases in sport and it was recurring themes such as these that three years ago led me to explore the literature on perfectionism and to investigate its incidence among athletes. I engaged a small group of committed and enthusiastic students in various projects and discussed the pros and cons of perfectionism with coaches of professional and elite amateur players across several sports. What follows in this chapter is a description of problems that can be associated with perfectionism and its underlying theoretical position at the present time. A composite case study will be described that is not based on one individual, but draws upon examples from several elite athletes whose perfectionist attitudes and behaviour have been partly beneficial, but also limiting to their progress. One particular player, 'Jane' (not her real name), has agreed to her experiences being described and discussed and I am most grateful to her for giving this permission.

The case of 'Jane'

Jane is an international badminton player. She is 25 years old and has been playing competitive badminton for more than 15 years. She has a good first degree and would be described as a 'natural athlete'. We have been working together for about two years and in that time have developed a mutual trust within our professional relationship. I have considerable respect for Jane as a player and as a person. She works hard to improve all aspects of her game and is held in high regard by those who coach her.

In badminton, as with several other sports, status is determined by national and international rankings, which reflect tournament success. However, although rankings provide a good form guide, the true situation can be blurred according to the prestige of tournaments entered. Jane has a high national ranking, but is constantly seeking to improve it, principally by working longer and harder. It is not surprising that injuries will occur from time to time and in Jane's case several have sometimes occurred more or less consecutively. She usually responds positively at these times, which is probably a reflection of her commitment to rehabilitation and a good relationship with her physiotherapist.

During our first meeting Jane described herself as 'an error machine', but also as a perfectionist, tending to emphasize her limitations as a player while disregarding her many achievements. In explaining that there were two broad categories of perfectionism, one that is motivating and the other debilitating, she felt that she was more of the former. Thus, at this stage it is important to emphasize that, contrary to the focus of much of the perfectionism research, having perfectionist tendencies may not be entirely negative. Research into negative perfectionism will be examined later in the chapter when considering its psychopathological nature, but there is also evidence that there is such a person as a 'positive perfectionist'. Slade and Owens (1998) have described them as those who demonstrate cognitions and behaviours that are directed towards achieving difficult goals to produce positive outcomes. They argued that a positive perfectionist is driven by a desire to succeed. Isn't that precisely what we observe in any ambitious and successful athlete? Without a positive approach to sport that reflects enjoyment, commitment and enthusiasm, the attainment of difficult goals is unlikely. By contrast, a negative perfectionist will be driven by the pursuit of success that is a reflection of a need to avoid failure. The psychopathology of perfectionism manifests itself in the latter condition and, although there are some athletes who 'compete to avoid defeat', most elite athletes reflect positive perfectionist characteristics.

That has been principally the situation with Jane; usually dedicated for the right reasons, but depressed on occasions when results were not as she would wish them to be. It is also symptomatic of many racket-sport players that they acquire irrational beliefs about certain opponents, namely that they can't beat them. There is usually a tendency to think about playing that person, rather than an opponent; in other words, they personalize the opposition. Jane's evaluation of a tournament performance is often typical of this and it has been helpful when she has talked about the draw in advance of playing so that we could identify and then attempt to change some of her irrational beliefs about a perceived outcome.

ACSI-28 SCORES

Jane's capacity for coping with her life as an elite badminton player was indicated by her results from the Athlete Coping Skills Inventory (ACSI-28) devised by Smith *et al.* (1995). Of the seven factors, she scored highly for goal setting, 'coachability' and confidence, moderately for concentration, peaking for a tournament and coping with disappointment. Her poorest score was for worry, which tends to reflect a relatively limited ability to cope with difficulties. We naturally discussed these data and I pointed out to Jane that she was probably better at coping than she thought, especially given some difficult situations that she was dealing with outside badminton at the time. An interesting strategy that she proposed, and which I agreed with, was for her to be a little more selfish and learn to say 'no' to some of the demands being placed upon her.

Perhaps one of the more obvious characteristics that Jane revealed was a tendency to be hard on herself. This is not unusual in one who shows fairly obvious negative perfectionist characteristics. Her speed around the court, power and flexibility were not in question, but it was fitness that she tended to work hardest on after a disappointing tournament, rather than, for example, the technical aspects of her game. She keeps a well-organized training diary, but mainly records details of her training programme. During our seventh meeting Jane said that she felt she needed to be more consistent. When asked to explain what she meant by this, she acknowledged for the first time that she would usually start well, win the first set and be leading in the second. She would then lose her concentration and let things slip, commencing, as she put it, 'the downward spiral'. Unfortunately, this usually went unrecognized and we agreed that 'triggers' were needed to bring her back on track; perhaps towelling down briefly so that she could begin to think 'smarter'.

From a personal construct analysis Jane described herself as dependable, ambitious, respected and organized. She tended to score highly on each of 10 constructs used to describe her ideal self. Despite this, however, her self-image continued to appear low. When we discussed the anomaly, she revealed a good deal in saying that she needed to have a good win to prove that she *can* do it. It was the start of a new tournament season in Olympic year and, realistically, Jane did not feel that she would be selected for the Great Britain team, but there was always a chance.

Given a 'good win', as she put it, she felt that psychologically she would then move to the next level. At the first major tournament of the season the win was achieved and this set her up for the following few months. There was continuing evidence that Jane rushed to finish her matches, was keen to maintain a good early start and then relied mainly on her fitness to win the match. As soon as an opponent demonstrated equal fitness, self-doubt crept in and points were quickly lost, often from a series of unforced errors.

SELF-BELIEF ISSUES

Jane's difficulty with self-belief, or self-efficacy, might have been associated with some of her perfectionist characteristics. In a study of male and female undergraduates, Hart *et al.* (1998) provided further support for the view that perfectionism can be adaptive as well as maladaptive. When excessively high standards are set by a player, or a player sets those standards for others, self-efficacy tends to be low. However, when high standards are set for a player by, say, a coach, self-efficacy is likely to be high. This is an important issue, since there is increasing awareness that a successful outcome is largely determined by high self-efficacy, and vice versa. Jane has tended to go into tournaments with many preconceptions, usually negative, about the possible outcome. When a desired result is not achieved she often responds by being even more determined to succeed in the next tournament, which has meant reaching a specific stage, for example the semi-final, depending upon the standard of the event. One of her shortcomings, perhaps, is that she keeps the pressure on herself and has said, 'Losing makes it hard to live with yourself'.

Rather than changing her strategy when necessary within a match, she does not accept that errors are inevitable and thinks, 'Here we go again'. A particularly telling comment from Jane after a solid performance, but one which fell below the standard she had set herself, was that she had '... snatched defeat from the jaws of victory'. Pressure is a word that Jane has used a good deal and she now recognizes that much of it is self-imposed. It became clear to her that much of the perceived pressure came from her belief that she was not playing to her potential. She frequently felt that she could do so much better. If she progressed to the semi-finals, it should have been the final; when she won a match, the number of points lost loomed larger than her victory. Thinking of this kind is typical of negative perfectionism and it can be most debilitating for a player.

To summarize Jane's situation, her strengths are that she is very well organized without being obsessive, and she sets high standards in all aspects of her life. On the other hand, she realizes that she worries unduly about making mistakes and when mistakes occur during a match she either fails to recognize what is happening, or does not change her game plan because of doubts that the change will be beneficial. An important attraction of sport, of course, is that the outcome of a competition is never wholly predictable. For Jane, uncertainty is difficult to deal with, although she is learning to 'expect the unexpected', as she puts it. Consistency is a word that often features in our conversations and, once again, she finds it difficult to accept that it will vary between matches for a variety of reasons.

It is invariably difficult to describe a player in one simple phrase, but in attempting to summarize Jane it would probably be that she tries too hard. Her commitment to badminton is unquestionable and she is prepared to do whatever is necessary to raise her already high standing in the game. She trains for approximately 21 hours a week for not less than three hours a day, often starting at 7.30am and programming three sessions across the day until 6.00pm. Her schedule includes on-court speed, agility and endurance work, weights, flexibility, badminton skills and drills. She also makes time for a daily evaluation of training or match outcomes and uses a variety of imagery and mental training techniques, which are carried out in the badminton hall and elsewhere. Given that Jane has an unhealthy as well as a self-expressed healthy perfectionist attitude, it is appropriate to examine these constructs in more detail, to identify the underlying theories of perfectionism and to evaluate the research, especially that which relates directly to sport.

Is perfectionism really a problem?

It is unfortunate that much of the work on perfectionism has focused upon its negative aspects. An early account by Hollender (1965) was published in a psychiatry journal and described the difficulties that perfectionist patients can experience. It is only over the past decade that the importance of perfectionism has been recognized in sport psychology research but, to date, there has been relatively little work in this area.

Perfectionism, then, is associated with behaviour that exceeds what is required of a situation. Perfectionists set personal standards that are always beyond reach and they are never satisfied with their performance. Hollender (1965) described a perfectionist as someone who seeks to 'perform perfectly', as distinct from one who seeks a 'perfect self-image'. The outcome of attempting to live up to others' expectations may be temporary depression and a feeling of despair and worthlessness. There is a focus upon faults and weaknesses, rather than upon personal attributes and skills.

A model of perfectionism that has implications for sport, although not originally associated with athletes, is the multidimensional model of Hewitt and Flett (1991). They identified three discrete components of the construct, namely (a) self-oriented, (b) other-oriented and (c) socially prescribed perfectionism. The first of these is fairly typical of the high-achieving athlete and Jane's personality reflects this in several ways. The benefits of self-oriented characteristics are having high standards and high achievement motivation. The disadvantages include being overcritical of one's performance and being unable to enjoy a successful performance for its own sake. Concern at being unable to control outcomes is also a reflection of this characteristic and has clear implications for competitive athletes.

The other-oriented dimension is where others are criticized for their poor achievements if certain criteria are not met. Criticism, blame and mistrust are typical features and sometimes include irrational beliefs that others 'should' and 'must' act in a certain way. As pointed out earlier, a high score on these two traits may be synonymous with low self-efficacy and they are, therefore, undesirable. The third dimension, socially prescribed perfectionism, emphasizes a striving to attain the standards that are perceived to have been set by others. Once again, a high score would tend to reflect a fear of failure and depression because of the unrealistic goals believed to be imposed by others. While this may be true, it is also possible that having high standards expected of you will lead to successful goal achievement, especially by those who are self-oriented perfectionists. Although the present discussion is associated specifically with a player, Jane, perfectionism has implications for coaches as well. Perhaps a coach who is considered to be high on each of the three dimensions would be largely ineffective owing to an inability to accept a very good performance from a player, while seeking one that is 'perfect'.

Thus far, the benefits of perfectionist thinking have been shown to be few and although it can have undoubted shortcomings for some, others have much to gain from their perfectionism. Hamachek (1978) has described positive and negative perfectionism, which, in terms of the cognitive appraisal of the outcome of a match, can also be referred to as 'healthy' and 'unhealthy' perfectionism. The former emphasizes strengths and achievements, while the latter is associated with behaviour that is designed to avoid losing. Terry-Short et al. (1995) designed an instrument that measures both dimensions as well as personal perfectionism and socially prescribed perfectionism, called the Positive and Negative Perfectionism Scale (PANPS). Their study of just 20 successful athletes revealed that they scored high on positive and low on negative perfectionism, indicating that being a perfectionist is not necessarily detrimental to an athlete. However, it is the instrument used to evaluate the construct that now requires careful scrutiny and there may be a case for developing a sport-specific perfectionism measure.

An important issue for sport psychology research to consider is how positive perfectionism might be transformed into negative perfectionism as a consequence of it being contingent upon social pressures. Slade and Owens (1998) have suggested that after early successes and positive reinforcement, a player eventually becomes aware of the expectancies of others. That which was once approach behaviour and the pursuit of success, now becomes behaviour designed to avoid failure and the adoption of a negative perfectionist perspective. They also exemplified the positive–negative shift for a young athlete whose parents have competed at a high level. Failing to match their achievements can lead to striving towards a standard that the youngster knows will never be attained. There are many examples of this situation and it can be difficult for a young athlete to deal with unless they change to a different sport or achieve success in a different area.

DIMENSIONS OF PERFECTIONISM

The three-factor Multidimensional Perfectionism Scale (MPS) developed by Hewitt, Mittelstaedt and Wollert (1989) and Hewitt and Flett (1990) coincided with the production of a similarly named scale by Frost et al. (1990). The latter MPS identified six dimensions of perfectionism, although the principal one was 'concern about making mistakes'. The others were 'having high personal standards', 'perceiving high parental expectations', 'perceiving high parental criticism', 'doubting the quality of one's actions' and 'seeking a high level of order and organization'. The six factors were derived from various existing measures of perfectionism and it can be seen that only one is associated with what has been referred to here as normal, positive or healthy perfectionism, namely high personal standards. A factor analysis of each scale showed that concern over mistakes accounted for the greatest amount of variance (22.5 per cent), followed by organization (12.5 per cent) and high personal standards (6.6 per cent). However, since organization was the dimension least associated with the other five MPS sub-scales and other perfectionism measures, only those five factors were summed to calculate an overall perfectionism score. Organization was retained as a separate factor and was represented by six of the 35 items in the Frost *et al.* (1990) MPS scale.

In order to address the multidimensional nature of perfectionism, Frost *et al.* (1993) compared the two MPS scales and found that there was a large measure of overlap between them. They described the relationship between the scales as producing a 'conceptually clean two-factor solution', namely (a) maladaptive evaluation concerns and (b) positive achievement strivings. The former is linked to concern over mistakes, parental criticism, parental expectations, doubts about actions and socially prescribed perfectionism. The latter is associated with personal standards, organization, self-oriented perfectionism and other-oriented perfectionism.

The implications of each of the above dimensions for sport are clear. Accordingly, the two versions of the MPS (Frost *et al.* 1990; Hewitt and Flett 1991) and the PANPS (Terry-Short *et al.* 1995) are currently the measures that sport psychologists are most likely to relate to in their work. In attempting to disentangle the many strands that contribute to perfectionist behaviour, whether inherited or acquired, several concepts need to be considered. For example, motivation orientation, level of trait anxiety and the influence of significant others are just three areas that can contribute to the development and subsequent manifestation of perfectionist behaviour among athletes and coaches. Future research effort should focus upon both healthy and unhealthy aspects of perfectionism in studying the various interrelationships that occur in sport.

From an applied standpoint, interventions are frequently necessary for those who demonstrate irrational beliefs about what they feel they must attain or do. It is important to address such perceptions with an athlete and encourage a more rational mode of thinking. For example, Jane may win a tournament but dismiss her victory as being of limited consequence, because she believes that international events are much more important. On the other hand she may think perfectly rationally and be satisfied in defeat if she has taken a set from a player for the first time. Thus, perfectionism does not only vary between athletes, it also varies within an individual as well. What is important is to ensure that Jane adopts a positive style of thinking and acting. This has not been an issue in training, but during competition there is sometimes a need for her to realize that she will invariably make some mistakes – everyone does – and to recognize them and correct them. Because most of the work in perfectionism has focused upon its negative features, the next section will examine some of these aspects and attempt to draw some implications for sport, and for Jane in particular.

Some psychopathological features of perfectionism

It is probably reasonable to speculate that anyone affected by high negative perfectionism is unlikely to succeed at a high level in sport. However, given that elite athletes are positive perfectionists, there may be a fine balance between the two constructs, with one readily influencing the other. Flett *et al.* (1994) found an association between self-oriented perfectionism and Type A behaviour, exemplified by the need to achieve high standards consistently. Once again, although Type A behaviour is recognized as being undesirable, it does incorporate several of the characteristics that are desired in a successful athlete, for example competitiveness and possessing high standards. On the other hand, Flett *et al.* (1994) have pointed out that Type A individuals are also predisposed to anger, impatience and irritability, not an unusual observation among some elite athletes and sometimes evident in relationships with a coach. It was not surprising, therefore, that Flett, Hewitt and Dyek (1989) found a positive relationship between scores on the Burns (1980) perfectionism scale and trait anxiety. Life stresses were found to mediate the relationship, hence anyone seeking to reach a high level in sport is required to cope successfully with a variety of stressful situations, yet it is interesting that athletes often fail to acknowledge the potential influence of life events. It was pointed out that Jane had encountered a series of changes to her life and, while none was a major issue in itself, together they probably had an adverse effect on her badminton.

Injuries of various degrees of severity are incurred by most high-level athletes and the high-intensity training of full-time badminton players means that they also receive their share of problems. Although it is considered that the injury-prone athlete is more conjecture than reality, it is possible that some aspects of perfectionism may be linked to concerns about health and fear of injury. Saboonchi and Lundh (1997), for example, used Hope's (1990) modified Stroop task (Stroop 1938) with undergraduates and found that negative perfectionist characteristics tended to be associated with a fear of situations that might not occur, such as fear of injury. Should a badminton player think in this way, then there is a possibility that failing to go for shots and being tense during a match will increase the likelihood of an injury. 'Positive thinking' is a term much loved by coaches and it features almost as frequently as 'lack of confidence', probably the phrase that coaches use most to describe an underperforming player. Frost *et al.* (1995) showed that people high in concern over mistakes responded to making mistakes with reduced confidence and the feeling that they should have performed better. This outcome is unsurprising because many athletes react in such a fashion to a performance perceived to be below par. However, it is premature to suggest that the 'mistakes' dimension is the one that is associated most closely with low confidence. It may be that possessing high standards – a healthy perfectionist characteristic – is linked to loss of confidence. Thus, while it is likely that perfectionism and confidence are connected in some way, the way in which this occurs among athletes remains unclear.

An interesting approach to studying perfectionism, and one that has potential for early diagnosis of sub-clinical depression in athletes, was that of Lynd-Stevenson and Hearne (1999). They devised two scales from the Frost *et al.* (1990) MPS to evaluate 'passive perfectionism' and 'active perfectionism' and showed that depressive affect and procrastination were related to the former, but active perfectionism – striving to achieve – was unrelated to depression. Moreover, those individuals high in passive perfectionism, that is, concerned about making mistakes and doubting their actions, were affected more by stressful life events than those who were low in passive perfectionism. It was pointed out earlier that Jane had experienced difficult life events over several months and the Lynd-Stevenson and Hearn (1999) study suggests that life stresses can, indeed, influence depressive affect, notably among high-passive perfectionists. There is a tendency for some athletes, including badminton players, to express acute self-doubt and fear of making mistakes after a poor run of performances. Determining whether those players are high in passive perfectionism would provide a useful insight into the possible under-lying causes of unfulfilled potential. Also of interest was the finding that a high level of need for organization was associated with low depression, again an outcome that may have implications for both research and subsequent interventions with athletes. Accordingly, this study showed that perfectionism per se is unrelated to depressive affect and it is certain features of passive, but not active, perfectionism that influence depres-sion. At a clinical level it is clear that depression has a powerful effect upon the life of an individual suffering from it. Athletes tend to experience relatively mild symptoms, prin-cipally of self-doubt that may be brought on by career-threatening injury, the end of a full-time athletic career, or even being rejected from a squad or team. Although there have been instances of severe depression among athletes, there are fortunately few.

To conclude this section on the psychopathology of perfectionism, Blatt (1995) proposed that the antecedents of depression stemming from self-criticism may be derived from early experiences. To address them fully, he highlighted the need for longi-tudinal studies, autobiographical accounts and clinical reports of early life experiences. In respect of athlete behaviour, it is possible that perceived pressure from coaches, as much as from parents, can influence subsequent attitudes and behaviour. This area has not been addressed by researchers and, given the continuing reduction of the age at which sport becomes 'serious', studies in this area are timely.

Perfectionism, the elite athlete and suggestions for Jane

Elite athlete is a term that is often used, but frequently misunderstood. For the purpose of this discussion an elite athlete is one who is either a full-time professional, or an amateur who trains for 20 hours or more each week and is probably competing at national and international level. The remainder of this chapter will draw together what are seen to be key issues for the perfectionist player and suggestions will be made with reference to Jane. Alongside her own unique characteristics, she will be considered to possess attitudes and behaviours that may be attributed to other elite-level players. Thus, this section illustrates a composite profile, rather than that of a specific individual.

In emphasizing once again that perfectionism has positive as well as negative connotations, it is important that Jane also recognizes this and she should attempt to focus upon her positive perfectionist qualities rather than the negative elements. It is sometimes evident that high-achieving players see themselves as reaching a high standard under false pretences; this is the so-called 'imposter phenomenon' (IP), a term used by Clance and Imes (1978) to describe high achievers. There have been occasions when Jane has felt overawed when playing against those whose names were very well known in badminton. She would tend to question what she was doing playing against such exalted opposition, or in a world-class tournament. This kind of thinking is not uncommon among athletes, especially at occasions such as the Olympic Games. For them, the goal is to be selected, a major achievement in itself, and the reality of having to actually compete against the best can prove stressful. An investigation by Henning, Ely and Shaw (1998) of IP in students from the health professions found that high levels of perfectionism led to the experience of IP and placed them at risk of psychological distress. Although Jane was not particularly susceptible to IP, she did appear to benefit from discussing both her current situation as a player and her future aspirations. The recommendation by Henning, Ely and Shaw (1998) that peer discussion groups, workshops and counselling may benefit IP sufferers is valuable. There are occasions when group discussions and workshops will show a player that others also experience similar feelings of self-doubt and inadequacy, just as they do.

It has been pointed out that there have been few studies of perfectionism in athletes, a statement that has been reiterated by Hall, Kerr and Matthews (1998). They referred to an experiment by Frost and Henderson (1991) that examined the incidence of anxiety, confidence, attitudes to competition and thoughts before competing among women athletes. Jane's concerns about letting others down was reflected in the results of that study and of special interest was the observation that negative features of perfectionism correlated with coaches' assessment that those with a high concern about mistakes do not recover easily from competition errors. Although Jane discusses her game with her coaches, three-way discussions between player, coach and sport psychologist now feature in her preparation and this kind of session has been shown to be beneficial. Hall, Kerr and Matthews (1998) examined goal orientation alongside perfectionism and they offered a way forward for alleviating pre-competition anxiety. Perfectionism is a robust personality characteristic that leads to chronic maladaptive behaviour, and therefore it is important to change what is possible, namely goal orientation. It is rarely straightforward to change a player's focus from an ego to a task orientation owing to the constant emphasis on tournament success and world ranking, but Jane has attempted to do this.

Reassurance from her badminton coaches and advisers has been valuable and commensurate with a noticeable change in her tournament behaviour. Emphasis has been placed on controlling that which is possible, while trying to disregard that which is not. In particular, preconceptions about an opponent have been debilitating and Jane now tries to see her opposition merely as opponents, rather than named individuals.

ATHLETE BURNOUT AND DISORDERED EATING

There are two other important issues worth reporting that are relevant to perfectionism in sport, namely burnout and eating disorders. The two are related as the incidence of fatigue in burnout, which is attributable to excessive training, is closely associated with eating disorders (Bamber, Cockerill and Carroll 2000). Of equal importance is the concern that young athletes, in particular, may be overtraining and in some sports there is considerable emphasis on what can be described as the 'aesthetic element' in performance. Unlike gymnastics and diving, badminton scoring does not incorporate this element, but the importance of an appropriate diet and weight could lead to an inappropriate focus by some players. Jane eats well and her weight and body composition do not present any problems for her. She does, however, train extremely hard and, from time to time, experiences excessive fatigue and heightened self-doubt, both symptomatic of burnout. The term was used by Freudenberger (1974) in relation to occupational stress, and burnout is most often measured by the Maslach Burnout Inventory (MBI) by Maslach, Jackson and Leiter (1996) to evaluate emotional exhaustion, depersonalization and personal accomplishment.

There has been little work on burnout in professional athletes, yet this group is likely to be highly susceptible to the condition, and none as far as is known that associates burnout with perfectionism in athletes or coaches. Magnusson, Nias and White (1996) studied fatigue in nurses and found that negative perfectionism was associated with physical, and especially mental, fatigue. They proposed that it may be possible to meet high standards providing that one is healthy and not under undue pressure. Although Jane possesses more healthy than unhealthy perfectionist characteristics, as with elite athletes generally, it is difficult for her to recognize potential burnout symptoms. Magnusson and her colleagues recommended the implementation of cognitive behaviour therapy as used by Sharpe *et al.* (1996) for treating chronic fatigue syndrome. Jane's experiences of short-term burnout have also benefited from a similar intervention in order to discourage irrational thinking.

In two of a series of studies of competitive junior tennis players, Gould *et al.* (1996a; 1996b) adopted both quantitative and qualitative approaches to examine burnout. They emphasized the intensity of expectations placed upon young athletes to succeed. That really means winning tournaments week-in, week-out. They reinforced findings from other research in sport and elsewhere that while life events and various situational variables will contribute to burnout, perfectionism – a robust personality characteristic – is of considerable importance. Qualitative approaches to studying perfectionism tend to reveal that 'nice' people who have concern for others may experience more problems with negative, or neurotic, perfectionism than those who are less sensitive. Jane can be described as a nice person. As mentioned earlier, she relates well to other players and to coaches and she is highly thought of as a coach herself. In trying to please others and fulfil their expectations of her, she tends to take on too many commitments; what she believes are obligations. Encouraging Jane to be more selfish in terms of doing more for herself has proved partially successful. At least she now recognizes the large amounts of time she has spent dealing with the problems that others have brought to her.

An issue that has been found to influence the impact of negative aspects of perfectionism is the effect of parents on young athletes. Gould *et al.* (1996a) have argued that burnout in players has its antecedents in high levels of parental expectations and parental criticism. While this may be true in some cases, it could be less widespread than hitherto supposed, or else is specific to certain sports; for example individual sports such as badminton and tennis. Perfectionism data from young professional footballers (Cockerill, in press) suggests that in team sports there is either less pressure from parents to succeed, or parent-related items from the Frost *et al.* (1990) MPS were not answered truthfully.

Conclusions and future directions

Despite a general consensus that perfectionism is usually defined according to the context in which it is used, there is little doubt that both the healthy and unhealthy aspects of the construct require close scrutiny by sport psychologists. Researchers need to examine its various dimensions across a range of populations, while practitioners should be aware of its presence in some form among competitive athletes and coaches. There are many areas of applied psychology that interact one with another, but none more so than the construct known as perfectionism. In particular, a sport psychologist is closely associated with issues of motivation, anxiety, goal setting, lifestyle management, player–coach relationships, deselection, coping with injury and so on. Perfectionists will respond to these issues in quite specific ways according to an adaptive or a maladaptive predisposition.

Jane's story has been used to illustrate her perception of herself as an elite badminton player, but examples from other players in different sports, both male and female, have been used to link theoretical positions with applied work. There are a number of key issues that have been addressed with Jane over a two-year period. Some interventions have been successful, others less so, but each has enabled this player to focus more precisely upon her principal concerns and to recognize her many strengths and positive attributes. In particular, she now has a more realistic acceptance of what she is likely to achieve as a player and is beginning to consider her longer-term objectives more fully. It may still prove quite difficult for Jane to be more forgiving of herself and to be less self-deprecating, but there is evidence to suggest that she is more settled in her life. There is also good reason to indicate that given her coaching potential, she will be able to guide others successfully in their quest to achieve their goals in badminton.

To illustrate the point that imperfection can be worth more than something that is perfect, Pacht (1984) has used the analogy of two objects, one hand-made and the other machine-made. Despite its flaws, the hand-made object was more expensive than the perfectly formed one. It was the imperfections that made one object a thing of beauty and a true work of art. Pacht stated that perfectionists never win because the goals they set for themselves are always out of reach. Not very long ago a lower second-class honours degree represented a good performance, these days anything less than an upper second seems to indicate failure! What is worse, irrational beliefs suggest that the 'failure' will be reflected in everything that the perfectionist does, both now and into the future. Barrow and Moore (1983) have proposed that perfectionist behaviour is acquired. For example, an overcritical coach can easily effect undue concern with a player's weight that could lead to an eating disorder, while the successful parent can demand too much from their less-talented offspring. The extent to which perfectionism in parents will manifest itself in their children remains to be determined. Barrow and Moore (1983) inferred that in seeking high standards parents should support, respond to and be available for their children. In that situation there is every opportunity for the development of healthy perfectionist characteristics. Finally, it is possible that there may also be errors and inconsistencies in the arguments expressed in this chapter, but then 'Who's perfect?'!

(📖 References)

Bamber, D., Cockerill, I. M. and Carroll, D. (2000) 'The pathological status of exercise dependence', *British Journal of Sports Medicine* 34:125–132.

Barrow, J. C. and Moore, C. A. (1983) 'Group interventions with perfectionist thinking', *Personnel and Guidance Journal* 61:612–615.

Blatt, S.J. (1995) 'The destructiveness of perfectionism: implications for the treatment of depression', *American Psychologist* 50:1003–1020.

Burns, D. (1980) 'The perfectionist's script for self-defeat', *Psychology Today* 34–51.

Clance, P. and Imes, S. (1978) 'The imposter phenomenon in high achieving women: dynamics and therapeutic intervention', *Psychotherapy: Theory, Research and Practice* 15:241–247.

Cockerill, I. M. (at press) 'Psychological features of overtraining and the overtraining–perfectionism relationship in sport', *Kinesiology*, (Greece), in press.

Flett, G. L., Hewitt, P. L., Blankstein, K. R. and Dynin, C. B. (1994) 'Dimensions of perfectionism and Type A behaviour', *Personality and Individual Differences* 16:477–485.

Flett, G. L., Hewitt, P. L. and Dyck, D. G. (1989) 'Self-oriented perfectionism, neuroticism and anxiety', *Personality and Individual Differences* 10:731–735.

Freudenberger, H. J. (1974) 'Staff burnout', *Journal of Social Issues* 30:159–165.

Frost, R. O., Heimberg, R. G., Holt, C. S., Mattia, J. I. and Neubauer, A. L. (1993) 'A comparison of two measures of perfectionism', *Personality and Individual Differences* 14:119–126.

Frost, R. O. and Henderson, K. J. (1991) 'Perfectionism and reactions to athletic competition', *Journal of Sport and Exercise Psychology* 91:323–335.

Frost, R. O., Marten, P., Lahart, C. and Rosenblate, R. (1990) 'The dimensions of perfectionism', *Cognitive Therapy and Research* 14:449–468.

Frost, R. O, Turcotte, T. A., Heimberg, R. G., Mattia, J. I., Holt, C. S. and Hope D. A. (1995) 'Reactions to mistakes among subjects high and low in perfectionistic concern over mistakes', *Cognitive Therapy and Research* 19:195–205.

Gould, D., Udry, E., Tuffey, S. and Loehr, J. (1996a) 'Burnout in competitive junior tennis players: I. A quantitative psychological assessment', *The Sport Psychologist* 10:322–340.

Gould, D., Tuffey, S., Udry, E. and Loehr, J. (1996b) 'Burnout in competitive junior tennis players: II. Qualitative analysis', *The Sport Psychologist* 10:341–366.

Hall, H. K, Kerr, A. W and Matthews, J. (1998) 'Pre-competitive anxiety in sport: The contribution of achievement goals and perfectionism', *Journal of Sport and Exercise Psychology* 20:194–217.

Hamachek, D. E. (1978) 'Psychodynamics of normal and neurotic perfectionism', *Psychology* 15:27–33.

Hart, B. A., Gilner, F. H., Handal, P. J. and Gfeller, J. D. (1998) 'The relationship between perfectionism and self-efficacy', *Personality and Individual Differences* 24:109–113.

Henning, K. Ely, S. and Shaw, D. (1998) 'Perfectionism, the imposter phenomenon and adjustment in medical, dental, nursing and pharmacy students', *Medical Education* 32:456–464.

Hewitt, P. L. and Flett, G. L. (1990) 'Perfectionism and depression: A multidimensional analysis', *Journal of Social Behavior and Personality* 5:423–438.

Hewitt, P. L. and Flett, G. L. (1991) 'Perfectionism in the self and social contexts: Conceptualization, assessment and association with psychopathology', *Journal of Personality and Social Psychology* 60:456–470.

Hewitt, P. L., Mittelstaedt, W. and Wollert, R. (1989) 'Validation of a measurement of perfectionism', *Journal of Personality Assessment* 53:133–144.

Hollender, M. H. (1965) 'Perfectionism', *Comprehensive Psychiatry* 6:94–103.

Hope, D. A. (1990) *The Revised Stroop Color-Naming Task for Social Phobics and Panickers*, Lincoln: University of Nebraska.

Lynd-Stevenson, R. M. and Hearn, C. M. (1999) 'Perfectionism and depressive affect: The pros and cons of being a perfectionist', *Personality and Individual Differences* 26:549–562.

Magnusson, A. E., Nias, D. K. B. and White, P. D. (1996) 'Is perfectionism associated with fatigue?', *Journal of Psychosomatic Research* 41:377–383.

Maslach, C., Jackson, S. E. and Leiter, M. P. (1996) *Maslach Burnout Inventory Manual, Third Edition*, Palo Alto, CA: Consulting Psychologists Press.

Pacht, A. R. (1984) 'Reflections on perfection', *American Psychologist* 39:386–390.

Saboonchi, F. and Lundh, L.-G. (1997) 'Perfectionism, self-consciousness and anxiety', *Personality and Individual Differences* 22:921–928.

Sharpe, M., Hawton, K., Simkin, S., Surawy, C., Hackmann, A,. Klimes, I. *et al.* (1996) 'Cognitive behaviour therapy for the chronic fatigue syndrome', *British Medical Journal* 312:22–26.

Slade, P. D. and Owens, R. G. (1998) 'A dual-process model of perfectionism based on reinforcement theory', *Behavior Modification* 22:372–390.

Smith, R. E, Schutz, R. W., Smoll, F. L. and Ptacek, J. T. (1995) 'Development and validation of a multidimensional measure of sport-specific psychological skills', *Journal of Sport and Exercise Psychology* 17:379–398.

Stroop, J. R. (1938) 'Factors affecting speed in serial verbal reactions', *Psychological Monographs* 50:38–48.

Terry-Short, L. A., Owens, R. G., Slade, P. D. and Dewey, M. E. (1995) 'Positive and negative perfectionsim', *Personality and Individual Differences* 18:663–668.

part (three)

Cognitions and confidence

chapter seven

Sport participants' reflections on past events: the role of social cognition

SANDY WOLFSON

The world is a stimulating but puzzling place for sports participants, who regularly experience the joys of success and the pains of failure. Psychological research has demonstrated that people are motivated to come to terms with these events by explaining their results and imagining alternatives to their existing reality, particularly when a disappointing outcome is encountered.

Much of the inspiration for the study of social cognition – the area of psychology that attempts to understand the role played by thought processes in people's understanding of the world – emanated from the work of Fritz Heider (1958), who suggested that people have a basic need to explain the events that occur around them. According to Heider and many other theorists since, we do not like to exist in a state of uncertainty and are uncomfortable with unpredictability and chaos, so we don't like to witness events that appear random and inexplicable. Heider believed we act as amateur scientists in our search for explanations. Just as a scientist will try to understand what causes a disease, the typical human will look for reasons for why an important competition was won or lost. We put together information like the pieces of a puzzle until we come to a conclusion that seems reasonable and acceptable to us.

Unfortunately, we are not truly scientific when we search for causality. This may be partly due to the fact that we are 'cognitive misers' (Taylor 1981), characterized by a tendency to be lazy and an inability to process information efficiently. We do not always spend sufficient time and energy on our analyses, usually preferring to come up with the easiest and most expedient explanations. This may involve focusing on the most obvious, prominent or enticing information, at the expense of data that may be equally influential but more difficult to integrate into our analyses. So in the end, because a full causal analysis would be time-consuming and effortful, we tend to take shortcuts and jump to quick and easy conclusions.

To complicate matters, humans have a tendency to see what they want to see. Just ask any referee! Evidence suggests that we are generally motivated to interpret stimuli in such a way as to maximize our self-esteem and look good to others. Again, we may ignore vital clues and distort information to suit our needs.

Attributions

The search for explanations can be readily seen when someone experiences a negative outcome. Suppose, for example, Tom has just lost an important tennis match which he had hoped to win. Tom will be inclined to try to explain this event. He might offer his coach, Mark, the following explanations:

1. The court was far too hot; it was impossible to play well in that weather.

2. The line judge made some outlandish decisions against me.

3. I react badly to that opponent's gamesmanship. He spent ages dallying around before every serve, and then grunted loudly each time.

4. I guess I haven't really recovered from my bout of flu yet.

Coach Mark might have his own views on the subject. Whether or not he expresses them to Tom, he might think:

5. You spend too much time partying and not enough practising.

6. You lack the necessary level of skill.

7. Every time you're on the verge of succeeding, you blow it. You did that with your exam results too, and in your relationship with Cindy, come to think of it.

8. This kind of result shows that you do not have the temperament to succeed at the highest level.

It is clear that Tom and Mark have come up with many different and varied kinds of explanations for the event. These kinds of explanations are known as attributions. They are all attempts at understanding why an event has occurred. Attributions differ on many important dimensions. Internal attributions are explanations that relate to the person. Mark's attributions 6 and 8 are examples of internal attributions, as they focus on Tom's traits and characteristics. Tom's attributions 1 and 2 about the weather and the line judge are typical of external attributions, as they focus on the situation.

Attributions also differ in terms of their permanence. Stable attributions refer to relatively enduring factors, while unstable ones are more temporary in nature. Tom's attribution 4 is an unstable one, as Tom is unlikely to be troubled by flu over the long term. However, Mark's attribution 8 is stable, as it refers to a long-term personal trait that is unlikely to change.

Global attributions refer to explanations that are pervasive, covering a wide range of events, such as Mark's attribution 7 which refers to a general tendency for Tom to fail, whether in tennis, examinations or relationships. Specific attributions refer to a particular situation. Tom's Attribution 3 suggests that Tom's response is specific to this opponent.

Mark's attribution 5 is controllable in that Tom could train more and party less. The vagaries of the weather and the line judge noted in attributions 1 and 2, though, are uncontrollable and out of Tom's hands.

Attributions are not always easy to classify in these ways, as they mean different things to different people. For example, 'luck' is often cited as an example of an external, unstable, uncontrollable attribution. However, some people see luck as permanently residing within the individual ('He is generally a lucky person') and even, with the help of a rabbit's foot or superstitious pre-game routine, controllable. Thus it is conceivable that an attribution of luck could be perceived as internal, stable, global and controllable.

Attributional bias

David Beckham's sending off cost us dearly. I am not denying it cost us the game. It was unbelievable. We could not have asked more from the players. I don't know if destiny was against us. Everything went against us. But it is not a night for excuses.

(Glenn Hoddle, The Guardian Sport, *1st July, 1998, p.1*)

If it wasn't for bad refereeing we would have won that game.

(Glen Hoddle, Daily Mail, *2nd July, 1998, p. 78.*)

It is helpful to be aware of patterns which tend to emerge when a sports participant explains why an event has been won or lost. Three of the best-known biases, their causes and their functions will be briefly described in this section.

SELF-SERVING BIAS

The most widely researched bias in the context of sport is known as the self-serving bias. This is a tendency for people to focus relatively more on external factors following a failure and internal factors after a success. The bias occurs in a wide range of academic, social and work situations. In sport, evidence for the self-serving bias is overwhelming and inescapable (see Biddle 1993; McAuley and Duncan 1989; Lau and Russell 1980). England manager Glenn Hoddle's above comments, following England's defeat by Italy in the 1998 World Cup, are typical of people's attributions for a loss. Poor refereeing decisions, the state of the pitch, an injury-stricken depleted side, misfortune when the ball hit the post and the luck of the opponent's goalkeeper in thwarting a penalty kick are all common laments after a loss. But it is rare to hear a manager allude to these points after a victory. Suddenly luck is irrelevant, whereas training, skill, teamwork and good coaching are all critical reasons for the success.

Losing is difficult enough without torturing ourselves with thoughts of our short-comings. If our analysis leads us to conclude that we are unskilled or mentally weak, we just might become depressed and give up completely. So the self-serving bias helps us to maintain an acceptable level of self-esteem and offers a defence against feelings of inferiority. The bias may also be a tactic in impression formation, designed to ensure that we look good to others (see Greenberg, Pyszczynski and Solomon 1982; Riess, Rosenfeld and Melburg 1981).

Alternatively, Miller and Ross (1975) contend that the bias may not be a motivational strategy at all, but rather a result of information processing. People strive towards and put effort into succeeding, so when they do succeed they see a logical relationship between their efforts and their outcome. In such cases they will, of course, take credit through the use of internal attributions. When they fail, they are likely to be confused and conjure up a variety of internal and external attributions. Mullen and Riordan's (1988) survey of 22 studies of self-serving bias in naturalistic settings found support for the information processing explanation, with internal attributions generally occurring for successful outcomes, but external ones not consistently given for failure.

If the self-serving bias serves such positive functions as protecting our self-esteem and offering us protection from unpleasant information, why should sport psychologists be concerned about it? One obvious problem is that the self-serving bias might at times be taken too far in removing responsibility from the individual. If Tom consistently blames external sources such as the weather and the referee whenever he experiences a defeat, he may become complacent and fail to contemplate how to improve.

FUNDAMENTAL ATTRIBUTION ERROR AND ACTOR-OBSERVER BIAS

The fundamental attribution error (Jones and Harris 1967; Napolitan and Goethals 1979; Ross 1977) refers to our basic tendency to focus on internal rather than external factors when attempting to explain *other* people's behaviour. We overlook situational forces and instead decide that other people's actions represent their inherent personal characteristics. Thus, when coach Mark observes Tom losing a tennis match, he may ignore possible situational factors and conclude that Tom's defeat must be due to something to do with Tom – his temperament, lack of skill, questionable talent or failure to commit to training. Luginbuhl and Bell (1989) found that athletes tended to give internal reasons for another person's unexpectedly poor performance.

Research into the actor-observer bias suggests that the failure to incorporate situational factors only happens when observing others. When it comes to explaining what happens to ourselves, we are much more likely to consider external causes (Nisbett *et al.* 1973). The 'perceptual focusing' explanation for this is that people perceive salient (prominent and vivid) stimuli as causal factors (McArthur and Post 1977). If you observe a runner stumble and fall, it will be the runner who is salient in your perceptual field, so you will make internal attributions for the stumble, such as 'He's a rather clumsy and inattentive person'. If *you* stumble while running, however, the situation rather than you will be salient, and your explanation will be external, such as 'That crack in the road caused me to fall'.

The 'divergent perspectives' explanation, on the other hand, suggests that people do not have easy access to information about another individual, nor are they generally motivated to gain this insight. Empathizing with close acquaintances (Prager and Cutler 1990) or performers from within your own sport (Luginbuhl and Bell 1989) thus serves to decrease actor-observer bias. Access to our emotions and physiological state also brings us to believe that we are more multifaceted than others and thus more susceptible to situational influences (Sande, Goethals and Radloff 1988). Wolfson (1997) found that elite male and female swimmers perceived a wide range of factors as having a greater impact on their own results than on the results of their fellow competitors. For example, they tended to believe that the temperature of the water had a greater effect on themselves, even though they were all swimming in the same water at the same time.

The fundamental attribution error and actor-observer bias can be problematic for sports performers by leading to oversimplistic assessments of a player's character and future behaviour. Conflict and friction in relationships between players and their teammates or coach can also arise, as each individual may arrive at a different explanation for a result. Because they sincerely believe that they are right, each might then feel insulted by the other or make accusations of lack of insight.

Counterfactual thinking

I couldn't help having those 'if only' thoughts. It could so easily have been England they were coming to see, and I just couldn't get that out of my mind.

(Teddy Sheringham in 1998, referring to his thoughts as the crowds entered the Stade de France for the World Cup Final.)

An offshoot of *determining* a cause for an event can be the regret felt about that cause. '*If only* I hadn't missed that penalty kick' or '*What if* I had managed to stay alert' are typical of the recriminations that characterize people's thoughts about failures and losses. They occur not only in sport, but in a wide range of unfortunate situations such as failing an examination, buying a defective car or being rejected in a romantic pursuit. In such disappointing cases, people are likely to replay their actions mentally over and over again, imagining how the results might have been different.

The study of counterfactual thinking (CFT) (Roese 1997) examines people's tendency to construct *mental representations of alternatives* to past events. Counterfactual means contrary to the facts. CFT can occur in many and varied forms, and its effects on people can be both positive and negative.

Imagining an improvement on the existing reality, or how the past might have turned out better, is known as generating an 'upward counterfactual': for example, 'If only I hadn't gone to the pub last night, I'm sure I would have beaten her at squash this morning.'

A 'downward counterfactual' involves imagining how things might have been WORSE: for example, 'At least I won a bronze medal – thank goodness I didn't come away with nothing at all.'

'Additive counterfactuals' insert a new idea or concept to the objective reality: for example, 'If we'd had the money to buy a new defender, we wouldn't have been relegated.' With 'subtractive counterfactuals', people undo or take away something: for instance, 'Why did I argue with the referee? If only I'd kept my cool, I wouldn't have been booked.'

THE ACTIVATION OF COUNTERFACTUAL THINKING

Roese and Olson (1995) identified a number of conditions under which CFT is most likely to be activated. The more negative, unexpected and emotionally upsetting the outcome, the more likely people are to engage in counterfactual thinking.

England's failure to reach the semi-finals of the 1998 World Cup aroused considerable cognitive activity as people grappled to figure out how the disappointing loss could have been avoided. Although England and Italy had each scored two goals at the time David Beckham was sent off for kicking at the leg of his Italian opponent, and an England victory was by no means guaranteed, the media and fans held Beckham responsible for the defeat. Indeed, the newspaper comments were frenzied as the blame for the 'needless' loss was aimed at Beckham:

> Mirror
> *Beckham is a bloody disgrace. We would have won the game without extra-time if he had stayed on the pitch.* (1st July, quote from fan.)
> Daily Mail
> *Moment Of Lunacy That Cost Cup Hopes* (1st July headline.)
> Guardian Sport
> *Without being too harsh on David, it cost us the game. (*1st July, quote from Ian Wright.)
> Evening Standard
> *I do feel that if it had been 11 versus 11 last night we would have won without doubt…The sending off cost us the game.* (1st July, quotes from Glenn Hoddle.)

The focus on Beckham in these 'If only…' counterfactual thoughts may seem fully justified and appropriate to the many England football fans who were traumatized by the result, but an objective observer might well consider whether Beckham's behaviour itself was only the focus of attention because of its dramatic outcome. As stated by Richard Williams in *The Guardian Sport,* on 1st July, 1998, p.3: 'Beckham was stupid to flick his foot at Diego Simeone after the Argentinian captain had flattened him. But if Nielsen [referee] had wagged his finger and let it go, no one would have noticed. Was Beckham's sin really any worse than that of Batistuta, who hacked at Beckham and Ince, but escaped punishment?'

An additional possible reason for the vitriolic attack was that the defeat was perceived as a 'near miss' in which England so nearly reached the next stage of the championship. Performers and spectators are more likely to agonize over thoughts of 'If only…' after a 5–4 than a 5–0 defeat, even though the latter result is far more negative. The impact of near misses was illustrated in a study of 1992 Summer Olympics winners (Medvec, Madey and Gilovich, 1995). Judges who were uninterested in sport watched videos of silver and bronze medallists who had just finished their competition or were receiving their medals on the winners' podium. Without knowing the results or hearing any sound, the judges gave higher ratings on a 'Happiness Scale' to the bronze than the silver medallists. The researchers reasoned that third place winners were ecstatic because they nearly hadn't won anything at all. But the joy of those in second place – even though they had actually won a more prestigious medal – was tempered by the thought that they'd just missed being the outright winner. The researchers found similar results on asking bronze and silver medallists how they felt during the 1994 Empire State Games in New York.

We might wonder if CFT is simply an immediate reaction that will wear off after a short period. But Medvec, Madey and Gilovich (1995) cite a quote from Abel Kiviat, the 1500 metre silver medallist in the 1912 Stockholm Olympics who had been ahead until at the last moment Britain's Arnold Jackson 'came from nowhere' to beat him by one-tenth of a second: 'I wake up sometimes and say, 'What the heck happened to me? It's like a nightmare'. Kiviat said this in 1989, at the age of 91!

One of the most robust findings is that when things go wrong and people try to understand why, they turn their attention to any departure from a normal routine. This can reinforce superstitious behaviours and cause people to imagine how the result might have been different if their customary practice had been followed. The footballer who normally comes out of the tunnel behind the number nine player but misses his usual position and then has a dreadful game, might put some of the blame on the change to his usual habit.

Kahneman and Tversky (1982) found that people attributed a fatal car accident to a change to someone's usual route or time of journey, overlooking other prominent features of the accident. Similarly, mock jurors gave higher compensation to a victim of food poisoning who had eaten at a restaurant other than her regular establishment (Macrae 1992). Apparently they felt greater sympathy for her when they could mentally 'take back' her non-routine action.

CFT is also likely to occur when a person has intentionally exerted control and made an explicit choice, but results have gone drastically wrong. Suppose a football manager, Robby, has two expert goalkeepers, George and Stan. After considerable pondering, Robby chooses George to play in a critical semi-final cup match. Unfortunately, a terrible error by George leads to a goal, and Robby's team goes out of the tournament. Robby will no doubt toss and turn over his decision, imagining that his team might still be in the championships if only he had chosen Stan. However, the situation would be very different if Stan had suffered an injury the day before the match, giving Robby no choice in the matter. Robby would still be unhappy about George's error, but he would be far less tormented because he had not made an active decision to select George. Kahneman and Tversky (1982) showed that people perceived more unhappiness for an investor who lost money after switching stocks than one who lost the identical amount after staying with his original company. The first had initiated an action; the latter hadn't.

Finally, counterfactual thoughts arise when an action associated with a failure occurs later rather than earlier in a sequence. This is why actions that occur at the end of a football game defeat are usually the focus of blame. The media normally neglect to mention a striker who misses a fairly easy goal in the early stages of the match, but place great emphasis on a similar miss in the dying minutes of the game. Similarly, when England were knocked out of the 1998 World Cup in the penalty shoot-out against Italy, the newspaper reports focused on David Batty's miss. Yet moments earlier, Paul Ince had also missed his penalty shot, and this was largely overlooked.

FUNCTIONS OF COUNTERFACTUAL THINKING

CFT serves both positive and negative functions, which is why it is important to be able to recognize when it occurs and determine whether it should be encouraged, discouraged or ignored. On the positive side, downward CFT offers comfort and relief ('At least I only sprained my ankle – imagine if I'd broken it'). Things could have been worse, we assure ourselves, to the extent that our discontent, fear or embarrassment is put aside for the time being. At the very least this gives us some time out to adjust to the negative outcome. Unfortunately, downward CFT can lead to a defeatist attitude and a reluctance to improve in a similar future encounter. The chubby footballer who ignores a nutritionist's advice might say after failing to lose weight. 'At least I didn't put *on* any weight'. This can be demotivating and lead to a failure to consider alternative strategies for improvement.

Upward CFT can be upsetting and ego-damaging as people torment themselves with thoughts of what might have been ('If only I hadn't missed the putt, I'd have won that game'). However, CFT can also serve a preparatory function by offering cues as to how to improve. The golfer who is haunted by missing a 12-inch putt may decide to spend many additional hours practising short putts. Roese (1994) found that people who were encouraged to generate upward counterfactual thoughts after receiving negative feedback on an anagram task went on to solve more anagrams in their second attempt.

Of course, we can never guarantee that a counterfactual thought will prevent a similar behaviour from recurring. According to psychologist Oliver James (*Daily Express*, 2nd July, 1998, p. 3), before the 1998 World Cup David Beckham had previously been suspended in the Tournoi de France for impetuous behaviour: 'Rebuked by Hoddle, a contrite Beckham admitted his weaknesses and stressed the lessons had been learned. "It could've been worse, it could've happened in the World Cup and hopefully I will learn a lesson from the experience".' Unfortunately, it appears he did not learn his lesson – it happened again in the World Cup!

Individual differences in social cognition

All humans differ from one another in a variety of important ways that are associated with our cognitions. For example, Cacioppo and Petty (1982) noted that people with a greater 'need for cognition' are more motivated to think, hunt for solutions and resolve inconsistencies. People also differ in their 'locus of control' (Rotter 1966), with external and internal locus of controllers, respectively, more likely to make situational and dispositional attributions. Internal locus of controllers may be more likely to believe they will improve with practice, while those with an external orientation see little connection between their training and their results.

Buchanan and Seligman (1995) identified a pessimistic 'explanatory style', which is characterized by the use of internal, stable, global attributions to explain negative outcomes. For example, when Millie explains why she lost in the first round of a table tennis tournament, she may decide: 'I've lost because of my anxiety.' (internal: due to her own traits); 'This has always been a problem for me, and no amount of training will change me.' (stable: permanent, producing long-term consequences); 'My anxiety is going to affect everything I do, even my social life and education.' (global: applied to a wide range of events).

Chronic pessimistic explanatory style has been associated with a number of negative consequences. Using measurement tools such as the Peterson, Seligman and Vaillant (1988) Content Analysis of Verbatim Explanations (CAVE) technique and the Attributional Style Questionnaire (ASQ) (Peterson *et al*. 1982), researchers have found relationships between pessimistic style and cognitive deficits, anxiety, illness, loneliness and depression (Seligman *et al*. 1979; Sweeney, Anderson and Bailey 1986). Rettew and Reivich (1995) found that professional basketball and baseball players with an optimistic explanatory style performed better than those with a pessimistic style, particularly when under pressure, and recovered better after a defeat.

Cognitive interventions

The evidence suggests, then, that although susceptible to many cognitive biases, people are not all necessarily affected in the same way by the same processes. Cognitive therapy approaches (Beck 1976; Ellis 1994) focus on the individual's specific thought processes and emphasize the effect of the person's beliefs upon his or her emotions and behaviour. Albert Ellis (1994; 1995), who developed a cognitive technique known as rational-emotive therapy, contended that many difficulties stem from people's unrealistic ways of construing events around them. He suggested that problems might be viewed through the ABC principle, with 'A' symbolizing an Activating event, 'B' a Belief, and 'C' a Consequence. For example: Activating event – My team-mate scowled at me when I missed a shot; Belief – He thinks it's my fault that we lost, and it very well could be; Consequence – Self-blame and emotional distress.

It can be useful to encourage people to recognize this chain of events and see how their beliefs follow from an activating event and then lead to a consequence. Beliefs are all-important. A major process in cognitive therapy is to discuss and challenge people's beliefs in a constructive way and encourage them to consider the accuracy and implications of their cognitions. Through this process, problematic thoughts can be restructured so that people not only feel better, but may gain some insight into the processes underlying their psychological state.

An example of a cognitive intervention can be seen in a consultation with a professional footballer who spent a good deal of time dwelling on, and reacting negatively to, attributions and counterfactual thoughts. Hal was a highly paid midfielder who played regularly for the first team of a Premiership club. An initial meeting was recommended and arranged by a fitness consultant who was working with the team. Various other team members and club personnel were also seen during this time. The details have been modified in order to disguise the identity of the individuals involved.

The importance of establishing exactly who the client is in sport psychology consultancy has been widely discussed (Rotella, 1990; Biddle, Bull and Seheult 1992), and a cognitive approach in particular requires this to be made clear to all concerned. At the onset of this intervention, the 'client' was identified as Hal rather than the football club he played for. It was agreed that meetings with Hal would be private and confidential, and that any decision to divulge information about the sessions would emanate only from him. This was imperative for the progress of the meetings, as Hal was likely to feel inhibited if he believed that his thoughts were being conveyed to the management. For example, Hal may well have been motivated to conceal any perceptions of personal shortcomings if he thought that these would be made known to the very people who made decisions about his career.

Despite the fact that he had voluntarily come to a session and was assured of confidentiality, Hal was at first uncommunicative and guarded. He asserted that psychological interventions were for 'weak' people and noted that he was not in the habit of talking about his problems with others, even close acquaintances and family members. We discussed at length the possibility that revealing thoughts to others could be beneficial, whether or not any specific problems existed.

Following some informal, lively discussions of football anecdotes, he eventually began to relax and talk about himself, gradually developing a willingness, and even a desire, to talk about his perceptions during the ensuing weekly meetings. He admitted to experiencing tension and crises of confidence on and off the pitch. He was frustrated that he was being instructed to play in a position which he believed was not his best, and he also worried about the effects of a long absence through injury.

Hal had chosen a home well away from the club and training grounds and rarely joined his team-mates for social occasions after a match or training session. He was particularly bothered by the behaviour of a fellow player, Smith, who was known for his outbursts during a game. Hal placed a great deal of emphasis on 'blame' and 'fault' in his analyses of a game, often deliberating on the extent to which Smith, others, and he himself held him responsible for defeats. He was sometimes haunted by counterfactual thoughts of 'what might have been' after a poor result.

We discussed Hal's thoughts following his team's 2–0 defeat in which Hal had played 80 minutes of the game before being substituted:

Hal　I've played better. Wilson and Jones [opposing team players] were giving me real problems. Wilson's incredibly fast … he could be an Olympic sprinter. He went right through me. But I'm playing out of position. I'm not being given the chance to show what I can do. But I know Smith thinks I'm to blame.

Psy　To blame for what, exactly?

Hal　Losing. I had a good chance to score but shot wide. He told me off for not passing, in front of everyone. He shouldn't do that, not in front of everyone.

Psy　So you *know* that Smith thinks you're to blame for losing? Are you sure of that?

Hal　Smith probably thinks he would have scored if I'd passed to him.

Psy　Have you talked to Smith since the game?

Hal　Not about that, no.

Psy　So you don't know for sure what Smith thinks. Maybe he doesn't blame you. Were you the only person he was telling off?

Hal　[laughs] No, he's like that with everyone. He blames everyone except himself. I think he does it to get himself going.

Psy　So Smith blames lots of people. Maybe he's not blaming you in particular. Maybe he was just acting like his usual self, trying to get himself going. Why would you conclude that he holds you responsible for losing?

Hal　I could have played better. Like I said, I had a chance to score. If I hadn't missed, we could have gone on to win, so I guess he's right, it could be my fault.

Psy　You can't really be sure what he thinks. You can't read his mind. If he blames everyone, not just you, you can't assume that he holds you responsible for losing. So maybe we could put Smith aside for the moment and talk about what *you* think.

Hal　Okay, but he really does annoy me. I know I shouldn't let him annoy me.

Psy　We can get back to Smith shortly. Right now let's concentrate on *your* thoughts. You regret not scoring; that's natural. But are you saying that your team would have gone on to win if only you hadn't missed?

Hal　We might have. The whole game would have changed.

Psy　The score would certainly have changed. But how do you know that if you'd scored, you'd have won? If I recall correctly, the score was 2–0 at the time, and there wasn't a lot of time remaining.

Hal   It would have been 2–1, so we could have gone on to win. Once you pull one back, anything can happen.

Psy   Okay, that's a valid point – anything might have happened. Anything. You've said that [the opposing team] are a really good side. Would players like Wilson and Jones have just sat back if you'd scored?

Hal   No. The odds would've still been against us.

Psy   Were any goals scored by your team before or after you missed that shot?

Hal   No.

Psy   So what's the evidence that you'd have gone on to win, if only you'd scored?

Hal   We would have been back in the game. I'm not saying we would have won. We probably *wouldn't* have won … there wasn't much time left. I guess I really shouldn't care what Smith says.

Psy   Remember, we're going to forget about Smith for a moment and focus on what you think. You say that you missed an opportunity to score. But you're just part of the team. Where is the evidence that you're the person responsible for not winning? Are you the only person who could have scored or played better?

Hal   No, we didn't gel. We weren't having our best day.

Psy   Did anyone score after you were substituted?

Hal   No.

Psy   Did anyone else on the team say that if you'd scored you'd have won?

Hal   No.

Psy   Did [the manager]?

Hal   Not me in particular.

Psy   Did the newspapers have anything negative to say about you in particular?

Hal   No, all of us.

Psy   So we can question whether the defeat might be your fault. Could you be putting too much of the responsibility on your shoulders? It's not definite that your team would have gone on to win if you'd scored. And you're not the only person who didn't score. In fact, Smith didn't score! Let's talk further about how Smith's behaviour may set off some of your concerns…

Hal's comments indicated his concern with a number of issues, such as the position he was asked to play in, his role in the team's defeat and his relationship with Smith. Smith's behaviour was an important activating event which undermined Hal's confidence and triggered concerns about his expertise. Hal often alluded to Smith, taking his team-mate's antics very personally and translating them into self-accusations of blame. Hal needed to recognize Smith's effect upon him and try to disentangle his own perceptions from those he attributed to Smith.

An important element of our discussions involved reflecting on and challenging HAL's assumptions in terms of their accuracy and logic. Wherever possible, he was encouraged to incorporate a 'reality check' on his beliefs, answering questions such as: 'Would a scientist or objective observer agree with that?' Possible 'unhelpful' thinking patterns were also identified so that Hal could try to recognize these in himself when appropriate. Examples of unhelpful thinking patterns included:

- *All-or-nothing thinking:* Everything is seen in extremes. 'I was fantastic' *or* 'I was useless.'

- *Overgeneralization:* Sweeping statements. 'I'll never get the chance to show how good I am.'

- *Personalization:* Seeing everything in terms of oneself. 'If I'd played better, we would have won.'

- *Catastrophizing:* Jumping to conclusions about a negative future. 'I was awful in training yesterday. Tomorrow will be a disaster.'

- *Mind reading:* Drawing conclusions from assumed knowledge of other people's thoughts and intentions without evidence. 'They blame me for the defeat.'

- *Emotional reasoning:* Drawing conclusions from one's own feelings. 'I don't feel like part of the team. They probably dislike me.'

Not only do problematic beliefs need to be recognized and evaluated, but their ramifications should be considered. Although not showing a consistently pessimistic explanatory style, Hal's attributions for aversive events were sometimes internal, stable and global. It was important to highlight areas where Hal had the power to exert any change as opposed to those which were not in his control. For example, he could take active steps towards improving his fitness and goal scoring in his training. Physical tension before and during the game was also problematic, therefore relaxation training exercises were introduced to help him feel more in control of his physiological state on and off the pitch.

Inevitably, though, a lack of control in certain areas has to be accepted in a sports context. A professional footballer normally cannot get rid of a troublesome team-mate or demand to play in a particular position. Sometimes it transpired that Hal's perception of lack of control was justified. His wish to play as an out-and-out striker, for example, was unlikely to be granted in the near future. According to the head coach, the manager was well aware of Hal's preference, but was unlikely to change his plans. Feeling constantly frustrated was counterproductive, so it was useful for Hal to concede that some of the changes he most desired were not going to come to fruition. Mechanisms for dealing with the status quo were discussed, such as the possibility of viewing his midfield role as a challenge, which, if met, would increase his versatility as a footballer.

We thus put a great deal of emphasis on the usefulness of separating out the areas within his control from those that he had to resign himself to accept. This involved the use of cognitive restructuring, wherein problems outside his control could be identified and accepted or reinterpreted, while those within his control could be acted upon to improve the situation. For example, in a session where the focus was on his relationships with his team-mates, Hal indicated that he felt alienated from the others and asserted: 'If my house weren't so far away, I'd spend more time with them.'

Again, we discussed this perception and his capacity to control the situation:

'Have you considered moving?'

'Would arriving home a few hours later really be so problematic?'

'Could you talk to [wife] about not being able to spend so much time at home?'

Hal was adamant that he did not want to move, but he did decide to make some efforts to socialize more with the team, despite some inconvenience. His relationship with Smith, though, remained a recurring problem for some time. Discussions with other team personnel revealed that Smith was known for publicly berating his fellow players, not just Hal, and was under no pressure to change. Hal's tendency to personalize led him to believe that he was a target victim, and Smith's comments and non-verbal gestures had a distracting and upsetting effect. It was important for Hal to accept this aspect of Smith's character and to recognize that he was not being singled out by Smith. Furthermore, because Hal viewed his vulnerability to Smith's behaviour as a personal shortcoming and said that he wished he were more 'thick-skinned', we discussed the fact that it would be unnatural for any individual *not* to feel disturbed over criticism and negative evaluation, particularly in front of television cameras and a crowd of thousands of people.

Hal's awareness and acceptance that his response was normal and expected rather than a personal weakness proved helpful. In the future, when he noticed Smith scowling at him, he could interpret this as 'Smith's personality' rather than as 'my poor performance'.

This is an example of reattribution training, where people are guided into changing their attributions from an internal to an external orientation. Wilson and Linville (1985) carried out a study which showed that reattribution training could be successful in improving the outlook of first-year college students who were worried and dissatisfied about their academic performance. Some of the students were given statistical and video evidence that demonstrated that the first year can be especially problematic and that marks can often improve over time. This was designed to remove some of the self-blame from the students' attributions and provide them with more external, unstable and specific attributions, such as 'It's the first year of college that causes bad grades – the problems don't just affect me and won't necessarily extend to other years.' Students given this reattribution training were more likely than a control group who did not receive the training to improve and stay in college.

Hal's performance and standing within the team improved over the next year. He stated that he felt more calm and confident and this was reflected in his performance and in statements from other team personnel. Notwithstanding, it is difficult to establish the extent to which other factors might have been just as responsible for the change. For example, Smith eventually left the team, new players were brought in and their presence had a positive impact on team relationships. All of these factors had personal and professional implications for Hal and were clearly of importance in his improvement. Evaluations of any psychological intervention need to take such variables into account.

In summary, the cognitive approach to dealing with sports performers' attributions and counterfactual thoughts can be extremely useful. While there were early problems in the consultancy with Hal, who approached our first meeting extremely cynically, we were soon able to communicate openly and challenge each other's views. This was accomplished by early informal chats about football and exchanges of a non-personal nature. It can often take some time before an appropriate atmosphere develops, so it is useful to persevere. Empathy and flexibility are vital, and it is imperative to recognize the enormous pressures under which elite performers operate.

However, it remains true that despite the best intentions, cognitive methods may not be appropriate for every individual. Hal was an articulate, intelligent person, but if he had remained begrudging and aloof, it is likely that the sessions would have been unsuccessful. In the end, the consultancy proved productive and may have helped to bring about some beneficial cognitive and behavioural changes.

References

Beck, A. T. (1976) *Cognitive Therapy and the Emotional Disorders*, Harmondsworth: Penguin.

Biddle, S. (1993) 'Attribution research and sport psychology'. In R. N. Singer, M. Murphey and L.K. Tennant (eds.), *Handbook of Research on Sport Psychology*, pp. 437–464, New York: Macmillan.

Biddle, S. J. H., Bull, S. J. and Seheult, C. L. (1992) 'Ethical and professional issues in contemporary British sport psychology', *Sport Psychologist* 6:66–76.

Buchanan, G. M. and Seligman, M. E. P. (1995) *Explanatory Style*, Hillsdale, NJ: Lawrence Erlbaum.

Cacioppo, J. T. and Petty, R. E. (1982) 'The need for cognition', *Journal of Personality and Social Psychology* 42:116–131.

Ellis, A. (1994) *Reason and Emotion in Psychotherapy*, revised and updated edition, New York, Birch Lane Press.

Ellis, A. (1995) *Better, Deeper and Enduring Brief Psychotherapy: The Rational Emotive Behavior Therapy Approach*, New York: Brunner/Mazel.

Greenberg, J., Pyszczynski, T. and Solomon, S. (1982) 'The self-serving attributional bias: Beyond self-presentation', *Journal of Experimental Social Psychology* 18:56–67.

Heider, R. (1958) *The Psychology of Interpersonal Relations*, New York: Wiley.

Jones, E. E. and Harris, V. A. (1967) 'The attribution of attitudes', *Journal of Experimental Social Psychology* 3:1–24.

Kahneman, D. and Tversky, A. (1982) 'The simulation heuristic'. In D.Kahneman, P. Slovic, and A. Tversky (eds.), *Judgment Under Certainty: Heuristics and Biases,* pp. 201–208, New York: Cambridge University Press.

Lau, R. R. and Russell, D. (1980) 'Attributions in the sports pages: A field test of some current hypotheses about attribution research', *Journal of Personality and Social Psychology* 39:29–38.

Luginbuhl, J. and Bell, A. (1989) 'Causal attributions by athletes: Role of ego involvement', *Journal of Sport and Exercise Psychology* 11:399–407.

Macrae, C. N. (1992) 'A tale of two curries: Counterfactual thinking and accident-related judgments', *Personality and Social Psychology Bulletin* 18:84–87.

McArthur, L. Z. and Post, D. L. (1977) 'Figural emphasis and person perception', *Journal of Experimental Social Psychology* 13:52–533.

McAuley, E. and Duncan, T. E. (1989) 'Causal attributions and affective reactions to disconfirming outcomes in motor performance', *Journal of Sport and Exercise Psychology* 11:187–200.

Medvec, V. H., Madey, S. F. and Gilovich, T. (1995) 'When less is more: Counterfactual thinking and satisfaction among Olympic medalists', *Journal of Personality and Social Psychology* 69:603–610.

Miller, D. T. and Ross, M. (1975) 'Self-serving biases in the attribution of causality: Fact or fiction?', *Psychological Bulletin* 82:213–225.

Mullen, B. and Riordan, C. A. (1988) 'Self-serving attributions for performance in naturalistic settings: A meta-analytic review', *Journal of Applied Social Psychology* 18:3–22.

Napolitan, D. A. and Goethals, G. R. (1979) 'The attribution of friendliness', *Journal of Experimental Social Psychology* 15:105–113.

Nisbett, R. E., Caputo, C., Legant, P. and Maracek, J. (1973) 'Behavior as seen by the actor and by the observer', *Journal of Personality and Social Psychology* 27:154–164.

Peterson, C., Seligman, M. E. P. and Vaillant, G. E. (1988) 'Pessimistic explanatory style is a risk factor for physical illness: A thirty-five year longitudinal study, *Journal of Personality and Social Psychology* 55: 23–27.

Peterson, C., Semmel, A., von Baeyer, C., Abramson, L. Y., Metalsky, G. I. and Seligman, M. E. P. (1982) 'The Attributional Style Questionnaire', *Cognitive Therapy and Research* 6:287–300.

Prager, I. G. and Cutler, B. L. (1990) 'Attributing traits to oneself and others: The role of acquaintance level', *Personality and Social Psychology Bulletin* 16:309–319.

Rettew, D. and Reivich, K. (1995) 'Sports and explanatory style'. In G. M. Buchanan and M. E. P. Seligman (eds.), *Explanatory Style*, pp. 173–185, Hillsdale, NJ: Lawrence Erlbaum.

Riess, M., Rosenfeld P., and Melburg, V. (1981) 'Self-serving attributions: Biased private perceptions and distorted public descriptions', *Journal of Personality and Social Psychology* 41:224–231.

Roese, N. J. (1994) 'The functional basis of counterfactual thinking', *Journal of Personality and Social Psychology* 66:805–818.

Roese, N. J. (1997) 'Counterfactual thinking', *Psychological Bulletin* 121:133–148.

Roese. N. J. and Olson, J. M. (eds.) (1995) *What might have been: The social psychology of counterfactual thinking*, Hillsdale, NJ: Lawrence Erlbaum.

Ross, L. (1977) 'The intuitive psychologist and his shortcomings: Distortions in the attribution process'. In L. Berkowitz (ed.), *Advances in Experimental Social Psychology*, pp. 174–221, New York: Academic Press.

Rotella, R. J. (1990) 'Providing sport psychology consulting services to professional athletes', *Sport Psychologist* 4:409–417.

Rotter, J. B. (1966) 'Generalized expectancies for internal versus external control of reinforcement', *Psychological Monographs,* 80 (1, Whole No. 609).

Sande, G. N., Goethals, G. R. and Radloff, C. E. (1988) 'Perceiving one's own traits and others': The multifaceted self', *Journal of Personality and Social Psychology* 54:13–20.

Seligman, M. E. P., Abramson, L. Y., Semmel, A. and von Baeyer, C. (1979) 'Depressive attributional style', *Journal of Abnormal Psychology* 88:242–247.

Sheringham, T. (1998) *My autobiography*, London: Little, Brown and Company.

Sweeney, P. D., Anderson, K. and Bailey, S. (1986) 'Attributional style in depression: A meta-analytic review', *Journal of Personality and Social Psychology* 50:974–991.

Taylor, S. E. (1981) 'The interface of cognitive and social psychology'. In J. Harvey (ed.), *Cognition, Social Behavior, and the Environment*, pp. 189–211, Hillsdale, NJ: Lawrence Erlbaum.

Wilson, T. D. and Linville, P. W. (1985) 'Improving the performance of college freshmen with attributional techniques', *Journal of Personality and Social Psychology* 49:287–293.

Wolfson, S. (1997) 'Actor-observer bias and perceived sensitivity to internal and external factors in competitive swimmers', *Journal of Sport Behaviour,* 20:477–484.

chapter eight

Confidence and the pre-shot routine in golf: a case study

DAVID SHAW

The problem

Approximately 12 months ago I was contacted by Mark, a 30-year-old professional golfer, who thought he might benefit from help with the psychological side of his game and in particular with his concentration. He said he had reached a point in his career where he wanted to take his game to the next level and that overcoming problems with concentration would be an important step in achieving this. We agreed to meet and discuss possibilities.

At the first meeting I confirmed that we were dealing with a psychological rather than a technical problem, and that it was related to concentration and not to some other issue. Mark assured me that, in general, he was hitting the ball as well as he had ever done, but on occasions during a round he would find himself 'not focusing' on the shot he was about to play. For example, he said that one particularly annoying thing that happened was that a tune would come into his head as he addressed the ball. I checked what he meant by loss of concentration and asked what he felt like when he had good concentration. He described this as feeling 'calm in myself'. When asked if there were specific situations when the problem arose, he replied that he didn't think that there were.

At the end of the first meeting we did a bit of 'contracting'. I wanted to ensure that I did not promise too much and to understand Mark's expectations concerning the help I might offer him. I explained that while I had a background in academic sport psychology, and many years' experience of consultancy work in organizations, I had limited consultancy involvement in sport. I explained that I would be happy to work with Mark, to understand golf-specific issues and hope to apply my knowledge and skills to that sport. For him, potential benefits were that he could understand something about sport psychology and hopefully solve his concentration problem. Mark said that he was happy to proceed on this basis.

Before our second meeting I located many published articles on concentration and went armed with ideas and work sheets for Mark to complete and reflect upon in relation to pre-event planning, in-event routines and refocusing routines. Again, the meeting involved much information gathering as I enquired about his pre-match routine and asked him to expand on what he meant when he used the expression 'calm in myself' and how he thought he could attain it. I showed him some of the material I had found on techniques that might be of use to us, for example Bull, Albinson and Shambrook (1996) *The Mental Game Plan* and Orlick (1986) *Psyching for Sport*. At the end of the session he took home various information sheets and questionnaires for completion and future discussion. The third meeting involved me observing Mark in competition, which I videotaped and subsequently analysed. It was revealed that Mark had a consistent physical pre-shot routine in terms of the number of practice swings and half swings and the time taken to perform them.

It was not until just before our fourth meeting that I began to feel encouraged that I had found something specific and particularly useful that I could offer. I had discarded anything based on the sort of attentional intervention that might have been guided by Nideffer's (1992) ideas on broad/narrow and internal/external focus. I had also decided that I did not want Mark to try and improve his concentration by using concentration grid exercises (Schmid and Peper 1998). I wanted something specific to golf and, crucially, that possessed high face validity. What was interesting in terms of a potential intervention were ideas from Rotella (1995), a sport psychologist who has worked with some of the world's top golfers for many years. The major tenet which drives his applied work is that the best thing skilled golfers can do as they are about to hit a shot in competition is to allow their bodies to take over and go into 'auto-pilot' (Rotella 1995). In other words, they need to have a level of concentration to the extent that they avoid focusing so much on technique that they tighten up. Equally, they need to avoid being so unfocused as to be easily distracted. Rotella's solution lies in the pre-shot routine, a sequence of physical and mental actions carried out immediately prior to performance. He emphasizes the importance of a sound pre-shot routine as the foundation to consistency, claiming that it allows the golfer to trust their swing, to be decisive and to be focused. I also found some useful suggestions on the practicalities of how to develop pre-performance routines in the work of Boutcher and Rotella (1987), Ravizza and Osborne (1991) and Loehr (1994).

Following our discussions of these issues, we decided that the most useful way forward was to develop Mark's pre-shot routine, which was mainly physical, to one that would be personally tailored to incorporate mental components designed to produce a relaxed, yet highly focused performance state. In a later section I will describe how we did this and what was incorporated within the routine. First, the theoretical underpinnings of pre-shot routines will be discussed, followed by a review of the literature concerning their effectiveness.

The theory

In attempting to answer the question, 'How does the pre-shot routine have an effect on performance?' it should be borne in mind that routines consist of a series of subcomponents, each with its own set of possible explanatory mechanisms. A detailed account of these is beyond the scope of this chapter, but given that the main focus of the intervention was Mark's ability to concentrate, it is appropriate to discuss those theories that are relevant to the mechanisms by which the concentration components of pre-shot routines might affect performance.

There are perhaps three main ways in which pre-shot routines might operate. First, they have been conceived of as having an informational role (schema theory and the direct-perception approach). Secondly, they have been characterized as having a preventative role (attentional-control theory and automaticity theory). Thirdly, they have been seen in a priming role (set theory). Schema theory (Schmidt 1975) proposes that golfers have schemata or abstract rules stored in memory for each type of golf shot. Schemata control the running of a motor programme which is 'fired off' in the execution of a shot (Magill 2001). According to this view, what the pre-shot routine does is to help in the selection of fundamental movement parameters, such as overall timing and overall force, which are implemented by a general motor programme. Thus, during the pre-shot routine, the golfer is initially engaged in recognizing the desired movement outcome and determining the initial conditions that exist before the shot is played, such as body position relative to the ball and distance to the hole. The recall schema is then employed to furnish the general motor programme with those parameters that will best meet the needs of the shot (Cohn 1990).

An alternative theory that relies on information, in this case on information obtained directly from the environment, to explain the benefit of pre-shot routines, comes from the direct-perception approach. Here, it is proposed that rather than employing a store of schematic representations, golfers respond directly to information in the environment (Williams, Davids and Williams 1999). It is argued that the requirements of the performance in terms of muscle force, angles and kinematic information are 'picked up' directly from the environment, the optic array (Gibson 1966). The value of a pre-shot routine, therefore, is that it may pre-sensitize the movement system to the appropriate perception–action coupling between environment and player. Thus, it can provide depth and positional information about the target and important invariances in the optic array and for the movement sequence that is to follow. While both theories compete to explain the specific mechanism involved in executing a shot, both agree that the fundamental purpose of the pre-shot routine is that of information provider.

In terms of the preventative role of pre-shot routines, again there appear to be two differing views. In the attentional-control approach (Boutcher 1990), the routine is said to direct attention to relevant stimuli, for example the ball or target, thereby preventing the mind from wandering. The second preventative theory of the value of pre-shot routines has its origins in the notion of stages of skill development (Fitts and Posner 1967). The automaticity explanation is that skilled behaviour develops from an earlier stage where conscious processing is necessary for execution, to one where actions can be carried out unconsciously. Indeed, the theory emphasizes that by the time skills are so well learned as to be executed automatically, conscious processing may interfere and disrupt performance. The tale of the centipede is relevant here: when asked how it coordinated his 100 legs, the creature stopped to think about it and was unable to move, illustrating the notion of 'paralysis by analysis' implicit within automaticity theory. According to the Bliss-Boder Hypothesis (Boutcher 1990), skilled performers will play better if they can allow their automatic subconscious processes to function. There is both experimental (Langer and Imber 1979; Baumeister 1984) and anecdotal evidence for this. A golfer may use the term 'wounded-tiger syndrome' to explain how someone with an injury is sometimes known to play better, attributing success to the pain of the injury distracting conscious thought from the mechanics of the shot. In one example, Rotella (1995) described how Walter Hagen won his first American Open despite being doubled up with pain from food poisoning. He argued that Hagen would not have been concerned about the way he was swinging, thereby allowing himself to play 'automatically'. Similarly, it is argued that a pre-shot routine might also operate to prevent a golfer from focusing on the technical aspects of the shot.

Finally, set theory is based on the idea that a pre-shot routine primes the performer both physiologically and psychologically. It was originally employed to explain the warm-up decrement effect, where there is a reduction in levels of skill immediately following brief periods of rest. The theory maintains that optimal performance requires the athlete to have a mental 'set', or readiness, prior to an action (Boutcher 1990). In a tennis rally, for example, where strokes follow quickly one after the other, the 'set' may be continuously useful. However, in golf, where professionals will play fewer than 80 shots in a four-hour match, performance may deteriorate during a round because the mental 'set' has been lost between shots. Proponents of the theory suggest that what pre-shot routines might do is to establish the correct 'set' for each shot. In a similar way mental rehearsal, which is a component of pre-shot routines for some players, might work to prime the golfer by establishing a successful mental 'set'.

Review of the literature

Crews and Boutcher (1986a) defined the pre-shot routine as 'a set pattern of cue thoughts, actions and images consistently carried out before performance of the skill'. This is straightforward enough, although it might be preferable to add something about the purpose of a routine. An alternative definition might be 'a set pattern of physical and/or mental activities carried out immediately prior to performance with the purpose of aiding that performance'. It should be noted that although the definition includes both physical and mental components, most studies have investigated only physical aspects.

Research using correlational designs has provided information about the basic aspects of routines. For example, it appears that better performers have longer routines (Crews and Boutcher 1986a), that their routines are more complex (Boutcher and Zinsser 1990) and that lower variability in the timings of pre-shot routines are associated with better performance (Wrisberg and Pein 1992). Also, consistency in relative timings of the parts of the routine is more important than consistency in overall timing (Southard and Miracle 1993; Southard and Amos 1996) and consistency in timing is less evident when task difficulty varies (Jackson and Baker 2001).

We know that pre-shot routines are used widely in sport, that they have face validity and there is anecdotal evidence that they are beneficial (Hardy, Jones and Gould 1996; Moran 1996), and especially in golf (Yancey 1977; Kerr 1997). In one example, Kerr (1997) described how golf experts had reported that Greg Norman's dramatic 11-shot final round collapse to Nick Faldo in the 1996 Augusta Masters was accompanied by a change in his pre-shot routine. Of course, we cannot be sure whether that change was the cause of the collapse or the consequence of it. Neither this type of anecdotal evidence, nor findings of correlational research, allows us to infer a causal relationship between the use of a pre-shot routine and subsequent performance enhancement. To do this it is necessary to consider experimental studies that have involved the manipulation of routines.

There are few experimental studies that have investigated the practical value of pre-shot routines. Crews and Boutcher (1986b) investigated their efficacy among novice golfers involving 17 male and 13 female adult beginners who underwent an eight-week learning phase during which they were taught the full swing. This was followed by a further eight weeks when half the group were taught to use a pre-shot routine while practising and the other half practised without. The routine was almost entirely physical and the only mental aspect involved imagining a line drawn from the target to the ball. It was found that the use of the pre-shot routine led to improved performance for male, but not for female participants. A difficulty with the study was that the performance measure used was limited, consisting of only eight shots for each player. It is possible that the small number of trials led to a performance measure that lacked sensitivity, with low discriminatory power and low reliability.

In a study on the effectiveness of cognitive strategies embedded in pre-shot routines, Wrisberg and Anshel (1989) compared the effect of arousal control, imagery and both together on the free throw performance of 40 boys aged between 10 and 12. While imagery was not effective they found a difference in performance between the arousal control plus imagery group and the control group. Once again, the study used a very small number of throws as the dependent variable. Predebon and Docker (1992) considered whether the apparent benefits of using a routine would disappear if skilled players practised without one. They measured the free throw shooting performance of 30 skilled basketball players aged between 17 and 23 and then trained them over six weeks in one of three conditions. One group practised without their normal routine, a second group learned a purely physical routine and the third group practised a routine combining imagery with the physical routine. None of the conditions revealed a performance improvement from baseline levels. This suggests that the pre-shot routines did not aid performance, but it appears reasonable to suggest that perhaps the experimental procedures may have interfered with the player's well-established behaviour. That is, it is possible that the new routines had not had time to supersede the older ones.

In a study that employed a multiple baseline design with three skilled college golfers, Cohn, Rotella and Lloyd (1990) attempted to show whether pre-shot routines would benefit actual competitive performances, rather than just laboratory-based tasks. The design required the golfers to use a pre-shot routine at different times over an extended period. The logic of this approach was that if performance improved following the introduction of the pre-shot routine, and not at other times during the study, it might be assumed that the routine had produced the change, rather than some other factor. Performance measures included the number of fairways hit, greens reached in regulation, total number of putts and average number of strokes per round. There was no evidence of a consistent link between the introduction of the pre-shot routine and improved performance.

Drawing the evidence together, it appears that support for the efficacy of the pre-shot routine is both mixed and limited. Of the four relevant studies reported, one suggests that the performance of male (but not female) novice golfers produces an improvement, and another found that the basketball free throw shooting of young boys was enhanced. In contrast, the remaining two studies found no improvement in performance following the introduction of pre-shot routines. Consequently, it is clear that there is insufficient research upon which to base a considered answer to the question 'Do pre-shot routines aid performance?' As yet, researchers have only a limited understanding of the role and importance of pre-shot routines. Studies are needed that employ training phases of sufficient time to embed pre-shot routines, while performance needs to be measured more reliably by employing many more trials. A final suggestion for future studies is that researchers should focus on routines that include mental as well as physical components, because it is likely that any benefits will also facilitate the control of arousal, concentration and confidence.

Given the lack of evidence on the value of a pre-shot routine, it might appear that there is little point in coaches and psychologists continuing to advocate its use with golfers, yet there are sound reasons for proceeding. First, the present review does not show that pre-shot routines are ineffective. Rather, it shows that we do not yet understand their precise value. It seems reasonable to suppose that future investigations of routines that include mental components are likely to reveal performance enhancement. Secondly, there is no evidence to suggest that they are actually detrimental to performance, hence their use should be explored further. An additional reason for optimism stems from Rotella's (1995) opinion that the basis of consistency in golf is a sound pre-shot routine, because it leads to concentration and confidence in the swing. Even if future studies show that performance following pre-shot routines is not enhanced sufficiently to satisfy the demands of statistical significance, it may be that they are practically significant. In sport, winning often depends upon very small performance differences that may not be possible to confirm statistically, but which do exist.

The intervention

It may be prudent to exercise caution when making claims for the efficacy of a particular intervention procedure; indeed some would argue that caution is a prerequisite. On the other hand, as applied sport psychologists we are faced with coaches and players who seek help quickly. That was where I found myself with Mark and it seemed that I might help in a way that would make a difference to his game; it was on that basis that we proceeded.

It was during our fourth meeting that we really began to focus on the development of a pre-shot routine. What Mark appeared to need was something that included more than a physical dimension. On the one hand, he needed a set of mental activities that would focus his attention on the shot he was about to play and away from distractions. On the other hand, he had to avoid focusing on the shot to the point where he was thinking too much, suffering from 'paralysis by analysis'.

His existing routine was a purely physical one to judge distance, decide upon the route to the pin, select the club and take it from the bag, look at the target from behind the ball, move to the side of the ball looking at the target, take a practice swing, look at the target and step forward to address the ball, look at the ball, ground the club behind the ball, look at the target, take a half swing, glance briefly at the target, ground the club behind the ball, focus on the ball and, finally, play the shot. I identified the following list of mental strategies to be selected and integrated into his routine:

- *Reset time*: Here, the idea was that even before arriving at the ball, time needed to be set aside to leave the previous shot behind. This was designed to 'wipe the slate clean' to ensure Mark 'played in the present' and that he was ready to focus on the next shot. Not being able to forget about a bad shot is often found to be a big problem for golfers. This notion was captured nicely by Mark Twain who stated, 'The inability to forget is infinitely more devastating than the inability to remember.'

- *'Concentration on' time*: The function of the 'concentration on' time was to signal the beginning of a funnelling/focusing process. I felt that a trigger gesture might be useful to 'switch on' the routine. We decided the trigger activity would be for Mark to look at the manufacturer's logo on his golf bag. We also discussed using a mental 'bubble' or 'dome' that Mark could imagine around him to protect him from distraction. Some golfers mentally flick a switch that creates a protective bubble into which they step just prior to the execution of each shot.

- *Arousal level time*: I considered that a calming breathing exercise could be of value.

- *Decision time*: As the name suggests, this would be when Mark would assess distance, wind trajectory and lie, after which he would select the appropriate club and decide upon the precise objective of his shot.

- *Target time*: This would be when Mark identified his target, which should be small and precise. Note that the 'shot goal' and the target are not synonymous; for example a golfer may have a target of landing the ball on the green just over a bunker and a 'shot goal' of getting the ball in the hole. Similarly, from the rough to the right of the fairway the target may be a church spire to the left of the fairway, using a fade to avoid a tree so that the ball will come to rest in the centre of the fairway.

- *Confidence time*: Here, Mark would use positive affirmations to boost his confidence; for example, 'I have selected the shot I can execute best from here' or 'I have a good technique and this is a shot I excel at'. Alternatively, he could visualize the best shot he had ever hit with that club.

- *Mental rehearsal time*: This would be when Mark mentally rehearsed his swing and pictured the flight of the ball to its designated target.

- *Auto-pilot time*: This should signal the time to do what he had spent years practising, namely hitting the golf ball. By now he should have become focused, decisive and what he described as 'calm in myself'. It should mark the end of the mental components of his pre-shot routine and he should finish with his already well-learned physical routine that would take him through to the shot itself.

We discussed the potential efficacy of each of these aspects and those components with which he felt most comfortable. I was careful to ensure that Mark was happy with each of the mental techniques I was proposing. I was concerned not to employ psychological techniques with him too quickly, even though he was very open-minded about using them. Mark told the cautionary tale of a well-known British golfer who had told him that he had tried working with a sport psychologist, but quickly gave up because he had been asked to putt imaginary balls at an imaginary hole and report how well he had done. While it may be easy for a psychologist to justify such an exercise, it is important to remember that golfers might find it difficult to accept and see it as irrelevant, especially during the early stages of a working relationship. By the end of the meeting we had identified a set of options for the routine and had decided we would work on them together in the next session.

For the fifth session Mark came in to the laboratory where we found a space to work on the detail of each step in the routine. My role was to go through each phase with him, checking that he understood what was required. He recorded the details of each component and any trigger words or phrases on index cards. We changed the order of some things to create a more logical sequence. I demonstrated a breathing exercise to use in the 'arousal time'. It involved imagining that as he breathed in he was filling up a glass statue of himself with calming blue liquid, such that after three or four breaths the statue was full to the top. Finally, we discussed 'swing thoughts'. These are self-instructional cues that many golfers use (Mark included) as they are about to hit the ball to remind them of aspects of technique such as 'keep your head still'. Based on Rotella's (1995) view that they lead to too much focus on technique, Mark agreed to try to disregard them. By the end of the session the following components had been tried, tested and agreed, each with its own specific set of activities. Having decided on the 'shot goal' and appropriate club, Mark began the following pre-shot routine:

- *'Concentration on' time*: Mark would look intently at the manufacturer's logo on his golf bag to signal the switching on of the routine and would then imagine a protective bubble around himself into which nothing distracting could penetrate. Then he would repeat to himself 'focus, focus, focus'.

- *Relaxation time:* Mark would take four breaths using the blue liquid breathing exercise.

- *Confidence time:* Mark would repeat one of the following: 'I have a strong technique', 'I have hit this shot before', 'I am a solid striker', 'I am a good player'. Each statement was originated by Mark himself, so that he would feel comfortable using them.

- *Target time*: Mark would identify a small and precise target to aim for.

- *Mental rehearsal time*: Mark would visualize the shot he wanted to happen.

- *Auto-pilot time*: Mark would now execute his normal physical routine, including hitting the shot.

After the shot there was a card for 'Reset time' when Mark would refocus before the next shot.

The next step was to leave the laboratory to see how the procedure worked on the golf course. In a phone conversation before we met again on the course, Mark said things were going well. He had been third, third and first in his last three competitions. He said that he was surprised that he was not using 'swing thoughts' and that it seemed to be helping. I felt that this was a good sign, suggesting that he was not becoming bogged down in thinking about technique. It is possible that using the new routine had left no room for 'swing thoughts'. Mark also explained that he had not been using the breathing exercise, something he had earlier reported as being useful, but he did say that thinking 'focus, focus, focus' had helped. However, he had not felt comfortable with the confidence component or the imaginary bubble and I began to wonder whether I had tried to take him too far too fast. He believed that there was great merit in setting precise targets for each shot and in specifying clear 'shot goals'.

Our next meeting consisted of Mark playing nine holes, during which I watched and discussed with him what he was doing. This led to some alterations to the timing of components of the routine. At the end of the session Mark agreed to continue to practise his routine in normal play. The final meeting followed a phone call from Mark who wanted to have a session on the practice ground. He said that from playing in matches he had found some changes were necessary, feeling that there were too many parts to the routine and he wanted to try it with fewer. We met at the practice ground and narrowed it down to selecting the 'shot goal' using the trigger gesture of looking at the logo on his bag, thinking 'focus, focus, focus', implementing the breathing exercise and picking a specific target, followed by 'auto-pilot', which constituted his normal physical routine. We practised the new procedure for an hour or so and it was agreed that he would continue with it in competition.

REVIEW

It has been almost a year since the start of our collaboration and it is appropriate to consider how effective the pre-shot routine has been. It would have been useful to have objective data on Mark's performance over the year to show whether there had been any improvement. Unfortunately, he stopped recording specific shot data, saying that all it told him was that if he played well it was because he putted well. In terms of evaluating the intervention, it meant that we had to rely on subjective impressions and, in particular, on Mark's views on the whole experience. With this in mind, I phoned Mark to ask him to review things one year on. Before asking him about how useful he felt the routine had been, I tried to assure him that I was keen to find out what he truly felt and that I was more interested in him being honest than worrying about my feelings.

I should say that Mark has not been slow to mention when he was unhappy with any aspect of our collaboration over the year. Fortunately, he also had the social skills to do this in a way that was easy for me to understand and work on. He said that he did use the routine and that it had become ingrained so that he only became aware of using it when he was not playing well. When this happened he said he would deliberately and consciously go through the routine before hitting the ball. In particular, he found that visualizing where the ball would finish was useful, as it seemed to help him to hit it more accurately. I asked him about 'swing thoughts' and whether he was still using them less. He said he only used them at times when his technique was letting him down and that as soon as he was swinging well again he stopped using them. He said that this tended to be a subconscious response.

When I asked Mark what he had derived from the work we did, he was emphatic that the new routine had made him more focused for each shot and therefore less distracted by irrelevancies. He also felt the routine was useful when he couldn't see a shot in his mind. He explained that sometimes he couldn't visualize the appropriate shot to play and that using the routine helped him to decide which one to select. I asked him whether he thought his concentration had improved and he said that it had. I also asked if he was still distracted by songs coming into his head and he replied that it did happen occasionally, but not for the past three months. My final question was, 'Has the pre-shot routine helped?' to which he replied, 'Definitely'.

It appears that Mark had benefited from our work together. In particular, introducing a mental and physical pre-shot routine had been useful for his game, perhaps more so than I expected when we first began our work. I would have no hesitation in employing a similar procedure again. I was not entirely happy with my role overall, but I, too, learned from the experience. For example, if I were to repeat the intervention I would make some changes to my way of working. First, I would be more careful to ensure that the client kept a detailed diary of the stages of the intervention. Reflective logging would provide a detailed record of what took place and, hopefully, promote both deeper learning and engender greater ownership of the solution in the client. Secondly, I would take a more proactive role in the process of ensuring that the client initially over-learned the necessary skills and then adhered to the routine for long enough to give each component a fair trial. I would also be more vigilant in checking that the routine was being used regularly. Finally, I would try to be clearer about the need for continuous, objective recording of performance by asking the player to keep a record of crucial statistics, such as fairways hit, greens reached in regulation, putts taken per round and total scores.

Throughout the chapter I have advocated the use of a pre-shot routine as a potential solution to the problem of loss of concentration in golf. As we saw in the section on research into pre-shot routines, there are several ways in which their effectiveness might be explained, but so far there is little evidence to indicate which one will provide the clearest picture. Similarly, the literature suggests that research to demonstrate the efficacy of pre-shot routines is awaited.

References

Baumeister, R. F. (1984) 'Choking under pressure: Self-consciousness and paradoxical effects of incentives on skilful performance', *Journal of Personality and Social Psychology* 46:610–620.

Boutcher, S. H. (1990) 'The role of performance routines in sport'. In J. G. Jones and L. Hardy (eds.), *Stress and Performance in Sport.* pp. 231–247, Chichester: Wiley.

Boutcher, S.H. and Rotella, R.J. (1987) 'A psychological skills educational program for closed skill performance enhancement', *Sport Psychologist* 1:127–137.

Boutcher, S. H. and Zinsser, N. (1990) 'Cardiac deceleration of elite and beginning golfers during putting', *Journal of Sport and Exercise Psychology* 12:37–47.

Bull, S. J. Albinson, J. G. and Shambrook, C. J. (1996) *The Mental Game Plan*, Brighton: Sport Dynamics.

Cohn, P. J. (1990) 'Pre-performance routines in sport: Theoretical support and practical applications', *Sport Psychologist* 4:301–312.

Cohn, P. J., Rotella, R. J. and Lloyd, J. W. (1990) 'Effects of a cognitive-behavioral intervention on the pre-shot routine and performance in golf', *Sport Psychologist* 4:33–47.

Crews, D. J. and Boutcher, S. H. (1986a) 'An exploratory observational behavior analysis of professional golfers during competition', *Journal of Sport Behavior* 9:51–58.

Crews, D. J. and Boutcher, S. H. (1986b) 'Effects of structured pre-shot behaviors on beginning golf performance', *Perceptual and Motor Skills* 62:291–294.

Fitts, P. and Posner, M. I. (1967) *Human Performance*, Monteray CA: Brooks Cole.

Gibson, J. J. (1966) *The Senses Considered as Perceptual Systems*, London: George Allen and Unwin.

Hardy, L., Jones, G. and Gould, D. (1996) *Understanding Psychological Preparation For Sport: Theory and Practice of Elite Performers*, Chichester: Wiley.

Jackson, R. C. and Baker, J. S. (2001) 'Routines, rituals and rugby: Case study of a world class goal kicker', *Sport Psychologist* 15:48–65.

Kerr, J. H. (1997) *Motivation and Emotion in Sport: Reversal Theory*, Hove: Psychology Press.

Langer, E. J. and Imber, L. G. (1979) 'When practice makes imperfect: Debilitating effects of overlearning', *Journal of Personality and Social Psychology* 37:2014–2024.

Loehr, J. E. (1994) 'The development of a cognitive-behavioral between-point intervention strategy for tennis'. In S. Serpa, J. Alves and V. Pataco (eds.), *International Perspectives on Sport and Exercise Psychology*, pp. 219–233, Morgantown WV: Fitness Information Technology.

Magill, R. A. (2001) *Motor Learning: Concepts and Applications,* sixth edition, New York: McGraw-Hill.

Moran, A. P. (1996) *The Psychology of Concentration in Sport Performers: A Cognitive Analysis*, Hove: Psychology Press.

Nideffer, R. M. (1992) *Psyched to Win*, Champaign, IL: Human Kinetics.

Orlick, T. (1986) *Psyching for Sport: Mental Training for Athletes*, Champaign, IL: Leisure Press.

Predebon, J. and Docker, S. B. (1992) 'Free-throw shooting performance as a function of pre-shot routines', *Perceptual and Motor Skills* 75:167–171.

Ravizza, K. and Osborne, T. (1991) 'Nebraska's 3 R's: One-play-at-a-time pre-performance routine for collegiate football', *Sport Psychologist* 5:256–265.

Rotella, R. (1995) *Golf is Not a Game of Perfect*, New York: Simon and Schuster.

Schmid, A. and Peper, E. (1998) 'Training strategies for concentration'. In J. M. Williams (ed.) *Applied Sport Psychology: Personal Growth to Peak Performance*, pp. 316–328, Palo Alto, CA: Mayfield.

Schmidt, R. A. (1975) 'A schema theory of discrete motor learning', *Psychological Review* 82:225–260.

Southard, D. and Amos, B. (1996) 'Rhythmicity and pre-performance ritual: Stabilizing a flexible system', *Research Quarterly for Exercise and Sport* 67:288–296.

Southard, D. L. and Miracle, A. (1993) 'Rhythmicity, ritual and motor performance: A study of free-throw shooting in basketball', *Research Quarterly for Exercise and Sport* 64:287–290.

Williams, A. M., Davids, K. and Williams, J. K. (1999) *Perception and Action in Sport,* London: E and FN Spon.

Wrisberg, C. A. and Anshel, M. H. (1989) 'The effect of cognitive strategies on the free-throw shooting performance of young athletes', *Sport Psychologist* 3:95–104.

Wrisberg, C. A. and Pein, R. L. (1992) 'The pre-shot interval and free throw shooting accuracy: An exploratory investigation', *Sport Psychologist* 6:14–23.

Yancey, R. (1977) 'Develop a pre-shot routine and play better', *Golf Digest* 115–117.

chapter nine

Functional equivalence solutions for problems with motor imagery

PAUL HOLMES AND DAVE COLLINS

Imagery is perhaps the most common component of any sport psychology intervention. Most athletes use it, coaches advocate it and you could stock a shop with the tapes, CDs and books that promote the development of imagery skills as a key factor in performance enhancement. This universality also extends to the range of applications that are described within these materials, such as slow-motion, instant pre-play, confidence imagery, ideal as-if and positive-emotional promotion: the list is endless.

Despite such ubiquitous use, many imagery interventions lack a theoretical and empirical rationale, often being driven by what is convenient for the practitioner, rather than what is appropriate for the client. Since many sport psychologists appear oblivious to the mechanisms that drive imagery, some practices may even have a *detrimental* effect when positive motivational effects of the psychologist–athlete relationship are partialled out!

Thus, the key issue for authors, researchers, educators, practitioners and athletes is that understanding how something works is a crucial precursor to using it effectively. For example, knowing how muscle fibre recruitment is affected by movement speed and training load can be helpful when designing weight-training schedules. Accordingly, if a practitioner understands the operational mechanisms of imagery, they will find it easier to design and implement effective imagery strategies.

The problem: lack of clarity in the design and implementation of imagery interventions

Some may consider that we have taken these statements too far. Before offering practical guidelines for the design of mechanism-effective imagery interventions, it is worth considering the evidence for problems that can limit the efficacy of the world's favourite mental skill. The evidence is set out in the following three sub-sections.

THE RELAXATION EMPHASIS

Relaxation as an essential precursor to imagery is a telling example of the unquestioning acceptance of methodology from other fields. Relaxation plus imagery is fundamental to the use of imagery as a therapeutic tool, where clients/patients image stress-invoking scenes. They incorporate relaxation alongside an image to attack the learned panic response by developing a new association with calm and control. Thus, in this setting the juxtaposition of imagery and relaxation is both logical and theoretically sound, and forms a key component of many cognitive-behavioural approaches, for example in Young's (1990) work on early maladaptive schemas. This juxtaposition may be an important reason for imagery's inclusion in many sport-related interventions. Elsewhere, support for relaxation is less apparent and the only argument for relaxing before imagery is based on the notion that lower levels of muscle activity remove a block to smaller innervations that, according to the psycho-neuromuscular approach, are the means through which imagery operates. Relaxation is believed to 'clear the mind' of distractions that may interfere with imagery content. Not only is this position highly questionable theoretically, it also ignores a range of ways in which imagery is now used; consider 'instant pre-play', for example. How can an athlete about to compete become relaxed, then image, then increase arousal to optimum performance levels?

In short, the idea that relaxation helps the imagery process in any of its conventional *sporting* applications is unsupported. In fact, we suggest that this emphasis can have a negative effect. Athletes asked to relax will often consciously inhibit small, but significant, movement signals (efferent leakage), which cause the 'twitching' that can characterize effective imagery. Inhibiting inappropriate movements may limit both the vividness and the impact of imagery. Conscious inhibition can limit 'functional equivalence', that is, the relationship between imagery and one's actual performance. Paradoxically, while practitioners appear willing to apply therapy-based ideas directly to sport, they have also ignored many of the research findings and practices from clinical psychology that have identified rigorous, mechanism-driven, approaches to imagery interventions.

IMAGERY AS A COMPREHENSIVE TOOL

As mentioned earlier, the wealth of potential applications for imagery represents a rich source for the practitioner. The cynic and the critical sport psychologist may ask whether there can really be just one mental skill, which, once taught, can be universally employed. Research seems to suggest that there can, although it is necessary to clarify the precise ways in which imagery interventions should be fine-tuned for the performer to benefit. Mental imagery for preparation, as distinct from mental practice (MP) for learning and emotion/motivation-based imagery, may be as varied as the emotions and mental processes that are engendered by the intervention itself. However, few systematic explanations or recommendations have emerged to guide the practitioner in its use. Thus, it is reasonable to suggest that the outcome of many imagery interventions will inevitably be less than ideal.

A SENSE OF PERSPECTIVE

Imagery perspective, whether internal or external, raises an issue that fails to identify a theoretical and/or mechanistic basis for its use. In fact, a visual imagery perspective is somewhat better than other fundamental issues considered here, since there is debate as to how this interesting approach may be best used. The emotional imagery literature strongly supports the concept of an 'internal' perspective, while motor imagery is distinguished from visual imagery in terms of content, but may not easily be separated from the latter, because movements occur in a spatial environment and their consequences typically involve transformations within it. The internal perspective, therefore, proposes an internal-visual perspective with concurrent kinaesthetic processing.

However, there is also evidence (Hardy and Callow 1999) for the utility of an external-visual perspective in mental practice settings, especially when the form of the movement is a key feature, for example in gymnastic floor routines. Surprisingly, its supporters' contention of external-visual superiority also includes a real-time and a concomitant kinaesthetic component. Thus, a major reason why the phenomenon has been examined was based on anecdotal experiences of expert performers in slalom canoeing and skiing. Given the massive differences on many fronts that are known to exist between novices and experts, it is surprising that novices are reported to enjoy similar experiences.

This observation raises more questions about the nature of imagery effects and its operation. Research from clinical psychology, such as Lang's (1977; 1979; 1985) work in bio-informational theory, suggests that the issue of perspective may be inordinately overemphasized in both sport psychology literature and practice. The separate, but related, issue of the propositional structure of images may be more important for practitioners to consider and these concerns will be addressed later in the chapter.

There are a number of unanswered questions that relate to the nature of the optimum imagery intervention, such as timing, how close the external-visual imagery phenomenon is to observational learning, and the extent to which existing measures of imagery skill accommodate the counter-intuitive position of external-visual/kinaesthetic imagery. Once again, the main point here is that imagery procedures are being shaped without recourse to understanding how they work.

In summary, it is proposed that a greater understanding of the mechanisms that underlie imagery interventions will enhance their design. In the following sections a neuroscientific model is described to highlight similarities between the physical preparation and execution of a task and the motor imagery of it. Practical guidelines based on a theoretical framework are described to assist practitioners in the use of imagery skills in sport.

Theoretical perspectives: motor representation

Assuming that imagery is a cognitive representation of neuropsychological signals associated with movement, then the concept of the motor representation is crucial to its understanding. Motor representation as a neuronal structure integrating cognitive psychology with neurophysiological evidence has been popular for more than four decades. Until fairly recently, only limited physiological evidence was available to support cognitive approaches and the emergence of neuro-imaging based methods has supported a number of representational theories. These have included motor representations (Jeannerod 1994), neural networks (Rosenzweig 1996), parallel distributed processing (Rumelhart and McClelland 1986), and cortical cell assemblies (Wickens, Hyland and Anson 1994). While terminology may vary, the fundamental physiological concept of interacting neuronal groups firing in defined patterns and able to evolve and be structurally modified to become more effective, is implicit within each. Given this evidence, the notion of a motor representation is ideally positioned for use by sport psychologists as an integral part of a dynamical mechanism underpinning motor behaviour. As such, a motor representation can be used to explain the multifaceted and variable motor behaviour of elite sport athletes and to develop a mechanistic explanation for the effectiveness of imagery generally.

MOTOR REPRESENTATION AND IMAGERY

One should avoid the common confusion between motor representation and more traditional cognitive computer-based metaphors of the brain. The neurobiological approach adopted here considers a representation to be a network, map or collective of interconnected neurons and brain areas that are active during a particular event (Keil *et al.* 2000). Areas involved in the execution of a given task are said to display 'functional specificity' to that task, or group of tasks.

So where does imagery fit? Proponents of representational models – for example Farah (1985) – suggest that a representation of overt motor activity is also likely to be associated with many aspects of motor imagery, such as motor planning and some execution stages of behaviour. This kind of activity may extend to functionally specific areas of the brain and have influence on the representational strength through neuronal and synaptic plasticity. The high degree of overlap is termed 'functional equivalence'. That is to say, the same bits of the brain should fire or, technically, be innervated, whether a skill is performed or imagined. The key point is that the efficacy of imagery depends on how well similar brain areas are activated by imagery manipulation. A greater recruitment of the areas that fire during physical performance will, by definition, make imagery more effective in achieving a desired outcome. Furthermore, if physical and mental practice can be shown to possess high functional equivalence, then many procedures that are efficacious in physical practice should be relevant to mental practice as well. An athlete will benefit from central reinforcement, but without the usual fatigue and possible risk of injury associated with physical practice.

However, motor preparation/execution and motor imagery vary fundamentally and functional equivalence is incomplete. Motor preparation is associated with subconsciously controlled, coordinated overt performance, whereas motor imagery normally has full efference blocked, or largely suppressed at some level of cortico-spinal flow so that overt behaviour is either minimal or non-existent. Movements are smaller, but rhythmically similar, so it is not surprising that both motor preparation/execution and motor imagery show incomplete functional equivalence.

Imagery, therefore, is concerned with an imagined movement without complete movement. Inhibition represents a central task with neuronal correlates, or bits of brain activity, that are likely to cloud the central functional equivalence debate. Significantly, if the imagery process is conscious, then the task of remaining still may become the primary task, with imagery the secondary task. Thus, a boxer, through trying to remain still and relaxed, can actually inhibit the degree of functional equivalence that is central to the effectiveness of the imagery process. Ironically, then, the requirement that imagers remain still and relaxed may have a direct and negative influence on the process the imager wishes to achieve!

Cognitive neuroscience research described in the following sections supports shared memory representation and is drawn from three main areas of study. The first relates to central functioning during the cognitive steps to action; a preparation phase of intending (Loze, Collins and Shaw 1999), planning and programming and an execution phase. The terms motor preparation and execution are used to describe those cognitive processes which, respectively, precede and control movement during autonomous overt performance. The second area relates to research that considers the peripheral typology of motor imagery, while the final section proposes that behavioural correlates of imagery may also provide an interesting avenue for functional equivalence-based work.

Central indices of equivalence

Considerable evidence in support of the functional equivalence issue is provided by the analysis of those neural mechanisms active during motor preparation and execution and motor imagery. Regional cerebral blood flow studies have highlighted motor imagery/motor preparation and execution topology. There *are* regions that are related specifically to motor preparation and execution, for example the primary motor cortex, although Pascual-Leone *et al.* (1995) have reported attenuated primary motor cortex activation during motor imagery conditions. However, a significant number of areas show a pattern of activity during motor imagery similar to that of actual performance. These are highlighted in Figure 9.1. The keyed elements in the figure are as follows: (1) Anterior supplementary motor area and (2) Posterior inferior primary motor cortex,

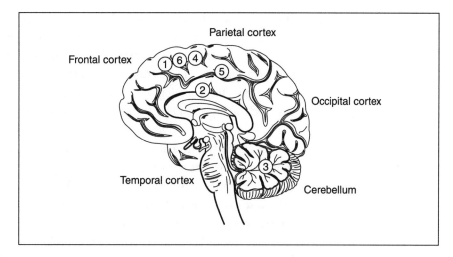

FIGURE 9.1   *Schematic of functionally active-brain areas common to motor preparation and execution and motor imagery (see text for details)*

Stephan *et al.* (1995); Montoya *et al.* (1998); (3) Cerebellum, Montoya *et al.* (1998); (4) Frontal lobe (and basal ganglia – not shown), Decety *et al.* (1990); (5) Anterior primary motor cortex and (6) Supplementary motor area, Delber *et al.* (1991); Roland *et al.* (1994).

Prefrontal areas, the supplementary motor area (SMA), cerebellum and basal ganglia have been shown to be active during motor imagery (Ingvar and Philipson 1977; Decety *et al.* 1990). A potentially more important finding is that brain activity is influenced by the nature of the imaginal task (Jeannerod and Decety 1995). For example, task requirements have been shown to recruit different portions of the SMA preferentially (Stephan *et al.* 1995). These and other studies provide strong support for a sport skill being imaged at any moment, while matching any attentional switches as the skill proceeds and modifying imagery scripts to consider the effects of learning.

What is clear from this work is that cortical and sub-cortical areas that are active during motor imagery pertain to neural networks known to be involved in at least the early stages of motor control (Decety 1996b). It supports the argument for common neural mechanisms of motor imagery and for motor preparation and execution. Therefore, if sport psychologists do not legislate for factors known to modify central topography, functional equivalence is likely to be severely compromised. Put simply, the task imaged must innervate the same brain areas as those involved during actual execution. Imagery interventions must reflect crucial considerations such as movement pace, muscular effort, emotion and level of learning, because each of these factors will determine precisely which networks and brain areas are involved.

Peripheral indices of equivalence

In addition to central measures indicating a close functional equivalence between motor preparation and execution and motor imagery, the peripheral cardiac and respiratory indices that anticipate muscular activity also increase during motor imagery. For example, some authors (Decety *et al.* 1991) have shown that heart rate and total ventilation increase proportionally with imagined incremental workloads for treadmill and ergometer exercising, even though no overt muscle activity was discernible. Similarly, in both pathologically and experimentally paralysed participants where no overt movement is possible, coupling of motor preparation and cardiac activation has been observed (Decety *et al.* 1990). On this evidence, motor preparation is arguably more akin to motor imagery. In a study of perspective effects on imagined exercise, Wang and Morgan (1992) also demonstrated peripheral activation, showing that ventilation and effort sense were higher when an internal imagery perspective was employed. Although there were similarities between internal and external conditions in metabolic and cardiovascular responses, it was concluded that internal (motor) imagery had the greatest resemblance to actual movement.

Some of the earliest studies to considered the physiology of imagery (Jacobson 1931; Shaw 1940) found functional equivalence in electromyographic (EMG) activity, and led to continued support for psycho-neuromuscular explanations of imagery effects. However, EMG activity has not always been associated with imagery (Yue and Cole 1992) and there may be two explanations for this. First, inhibition of movement may be more appropriate for some participants or conditions. Secondly, it has been suggested that the preparatory fibres involved are deeper and of the slow tonic type, so that usual surface EMG techniques are unlikely to record this activity (Jeannerod 1997). 'An incomplete inhibition of motor output (occurring as a consequence of instructions or of a participant's bias) would be a valid explanation for accounting for these muscular discharges' (Jeannerod 1997, pp. 110–111). This concept is similar to Lang's theory of efferent leakage (Lang 1979; 1985) and neatly emphasizes the critical importance of imagery instructions in enhancing functional equivalence. Thus, for the practitioner, accurate, overt movement is not an essential feature of effective imagery, although some physiological concomitant, albeit difficult to detect, would seem to be desirable.

Behavioural evidence for functional equivalence

It is obvious that the absence of an overt physical response is a problem for both research and applied work that focuses on behavioural indices of equivalence. However, investigation is possible with ingenuity, and Decety, Jeannerod and Prablanc (1989) have used timing to examine the extent of equivalence. Thus, the time taken to execute a movement in imagery varies in tandem with temporal parameters, for example distance walked (Decety, Jeannerod and Prablanc 1989), or complexity parameters such as degree of hand/foot rotation (Parsons 1987). There is also a variety of commonalties between physical and mental practice effects, as in contextual interference (Gabriele, Hall and Lee 1989), which support the contention that both forms of practice access similar, if not identical, systems and structures. Similarly, Farah (1985) has provided convincing evidence to show that interactions between imagery and perception imply a common locus of activity that consists of representational structures. Her data showed that imagery selectively facilitates perception through recruitment of attention to 'the same functionally spatial representational medium in which stimuli are encoded at an early stage of perceptual processing' (Farah 1985, p. 102). For example, imaging a complex tumbling skill or skating jump will facilitate attention to similar afference as experienced during actual execution. Using this technique, learners can prepare themselves to cope with the bewildering complexity of physical sensations that accompany the execution of a new skill, enabling them to select the relevant feedback for subsequent correction or modification of the movement. In a different context, behavioural evidence is available from qualitative studies. Harrigan and O'Connell (1996) have shown when examining facial gestures that re-experiencing anxious events through visuo-motor imagery leads to facial movements associated with fear expressions, more facial movement and increased arousal.

If such disparate aspects of behaviour are also functional equivalence elements, then sport psychologists may need to consider the congruence of motor imagery behaviour to preparation/execution behaviour, particularly experienced emotion and associated facial expression (Ekman 1992), as a possible window on the central and peripheral correlates mentioned above. Clearly, motor preparation and execution, and motor imagery share a number of socio-physiological processes in their occurrence. Thus, the use of a coping image, when the athlete mentally rehearses a competitive setting in association with the fear and arousal which accompanies pre-game apprehension, may be effective in increasing functional equivalence and developing coping skills in advance of a competition.

A possible solution: the PETTLEP model for motor imagery

Taking functional equivalence as a base, a model has been developed for optimizing this process (Holmes and Collins 2001a), with imagery used as an intervention. Seven elements were identified for sport psychologists to consider when delivering motor imagery-based interventions, as reflecting the most crucial considerations from a much longer list. The model comprises Physical, Environment, Task, Timing, Learning, Emotion and Perspective elements (PETTLEP) derived from neuroscientific functional equivalence literature, empirical studies in our own laboratories and clients' detailed personal experiences of those factors that relate to the construction of effective motor-imagery scripts.

All PETTLEP elements are subsumed by Langian theory (Lang 1977; 1979; 1985), with each one providing important response and meaning propositions. This approach is summed up by Carroll, Marzillier and Merian (1982) who stated '... it is the interaction between training mode and the propositional structure of the imagery presentation that is crucial' (p. 76). For readers unfamiliar with Lang's approach, a brief outline may be useful. For Lang, imagery is a process that increases the likelihood of locating and employing the correct motor programme. Thus, a key issue for the efficacy of the imagery process is that it recruits an appropriate programme by using the correct 'address' to find it, the memory trace. It has three addresses, one which relies on the environment where the movement is executed (the stimulus), one which relates to what is felt as the movement is performed (the response) and one that is based on the importance of the skill (the meaning). The Langian approach to effective imagery, therefore, depends on using scripts that include details about each of the three components and an ideal script will include stimulus propositions, response propositions and meaning propositions, each relating to an individual athlete's experience. Thus, using the PETTLEP approach maximizes the chances of accessing the most functionally equivalent memory trace by maximizing all three components.

The PETTLEP elements

PHYSICAL

The imagery approach described is in contrast to most performers' initial experiences of imagery training sessions – which typically begin with the instructions, 'Lying or sitting comfortably, visualize …' – and some authors (Weinberg, Seabourne and Jackson 1981; Miller 1991) advocate relaxation prior to imagery to clear the mind of distractions. However, support for the widespread use of relaxation seems, at best, equivocal and certainly not a critical mediating variable as some have suggested (Murphy 1994). As stated earlier, the relationship between relaxation and imagery emerges from the therapeutic history of relaxation techniques, typically represented by Wolpe (1958), rather than through empirical support from sport psychology research. Suinn's (1976) visuo-motor behaviour rehearsal (VMBR) is perhaps the best-known method employing relaxation prior to imagery.

While there is little doubt that relaxation strategies can have a positive cognitive imagery effect for some individuals, the technique does not take into account the somatic influences of relaxation that would seem to be totally contrary to the somatic state of the performing athlete. Rifle-shooters tested in one of our recent studies reported that relaxation-based scripts had left them feeling 'flat and lethargic', 'heavy and tired', ' very sleepy', '… definitely not like me when I am shooting well'. In addition, athletes' comments relating to poor image control during relaxation-based imagery were common: 'I can see myself shooting, but it's really hard to keep the picture, I'm off all over the place'. For 'stronger imagery effects' (Perry and Morris 1995, p. 376) such evidence provides support against pre-imagery relaxation. While shooters enjoyed being relaxed, they recognized the inappropriate nature of the strategy just prior to shooting. In fact, most relaxation techniques associated with imagery act principally on somatic systems (Davidson and Schwartz 1976).

If functional equivalence drives the effectiveness of imagery behaviour, manipulating the physical nature of imagery to approximate motor preparation and execution is appropriate. Indeed, Beisteiner *et al.* (1995) have proposed that the stimulation of peripheral receptors associated with task execution and activation of the cortico-motorneuronal system during motor imagery will increase the psychophysio-logical congruence of motor preparation/motor imagery at the central sites. The creation of a motor image utilizes shared brain regions that are clearly beneficial for strengthen-ing of the memory trace. This suggests that performers should be actively involved in the imagery experience by, for example, using equipment from the sport and making appro-priate movements as demonstrated by Mantle (1996). In these instances, afferent feed-back may serve as further reinforcement. Consequently, the term 'mental simulation with movement' may be a more appropriate description of this behaviour when referring to the imagery experience of athletes than Jeannerod and Decety's (1995) term 'mental simulation of movement' and it is certainly more useful for athletes than the simplistic label 'visualization'. Gould and Damarjian (1996) have supported imagery plus move-ment in their term 'dynamic kinaesthetic imagery' to assist athletes towards a clear recall of performance-related sensations. The postulate that PETTLEP elements may have an effect on imagery vividness is also relevant. If image vividness interacts with image controllability, as proposed by Moran (1993), then mental simulation accompanied by movement may address some of the image control concerns associated with relaxation-based procedures.

ENVIRONMENT

Lang's (1977; 1979; 1985) theory suggests that motor imagery should be personalized through full, multisensory involvement of the performer in the generation of the motor image content. This implies that unfamiliar environmental 'as if . . .' situations (Syer and Connolly 1987, p. 64) may not be effective for mental practice. On the other hand, the support of individual motor imagery with videotaped recordings of performance in familiar training and competition environments should access the correct motor repre-sentation, where neuronal connections already exist. Where performance is to take place at a new venue with limited representation of environmental cues, attempts should be made to provide multisensory support, including video footage, photographs and discussions with experienced performers. Because it may not always be convenient to conduce imagery sessions in a training or competition environment, facilitating envi-ronmental functional equivalence seems to be a useful investment.

TASK

It is surprising that most of the imagery-based interventions described in sport psychol-ogy texts fail to address the task-specificity issue. Even if a generic description of the skill is presented, key components of the task will vary substantially. Attentional varia-tion (what the performer attends to) occurs among performers, both between and within tasks. From a 'mechanisms' perspective, implications for functional equivalence are clearly apparent. Decety *et al.* (1994) have shown that different portions of the SMA are activated according to the nature of the task. For example, when a motor imagery task requires visually guided movements in the presence of a visual object, pre-motor neurones are especially active. With internally driven tasks, however, the ventral and mesial portions of SMA exhibit preferential activity.

Our shooting-based studies have shown preferential recruitment of the posterior parietal cortex in elite pistol and air-rifle shooters compared to three-position small-bore rifle-shooters. It was hypothesized that the more stable shooting environment of the air-range allowed greater dorsal stream involvement in visual processing. When considering these data in the light of findings by Konttinen, Lyytinen and Konttinen (1995), there is strong evidence that imagery techniques should be task-specific and different for elite performers by comparison with less-advanced shooters (Figure 9.2, route 1). Konttinen and his colleagues showed that for good performance, elite rifle-shooters focus primarily on motor control prior to triggering (internally driven), whereas the less-skilled were more concerned with visuo-spatial processing (externally driven). If functional-equivalence conditions are to be met, the content, and possibly the imagery modality, for elite shooters should be different until the less-skilled begin to display task characteristics of the elite. In one of the few studies to consider the nature of the task as an important factor in imagery interventions, Hardy (1997) provided evidence that task characteristics should determine the primary perspective of the imagery, although possibly not at the expense of individual perspective preference (Hall 1997). Where good form is emphasized, both Smith, Collins and Hale (1998) and Hardy and Callow (1999) have suggested that external visual imagery with kinaesthetic

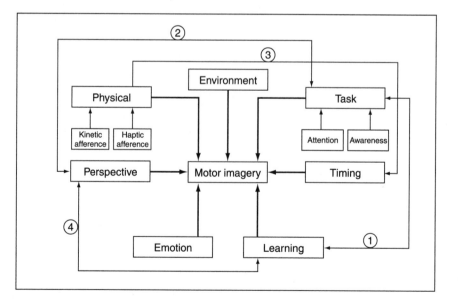

FIGURE 9.2 *Diagrammatic representation of the modified PETTELP model indicating modality interactions and sources (see text for details). Recent research from our own laboratories supports the inclusion of kinetic and haptic afference as critical elements within the Physical component and provides strong support for attention and awareness as elements of the Task component (Holmes and Collins, 2001b).*

imagery will lead to successful performance (Figure 9.2, route 2). In this instance an external visual image possesses greater information about the nature of the form than an internal image. Thus, the importance of the integration of information from task, learning and perspective is clearly evident.

TIMING

If motor preparation, execution and motor imagery access similar motor representations, then temporal characteristics should also be similar. A claim for functional equivalence seems reasonable, since both types of activity are characterized by a requirement to 'reconstruct or generate a temporally extended event on the basis of some form of memory' (Vogt 1995, p. 193). For example, when working with shooters it is essential to include the target-changing mechanism in the imagery conditions, together with all between-shot activity of reloading. These individuals have reported that they 'felt rushed' and experienced 'loss of control' if full reference to reloading was excluded from the script. Vogt's (1995) work supports the notion of temporal functional equivalence. He demonstrated that movement tempo and consistency of relative timing are similar for both physical and mental practice conditions and concluded that performance, observation and imagery of sequential patterns involve a common process. Similarly, the isochrony principle (Jeannerod 1997), according to which the tangential velocity of movements is scaled to amplitude, is maintained in both motor execution and motor imagery. Also, Decety, Jeannerod and Prablanc (1989) have shown that time is represented as a function of force (Figure 9.2, route 3), with estimated duration being derived from this level of centrally represented force (Jeannerod 1997).

Motor preparation and execution generally include greater force conditions than typical motor imagery. Consequently, where external force conditions are absent from imagery, athletes will perceive increases in felt force as an increase in movement duration according to their response and meaning propositions and image slower. Holmes and Collins (2001b) have shown that in basketball and golf studies, manipulating force available to an athlete in an imagery condition, for example changing posture and allowing sporting implements to be held, significantly reduces potential duration increases. These studies highlight the need to consider kinetic functional equivalence in imagery through either singular or interactional PETTLEP elements.

Motor imagery training that requires the performer to image internally in slow motion must be questioned, although an external visual perspective isolation approach with slow motion and freeze frame may be effective for some and provides an example of task–perspective–timing interaction. However, a study by Collins et al. (1997) has emphasized temporal rhythm rather than the achievement of key body positions as a feature of effective performance in the execution of closed skills. Realistic timing assumes great importance in imagery scripts. Consequently, where timing is important performers frequently refer to its key role when performing well. One elite field athlete has identified the rhythm of his run up as critical for optimal performance. His imagery script comprises auditory cues relating to his foot strike in the run-up phase, rather than a traditional written verbal script (Backley and Stafford 1996). Similar emphasis on the temporal elements of the task are emphasized in the Martin self-talk technique (Martin 1993). Where timing of a task is important, not only technically but also as a Langian meaning proposition for the athlete, specific reference to the timing element of PETTLEP might be considered for memory trace strengthening.

LEARNING

The importance of learning is apparent from electroencephalographic (EEG) data in our work with a pistol-shooter. A 14-month psychological intervention programme involving subconscious attentional shifts clearly showed a change in EEG profile at sites hypothesized to be associated with reduced awareness. The altered profile was also associated with improvement in shot quality. It follows that since motor representation changes over time as learning takes place, the content of a motor-image script must change to accommodate learning and to maintain functional equivalence. In support of this suggestion, Pascual-Leone *et al.* (1995) showed that motor imagery of finger movements increased in congruence with motor preparation and execution over a one-week period. Therefore, when motor imagery is combined with technical training or in intensive learning phases of a task, regularly reviewing the script content is essential to retain functional equivalence. Unfortunately, this kind of dynamic approach to imagery delivery is rarely seen in sport psychology literature.

EMOTION

Emotion has been referred to as 'the missing link' in sports performance (Botterill 1997), while (Loehr 1997) observed that 'the central core of mental training is emotional'. Similarly, Moritz *et al.* (1996) found that highly confident roller skaters mainly used mastery and arousal imagery, suggesting that emotions are an important imagery mediator. Some years ago, Lang (1985) proposed an underlying mechanism to describe the importance of emotions in the strengthening of the memory trace and stated that during emotional imagery the efferent pattern is even more elaborate than with non-emotionally relevant information.

When all modalities of PETTLEP, their integrations and Langian theory are considered as co-existing concepts, the associated emotional affect may be so great that relatively specific efference will show high congruence with overt behaviour. To return to a boxing analogy, a boxer should perceive greater movement when imagery content also includes appropriate emotional content. Furthermore, motor imagery scripts that create such efference should be encouraged if guidelines relating to 'the physical' are followed.

Affective response to a motor image is best shown through the autonomic system (Decety 1996a). Heart rate and respiration rate changes that accompany motor preparation and execution reflect alterations in the energetic state of a performer faced by psychological challenge (Smith and Collins 1992) as well as altered metabolic requirements. Such changes are important for imagery content and should be addressed by increasing the general physiological response (Carroll, Marzillier and Merian 1982). Fundamental research of this kind supports autonomic-biased stimulus and response propositions where cardiorespiratory control is required, for example in target sports (Holmes 1997). The inclusion of emotion as a motor imagery variable also challenges the common practice of preceding imagery with relaxation (Miller 1991; Weinberg and Gould 1999). Because sport is not performed in a hyper-relaxed, non-emotive state, then motor imagery of sport skills and situations should not be either.

PERSPECTIVE

It was suggested earlier that internal motor imagery is best, primarily for the promotion of kinaesthesis, but co-occurring with senses such as vision and audition. It is generally well regarded that this perspective, and similar response-propositional approaches (Lang 1979; 1985), lead to increased physiological response during the imagery process (Hale 1982; Perry and Morris 1995). As previously argued, this should lead to more effective learning and performance outcomes. However, recent findings have led to renewed interest in imagery perspective. Some authors (White and Hardy 1993; Smith, Collins and Hale 1998; Hardy and Callow 1999) have suggested using external visual imagery as an effective approach for certain skills in, say, gymnastics, diving or trampolining, allowing the performer to 'see' precise positions and movements. At first glance this may seem to challenge the functional equivalence approach, so why might an external visual perspective be effective and how can functional equivalence explain such effectiveness? In agreeing with Hardy's (1997) information-based position, it is proposed that a functional equivalence approach *can* offer support. Lang (1985) has stated that network activations can begin with *any* [our italicization] set of concepts and move within, or between, structural levels. Therefore, external visual imagery may contain sufficient prepositional (stimulus, response and/or meaning) information to access the motor representation to allow strengthening of memory traces and associated neural networks.

In the case of advanced performers, for whom a well-developed memory trace exists for a given task, it is plausible that an external visual perspective can access other elements of a representation concurrently with the visual. Theoretical perspectives that describe the multimodal, interactional coding of information in memory (Paivio 1986), cortical cell assemblies (Wickens, Hyland and Anson 1994), motor representations (Jeannerod 1994), parallel distributed processing (Rumelhart and McClelland 1986) or neural networks (Rosenzweig 1996), offer a mechanism for this effect. Also, both quasi-random and relatively task-specific movement may be discernible in experienced performers who adopt an external visual perspective. This contention is supported by Jeannerod (1997) and provides a theoretical underpinning to advice offered by some researchers (e.g. Hall 1997). It is suggested, therefore, that the perspective debate be further advanced to consider the use of interactional perspectives appropriate for both individual and task. It is further suggested that arguments should be based upon mechanistic, rather than outcome, perspectives. In short, consider what is causing an effect rather than just note that it occurs!

Traditionally, an image is defined as a cognitive production. Accordingly, processing response information may initiate associated kinaesthetic elements of the motor representations during visual imagery, but these factors cannot be consciously attended to simultaneously with a visual image (Pashler and Johnston 1998). It is possible, therefore, that some visuomotor elements experienced during performance are unavailable for conscious imagery, as discussed previously, but can be accessed via modalities containing sufficient response propositions, for example a self-model video. If this is so, then it is likely that meaningful visual images can access kinaesthetic elements of the representation at the subconscious level with associated efference. This situation is clearly different from conscious, internally based kinaesthetic imagery, although both approaches access a similar representation and may be equally effective. For the practitioner the message is clear. Use of video performance feedback is an effective way of increasing functional equivalence, especially emotional and attentional aspects. In fact it may work better than a traditional, written script-based approach and attentional problems can occur if an athlete is required to verbalize the image internally, for example if required to attend consciously to technical elements of an action.

Interactions between PETTLEP elements are likely to provide a way forward for practitioners, although some interactions are more obvious than others. While some are unidirectional, others will have more complex interactions. It is also likely that each will reveal considerable individual differences, as consistent with the Langian theory of propositional coding. A modification of the physical nature of the imagery experience will have a direct effect on the arousal level of the performer and, subsequently, on the emotional nature of the imagery. This may be particularly true for an internal visual/kinaesthetic imagery perspective in a relevant environment and a practitioner should consider all possible interactions when using a PETTLEP.

An interaction with the PETTLEP learning element is an important consideration for the sport psychologist (Figure 9.2, route 4). Smith, Collins and Hale (1998) have suggested that conscious attention to visual *then* kinaesthetic factors is the perspective most commonly employed by learners. Since the nature of a novice's representation is still at a formative stage, the learner must first perceive visual information and then estimate how the image may feel. Such attentional approaches offer a particular advantage to more cognitive tasks where symbolic learning is important (see Feltz and Landers 1983).

An application of the PETTLEP model.

Imagine a rhythmic gymnast using pre-performance imagery to prepare herself for a national competition. She is required to execute a dance-like, highly choreographed routine to music, while manipulating a hoop, a ball or a ribbon. Each separate element is physically demanding and possesses some of the characteristics of other gymnastic disciplines. Application of the PETTLEP system would be as follows:

Physical: The gymnast imagines being out of breath and the increasing fatigue which she will feel as the routine proceeds. In fact, the gymnast may even exercise before imagery to simulate her physical performance state. Imagery is completed standing, with physical movements that mirror the rhythm and pace of the actual routine. She wears a competition leotard, uses chalk and resin as for the competition and holds the implement – ball, hoop or ribbon – that she will use in her performance.

Environment: The gymnast images performance at the venue, using photographs, videos and audio tape of crowd noise, together with her accompanying music to create as closely as possible the environment in which she is to perform. Particular sensory features of the venue are also incorporated within the image.

Task: This component matches attentional demands and changes in the imagery condition to those attentional demands and changes that operate in the actual event *for that individual performer*. Thus, in this gymnastics example, the gymnast would focus very specifically on her performance, internal emotions/feelings and actual movements at a subconscious level. Prompts to 'attend to the crowd' would be inappropriate, at least during the routine itself, although they may be appropriate in a non-competitive, performance-as-entertainment situation.

Timing: The preparation for, and execution of, the routine are imaged in real time by utilizing appropriate kinetic stimuli and encouraging performers to experience the emotions associated with the successful performance.

Learning: Obviously the routine is well-learned. However, if there are difficulties envisaged, they may also be included to provide a more realistic situation. Note that imagery realism is essential for competition, but learning-based imagery would be different. For example, in mental practice designed for learning a routine, sections can be used in slow motion to best meet the requirements of the particular skill. As a routine is learned, other PETTLEP components will be modified to reflect changes in emotion, task-based attention and so on.

Emotion: Feelings of panic, worry, exhilaration should each be included if an athlete experiences these emotions in the real setting. Exercise-induced physical increases in emotion will also facilitate the vividness of an image.

Perspective: Since a gymnast is also assessed aesthetically, she should use an external visual-kinaesthetic perspective as if watching herself on film. Some might suggest that an internal visual-kinaesthetic perspective is preferable, as it represents her actual performance more accurately. The best approach may be to use two perspectives, with external imagery to promote confidence and internal imagery to rehearse the movement. As mentioned in the perspective section, very experienced performers can generate kinaesthetic sensations from an external visual perspective. However, this is where interactions between different components need to be considered. Internal visual perspectives may also promote better emotional and environmental reality, while an internal perspective may be more effective when a crucial concern is with functional equivalence as a means of generating an accurate reconstruction of the full performance.

This brief gymnastics example serves to exemplify the PETTLEP model in action. The key points are as follows. First, individual differences between athletes are so great that before applying the model it is important to check with each one, even if an opinion contradicts the theory! According to the Langian view, the meaning proposition is the key factor in promoting vividness for any individual. Secondly, knowing the components that are used within each factor of the model is crucial. That is, why are you doing what you are doing?

Conclusion

The suggestions presented in this chapter support the use of novel perspectives, but only on the basis of a clear understanding of their *modus operandi*. Both research and practice (Holmes 1996; Smith, Collins and Hale 1998) have identified a number of techniques that utilize a PETTLEP approach. For example, video 'step-in', emotional word sets and music-facilitated videos have each been used successfully to enhance sport performance. The theoretically based arguments presented here support new approaches and provide a sound rationale for practitioners in a way that anecdotal evidence from an athlete may not. While it is felt that the PETTLEP approach has much to offer sport psychologists working with imagery-based interventions, it is acknowledged that little applied work has undergone rigorous testing and evaluation. It is also recognized that some sport psychologists already adopt aspects of the approach in their work. However, it is rare to hear of scripts that include PETTLEP components, or that recognize personalized component interactions. As far as the future is concerned, our experiences with athletes suggests that along with an increased awareness of the benefits of psychological intervention strategies, comes a corresponding awareness of the advantages of the PETTLEP model.

References

Backley, S. and Stafford, I. (1996) *The Winning Mind: A Guide to Achieving Success and Overcoming Failure*, London: Aurum Press.

Beisteiner, R., Höllinger, P., Lindinger, G., Lang, W. and Berthoz, A. (1995) 'Mental representations of movements. Brain potentials associated with imagination of hand movements', *Electroencephalography and Clinical Neurophysiology* 96:183–193.

Botterill, C. (1997) 'The role of emotion in sport performance: The missing link?', *Journal of Applied Sport Psychology* 9:12.

Carroll, D., Marzillier, J. S. and Merian, S. (1982) 'Psychophysiological changes accompanying different types of arousing and relaxing imagery', *Psychophysiology* 19:75–82.

Collins, D. J., Morriss, C., Bellamy, M. and Hooper, H. (1997) 'Competition stress effects on kinematics and performance level in elite javelin throwers', *Journal of Applied Sport Psychology* 9:S38.

Davidson, R. J. and Schwartz, G. E. (1976) 'The psychobiology of relaxation and relaxed states: A multi-process theory'. In D. I. Mostofsky (ed.), *Behavior Control and Modification of Physiological Activity*, pp. 399–442, Englewood Cliffs, NJ: Prentice-Hall.

Decety, J. (1996a) 'Do imagined and executed actions share the same neural substrate?', *Cognitive Brain Research* 3:87–93.

Decety, J. (1996b) 'The neurological basis of motor imagery', *Behavioral Brain Research* 77:45–52.

Decety, J., Jeannerod, M., Germain, M. and Pastène, J. (1991) 'Vegetative response during imagined movement is proportional to mental effort', *Behavioural Brain Research* 42:1–5.

Decety, J., Jeannerod, M. and Prablanc, C. (1989) 'The timing of mentally represented actions', *Behavioural Brain Research* 34:35–42.

Decety, J., Perani, D., Jeannerod, M., Bettinardi, V., Tadary, B., Woods, R., Mazziotta, J. C. and Fazio, F. (1994) 'Mapping motor representations with PET', *Nature* 371:600–602.

Decety, J., Sjöholm, H., Ryding, E., Stenberg, G. and Ingvar, D. (1990) 'The cerebellum participates in mental activity: Tomographic measurements of regional cerebral blood flow', *Brain Research* 535:313–317.

Ekman, P. (1992) 'Facial expressions of emotion: New findings, new questions', *Psychophysical Science* 3:34–38.

Farah, M. J. (1985) 'Psychological evidence for a shared representational medium for mental images and percepts', *Journal of Experimental Psychology: General* 114:91–103.

Feltz, D. L. and Landers, D. M. (1983) 'The effects of mental practice on motor skill learning and performance: A meta-analysis', *Journal of Sport Psychology* 5:25–57.

Gabriele, T. E., Hall, C. R. and Lee, T. D. (1989) 'Cognition in motor learning: Imagery effects on contextual interference', *Human Movement Science* 8:227–245.

Gould, D. and Damarjian, N. (1996) 'Imagery training for peak performance'. In J. L. Van Raalte and B. W. Brewer (eds.), *Exploring Sport and Exercise Psychology*, pp. 25–50, Washington, DC: American Psychological Association.

Hale, B. D. (1982) 'The effects of internal and external imagery on muscular and ocular concomitants', *Journal of Sport Psychology* 4:379–387.

Hall, C. R. (1997) 'Lew Hardy's third myth: A matter of perspective', *Journal of Applied Sport Psychology* 9:310–313.

Hardy, L. (1997) 'Three myths about applied consultancy work', *Journal of Applied Sport Psychology* 9:107–118.

Hardy, L. and Callow, N. (1999) 'Efficacy of external and internal visual imagery perspectives for the enhancement of performance on tasks in which form is important', *Journal of Sport and Exercise Psychology* 21:95–112.

Harrigan, J. A. and O'Connell, D. M. (1996) 'How do you look when feeling anxious? Facial displays of anxiety', *Personality and Individual Differences* 21:205–212.

Holmes, P. S. (1996) *SCATT Recorded Centrefire Pistol Profiles of Elite Shooters*. Paper presented to the Great Britain National Centrefire and Standard Pistol Squad, Bisley, UK.

Holmes, P. S. (1997) *Psychological Support for Elite Pistol Shooters*. Paper presented at the Annual Meeting of the Great Britain National Shooting Squads. Bisley, UK.

Holmes, P. S. and Collins, D. J. (2001a) 'The PETTLEP approach to motor imagery: A functional equivalence model for sport psychologists', *Journal of Applied Sport Psychology* 13:60–83.

Holmes, P. S. and Collins, D. J. (2001b) *'Force-modified imagery and temporal functional equivalence in the basketball free throw and golf short iron play'*. Manuscript under review.

Ingvar, D. H. and Philipson, L. (1977) 'Distribution of cerebral blood flow in the dominant hemisphere during motor ideation and motor performance', *Annals of Neurology* 2:230–237.

Jacobson, E. (1931) 'Electrical measurement of neuromuscular states during mental activities', *American Journal of Physiology* 94:115–121.

Jeannerod, M. (1994) 'The representing brain: neural correlates of motor intention and imagery', *Behavioural and Brain Sciences* 17:187–245.

Jeannerod, M. (1997) *The Cognitive Neuroscience of Action*, Oxford: Blackwell.

Jeannerod, M. and Decety, J. (1995) 'Mental motor imagery: A window into the representational stages of action', *Current Opinion in Neurobiology* 5:727–732.

Keil, D., Holmes, P., Bennett, S., Davids, K. and Smith, N. (2000) 'Theory and practice in sport psychology and motor behaviour needs to be constrained by integrative modelling of brain and behaviour', *Journal of Sports Sciences* 18:433–443.

Konttinen, N., Lyytinen, H. and Konttinen, R. (1995) 'Brain slow potentials reflecting successful shooting performance', *Research Quarterly for Exercise and Sport* 66:64–72.

Lang, P. J. (1977) 'Imagery in therapy: An information processing analysis of fear', *Behavior Therapy* 8:862–886.

Lang, P. J. (1979) 'A bio-informational theory of emotional imagery', *Psychophysiology* 17:495–512.

Lang, P. J. (1985) 'Cognition in emotion: Concept and action'. In C. Izard, J. Kagan, and R. Zajonc (eds.) *Emotion, Cognitions and Behavior*, pp. 192–225, New York: Cambridge University Press.

Loehr, J. (1997) 'The role of emotion in sport performance: Emotions run the show', *Journal of Applied Sport Psychology* 9:S13.

Loze, G. M., Collins, D. J. and Shaw, J. C. (1999) EEG alpha rhythm, intention and oculomotor control', *International Journal of Psychophysiology* 33:163–167.

Mantle, H. (1996) *Demonstration of Dynamic Imagery Session with International Canoeist. Sport Psychology: Myth or Magic?* Grandstand, British Broadcasting Corporation, November.

Martin, G.L. (1993) 'Research on mental practice techniques: Comment on Palmer's study', *The Sport Psychologist* 7:339–341.

Miller, B. (1991) 'Mental preparation for competition'. In S. J. Bull (ed.) *Sport Psychology: A Self-help Guide*, pp. 84–102, Marlborough: The Crowood Press Ltd.

Montoya, P., Lotze, M., Grodd, W., Larbig, W., Erb, M., Flor, H. and Birbaumer, N. (1998) *Brain activation during executed and imagined movements using fMRI.* Paper presented at the 3rd European Congress of Psychophysiology: Konstantz.

Moran, A. (1993) 'Conceptual and methodological issues in the measurement of mental imagery skills in athletes', *Journal of Sport Behaviour* 16:156–170.

Moritz, S. E., Hall, C. R., Vadocz, E. and Martin, K. A. (1996) 'What are confident athletes imaging? An examination of image content', *The Sport Psychologist* 10:171–179.

Murphy, S. M. (1994) 'Imagery interventions in sport', *Medicine and Science in Sport and Exercise* 26:486–494.

Parsons, L. M. (1987) 'Imagined spatial transformations of one's hands and feet', *Cognitive Psychology* 19:178–241.

Pascual-Leone, A., Dang, N., Cohen, L. G., Brasil-Neto, J., Cammarota, A. and Hallett, M. (1995) 'Modulation of motor responses evoked by transcranial magnetic stimulation during the acquisition of new fine motor skills', *Journal of Neurophysiology* 74:1037–1045.

Pashler, H. and Johnston, J. C. (1998) 'Attentional limitations in dual-task performance'. In H. Pashler (ed.), *Attention*, pp. 155–189, Hove: Psychology Press Limited.

Paivio, A. (1986) *Mental Representations*, New York: Oxford University Press.

Perry, C. and Morris, T. (1995) 'Mental imagery in sport'. In T. Morris and J. Summers (eds.) *Sport Psychology: Theory, Applications and Issues*, pp. 339–385, Queensland: John Wiley and Sons.

Rosenzweig, M. R. (1996) 'Aspects of the search for neural mechanisms of memory', *Annual Reviews of Psychology* 47:1–32.

Rumelhart, D. E., McClelland, J. L. and the PDP Research Group (1986) *Parallel Distributed Processing: Explorations in the Microstructure of Cognition. Volume 1, Foundations*, Cambridge, MA: MIT Press.

Shaw, W. A. (1940) 'The relation of muscular action potentials to imaginal weightlifting', *Archives of Psychology* 247:1–50.

Smith, D. Collins, D. and Hale, B. (1998) 'Imagery perspectives and karate performance', *Journal of Sports Sciences* 16:99.

Smith, N. C. and Collins, D. J. (1992) 'The role of psychophysiology as a research and intervention tool in sport psychology', *Journal of Psychophysiology* 6:78.

Stephan, K. M., Fink, G. R., Passingham, R. E., Silbersweig, D., Ceballos-Baumann, A. O., Frith, C. D. and Frackowiak, R. S. J. (1995) 'Functional anatomy of the mental representation of upper extremity movements in healthy subjects', *Journal of Neurophysiology* 73:373–386.

Suinn, R. M. (1976) 'Visual motor behavior rehearsal for adaptive behavior'. In J. Krumboltz and C. Thoresen (eds.), *Counseling Methods*, pp. 320–326, New York: Holt, Rinehart and Winston.

Syer, J. and Connolly, C. (1987) *Sporting Body, Sporting Mind: An Athlete's Guide to Mental Training*, London: Simon and Schuster Limited.

Vogt, S. (1995) 'On relations between perceiving, imagining and performing in the learning of cyclical movement sequences', *British Journal of Psychology* 86:191–216.

Wang, Y. and Morgan, W. P. (1992) 'The effect of imagery perspectives on the psychophysiological responses to imagined exercise', *Behavioural Brain Research* 52:167–174.

Weinberg, R. S. and Gould, D. (1999) *Foundations of Sport and Exercise Psychology*, second edition, Champaign IL: Human Kinetics.

Weinberg, R. S., Seabourne, T. G. and Jackson, A. (1981) 'Effects of visuo-motor behavior rehearsal, relaxation and imagery on karate performance', *Journal of Sport Psychology* 3:228–238.

White, A. and Hardy, L. (1993) 'The effects of using different imagery perspectives on the learning and performance of two different motor tasks'. *UK sport: partners in performance. The contribution of sport science, sports medicine and coaching to performance and excellence.* Abstract s1, The Sports Council, pp. 98–99.

Wickens, J., Hyland, B. and Anson, G. (1994) 'Cortical cell assemblies: A possible mechanism for motor programs', *Journal of Motor Behavior* 26:66–82.

Wolpe, J. (1958) *Psychotherapy by Reciprocal Inhibition.* Stanford, CA: Stanford University Press.

Young, J. (1990) *Cognitive Therapy for Personality Disorders: A Schema Focused Approach*, Sarasota, FL: Professional Resource Exchange.

Yue, G. and Cole, K. J. (1992) 'Strength increases from the motor program: Comparison of training with maximal voluntary and imagined muscle contractions', *Journal of Neurophysiology* 67:1114–1123.

chapter (ten)

Case studies in confidence for elite slalom canoeists

HUGH MANTLE

Slalom canoeing involves paddling a canoe or kayak down moving white water through a series of gates in a set order. Contact with, or missing a gate incurs a time penalty that increases a competitor's run time and, of course, the competitor with the fastest time wins.

The problem

In his capacity as coach and sport psychologist to an elite squad of five canoe slalomists training together over a four-year period in preparation for international competitions including an Olympic Games, the author conducted a range of physiological and psychological investigations involving squad members. Research using the Competitive State Anxiety Inventory (CSAI-2) (Martens *et al.* 1990), for example, and relating this to performance, has shown no significant trends (Mantle 1997). The CSAI-2 indicated high confidence scores and relatively low scores on the cognitive and somatic anxiety scales. However, observation of the athletes' behaviour, and listening to their worries and concerns over a number of years during both training and competition, indicated that anxiety was a real issue. Therefore, it was postulated that the CSAI-2 was not reflecting the true feelings of these elite slalomists. It was possible that the instruments being used to measure anxiety in relation to performance at an elite level were too insensitive to identify discriminatory factors. Alternatively, the athletes might be denying significant problems as a coping strategy when going into a major competition.

As an alternative method of investigation the author adopted a case study approach, its purpose being to assess the individual's current attitudes and behaviour in relation to competition. Appropriate interventions were used and their effectiveness was evaluated to gain a greater understanding of the individual in the ecologically valid setting of preparation for major competitions. The two cases reported here are representative of the group in that it became clear that mental factors, including anxiety and loss of confidence, were having a significant effect on both preparation and performance. In both instances the sequence of interventions is summarized, with a brief indication of outcomes.

Research

Analysis of how the elite perform skills has been conducted for some time (Russell and Salmela 1992; Abernethy 1994; Abernethy, Neal and Koning 1994; Thomas and Thomas 1994). Research has indicated that elite athletes show psychological characteristics and behavioural tendencies that include self-confidence, competitiveness, coping style, internal locus of control, positive attribution style and the use of psychological strategies including mental imagery and positive self-talk (Cox 1990; Anshel 1994). It is also clear, particularly in canoe slalom, that some competitors are consistently more successful than others. Although the empirical literature tends to show that elite performers are better than non-elite at mental skills (Mahoney, Gabriel and Perkins 1987; Orlick and Partington 1988; Thomas and Thomas 1994), it does not demonstrate why or how these differences occur. Examination of the phenomenon may lead to insights into how elite athletes prepare for competition, how they feel during competition and how they evaluate their mental state in relation to current and forthcoming competitions.

Methodology

The chosen methodology was that of intrinsic case study (Stake 1994), an attempt to understand a particular case by using a qualitative approach, letting the case tell its own story (Coles 1989; Carter 1993) in order to gain insight into issues, contexts and interpretations. It is appreciated that a qualitative case study approach is not without some risk (Herriott and Firestone 1983; Lofland and Lofland 1984; Miles and Huberman 1984). Even taking into account the multiple sources of evidence that can form a chain of explanations, a certain amount of inference can take place (Yin 1994). A consideration of rival explanations might help to counteract this. It is appreciated that a case study is not exhaustive in its description and analysis of the person and situations; rather it is selective in that it chooses to concentrate on certain issues at the expense of others.

The author, as both coach and sport psychologist to the canoeists, was deemed to be a participant observer. The advantages and privileges of this position allowed the research to take on a grounded-theory approach where there was continual interplay between analysis and data collection and, thereby, constant comparative analysis (Glasser and Strauss 1967). At the same time the author was aware that as a participant observer he was open to changing the athletes' behaviour because of the close relationship he had with them, and there was also the possibility of changing himself (Clandimin and Connelly 1994). The study had, as its working principle, Bromley's

(1986) view that a psychological case study is an account of how and why an individual behaved as he or she did in a given situation. There has been no other attempt to use case study methodologies that incorporate both content analysis and levels of comparison.

The study adopted a non-experimental protocol based on single-subject design (Hersen and Barlow 1976; Kazdin 1982; Bryan 1987). Qualitative methodology was mainly used but with some incorporation of quantitative methods as described by Steckler *et al.* (1992). Note was taken of Bromley's (1986) suggested rules for the preparation of a psychological case study, namely truth, clear aims and objectives, prolonged enquiry and ecological context. These are similar to the concept of 'trustworthiness' as proposed by Lincoln and Guba (1985). It was felt that an idiographic approach would allow examination of changes within individuals. It was not the purpose of the investigation to seek and analyze between-subject variations (Smith 1989). Ecological validity was seen to be a prime focus in the study because of the unique opportunity to study elite performers over a prolonged period of time in their training, travelling, living and competitive environments. The author immersed himself in this environment feeling that this method matched the particular question of interest in this research (Hardy, Jones and Gould 1996).

ASSESSMENT PROCEDURES

Three assessment procedures were adopted. First, the Sports-Related Psychological Skills Questionnaire (SPSQ) (Nelson and Hardy 1990) was used to assess the current mental skill level of the subjects. The sub-scales measured were imaginal skill, mental preparation, self-efficacy, cognitive anxiety, concentration skill, relaxation skill and motivation. The scale consists of 56 items with eight items in each of the seven sub-scales. Responses are scored on a Likert Scale ranging from six (strongly agree) to one (strongly disagree). It has been reported that Cronbach's alpha for the selected items in each of the seven categories exceeded 0.78 (Nelson and Hardy 1990).

Secondly, the Performance Profile (Butler and Hardy 1992), with origins in personal construct theory (Kelly 1955), was used to identify the subject's personal viewpoint. Each athlete was asked to identify those qualities he believed to be most important for elite performance in his sport, to rate the relative importance of each quality and to assess his own current status in each. Finally, an interview, which had a structure based on gaining descriptions of current medical symptoms (Macleod 1973), and adapted for use with psychological emotional symptoms (Stern and Drummond 1991), was used to explore specific aspects in greater detail.

⟨ Case Study I ⟩   **'William'**

William was a highly talented paddler who had produced a number of very good international results at junior level, but was relatively new to the senior squad. His approach to preparation was somewhat haphazard and he tended to depend upon others to organize him. William had not previously involved himself in any mental training, although he was an outstanding competitor and showed few signs of anxiety. However, since joining the senior squad his results were not as good as had been predicted by the junior squad coach. The SPSQ (Table 10.1) indicated that William was confident, highly motivated and very relaxed, with good concentration and low cognitive anxiety. The lower scores for imaginal skills and mental preparation reflected how William approached competition. He rarely used mental rehearsal, did not like to imagine skills before practising them, did not practise relaxing and did not set goals or analyze his performance. The Performance Profile elicited the responses shown in Table 10.2.

Table 10.1   Scores from the SPSQ for William

Category	Score (max. score = 48)	(Deficit) = max. score less William's score
Imaginal skills	34	(14)
Mental preparation	34	(14)
Self-efficacy	48	(0)
Cognitive anxiety control	43	(5)
Concentration skills	43	(5)
Relaxation skill	46	(2)
Motivation	46	(2)

Table 10.2   Performance Profile as defined by William

Construct	William's definition	Current score (10)
Concentration	Ability to concentrate on the situation in hand.	7
Relaxed	Relaxed and controlled in unnatural and sometimes annoying situations.	8
Determination	Determined never to quit; keep going when things are down.	9
Arrogance	Arrogance, but kept to yourself	8
Competitive	Positively stimulated by competitive situations	8
Motivated	Motivated when defeated.	9
Motivated	Motivated when winning.	8
Respect	Respect other competitors, until competing against them, but again kept to yourself.	7
Self-importance	Self-importance, but kept to yourself in race situations	10

During the interview William pointed out that he had no experience of mental prepa-ration. He felt he was a good competitor, loved racing, rarely became nervous and did not have any problems. However, he said that he would like to be a little better orga-nized and thought that his concentration could be improved. This was surprising as his score on the SPSQ was reasonably high. Further exploration revealed that William felt he had skills, but there were times when he was indecisive about which ones to use to complete a certain gate sequence. He also lost concentration during certain races. William was conscious of a lack of improvement since being in the senior squad. He was also aware that another squad member was scrutinizing his prepara-tion; although this other person was extremely helpful in William's planning, he was also very critical and, as William saw it, very judgemental.

In discussion, William seemed to like the idea of an intervention programme and was prepared to experiment with anything that would move him off his plateau in performance. He admitted to feeling rather helpless. William was asked to record any critical interactions with other squad members at training sessions or social occa-sions. He was also asked to reflect on his relationship with the squad member he had characterized as helpful, but critical, on his feelings when receiving criticism, and on possible conflicting perceptions in himself and by the other person.

In further discussion William revealed that the reason he felt uneasy in the squad was partly because the other members were highly organized, very committed and very serious. In order for him to make an impression in the group he would have to conform to this approach, which he did not welcome. The identity of the particular squad member with whom there was a conflict between help and criticism was now revealed. This person, Sam, was much more experienced and, in William's view, trying to do the best for both of them. William felt that in some ways Sam represented a father-like figure. William had not followed the intervention recommendation to record incidents and feelings or to make evaluations of Sam's behaviour. Instead, he just wished to talk about the problem and try to clarify his thoughts and feelings.

Using Macleod's (1973) outline to structure the interview, the main factors presented were that William revealed that his self-confidence had always been low, as he felt that the only reason he was good at paddling had been as a result of Sam's input. He felt that he was treated as the 'little boy', and had become very fed up with the situation. At times he was irritable and uncooperative with Sam and resented his competence, which had been observed by the coach. Sam then reacted, so now William felt guilty because he should really be grateful for Sam's help and advice. He could not broach the subject, so he asked the author to act as an intermediary in what was proving a difficult situation. Sam was approached and it was found that much of what William had said was valid but could also be seen from the other's perspective.

According to the cognitive model (Beck *et al.* 1979), assumptions, inappropriate beliefs and illogical thinking errors play a primary part in maintaining problems in relationships. It is also interesting to note that certain therapists (Lederer and Jackson 1968; Treacher 1985) regard interventions with individuals as unlikely to have a lasting effect unless the whole 'family' is involved in the intervention. On this basis it was decided to ask both William and Sam to keep separate two-week diaries of critical incidents and to describe emotions and automatic thoughts (Beck *et al.* 1979). Typical extracts are shown in Table 10.3.

Table 10.3 Typical diary extracts from William and Sam

Day/time	Situation	Emotion	Automatic thoughts
	What were you doing or thinking about?	What did you feel? How bad? (0–100)	What exactly were your thoughts?
William			
Wednesday 8.00am	Sees Sam training with two others of the squad.	Despair (45) Anger (80)	They don't like me. I am not good enough. They regard me as the 'little boy'.
Wednesday 2.00pm	Sees Sam going through BOMC test results.	Guilt (60) Anger (80)	He is so organized. I should model him. He has stopped me developing physiology knowledge.
Sam			
Wednesday 8.00am	Training with two others of squad. Sees William.	Hurt (45)	Why doesn't he take notice of my advice and train with us?
Wednesday 2.00pm	Doing BOMC (British Olympic Medical Centre) test results.	Annoyed (85)	He doesn't care about getting the peaking right.

Following this intervention William was visibly happier and felt he was communicating his feelings better with Sam (and vice versa). There was open appreciation of each other's qualities and they appeared to be working better as a pair. They had made a pact not to discuss canoeing matters when they met socially and this helped their relationship.

Evaluation of William's relationship with the rest of the squad was good, although he started to raise some issues about the 'relationship with himself'. He had competed in some internationals with reasonable results and his CSAI-2 scores, whatever his performance results, always showed high confidence levels with little anxiety (Mantle 1997). Yet he admitted that a few days before competition he was starting to feel anxious, not about the race, but about himself as a person. Further enquiry revealed that he still felt over-attachment to Sam and continual comparison with the rest of the squad. As a result he experienced a predictable lowering of his self-image and self-esteem when he performed below par, but when he did well he tended to feel surprise rather than enhanced self-esteem. Had he really achieved success on his own merit, or were his results achieved through other people's efforts? William did not see himself as an equal and this view needed changing if he was to be fully integrated in the squad and able to overcome the perceived barriers inhibiting his growth as a performer (Syer 1986). Anxiety about integration, dependency on the other person and the ways in which he thought he was perceived by other squad members (leading to inappropriate behaviour) underpinned William's problems.

With Olympic selection imminent, it was imperative that William was confident and had generally high self-esteem, along with positive and realistic expectations about his preparation for the selection events. It was felt that William needed to discuss the issues further to clarify both functional and dysfunctional thoughts, emotions and behaviours (Trower, Casey and Dreyden 1988). This was done within a gestalt consultation model (Ferrucci 1990; Clarkson 1992). The aim of the gestalt model is to use initial questioning in order that the individual may discover, explore and experience a personal shape, pattern and wholeness. Analysis may be part of the process, but the aim of gestalt is the integration of all disparate parts. The long-term aim of the model is to allow individuals to become totally what they already are and what, potentially, they can become. Each athlete would then possibly understand that this fullness of experience could be available in the course of a canoeing career and in the experience of a single moment.

Questioning focused specifically on 'disidentification', where William would identify with only one aspect of himself to the exclusion of others, and possibly blocking out his ability to respond to situations in creative ways, and awareness. It would allow William to avoid evaluation and labelling and, instead, for him to accept his thoughts and feelings, thus reinforcing functional, rather than dysfunctional, behaviour. A further examination of the accuracy of perceptions was made, along with an assessment to identify possible projections that were being made onto significant others; for example, William's projection onto Sam of the role of 'domineering father' in order to validate his own role of 'child'. The ways these projections can limit self-development were explored in order to identify potential opportunities for change within the subject. For further information the reader is referred to Mackewn (1997). William was selected for only one international race and placed in the top 10. In the Olympic selection races he was unsuccessful, but did well in domestic events with a national top 10 classification for the season, a good result in a country with a high standard in the sport.

Measuring the success of the intervention programme as a whole showed it to be partially successful. William's preparation and decision making improved. His concentration did not, but perhaps that was not his real problem. In terms of the way he integrated within the squad, observation of William and other members of the group seen at close quarters over a period of 12 months indicated that he was at ease. He felt happier and acknowledged that he was making a contribution. He felt more of an equal and accepted that, technically, he was learning quickly. Whether this development and growth would have taken place anyway remains conjecture. The relationship with Sam was much improved; each recognized the other's needs and there was a degree of mutual respect. Sam made the Olympic Team, which was expected, so perhaps in the end he had to concentrate on his own preparation and this naturally eased William's problem because Sam devoted less time to him.

Case Study 2

'Peter'

Peter had an excellent international record and had won the Junior World Championships, but his results in the previous two years had been inconsistent at senior level. Peter organized his training and preparation with military precision and was up to date on research related to physical conditioning. He was sceptical about sport psychology and doubted the value of questionnaires for either assessment or monitoring progress. For this reason it was decided to use an informal interview as the first stage of assessment. A holistic gestalt approach (Clarkson 1992) was used, enabling Peter to be more aware of the issues surrounding his description of problems he had encountered.

It emerged that Peter perceived himself as a failure, but felt that his role as a senior athlete within the squad gave status and empowerment to compensate. However, to maintain this status he set himself overambitious standards and became disheartened when he could not meet them, which affected his confidence. Also, he felt that other squad members were watching him to monitor his form. Peter knew he was skilful, yet still did not believe in himself. He felt that he needed to cope better with his perceived failure and to set standards of performance that were more in line with his current assessment of his form. Peter felt his previous year's training return graphs were close to an ideal training shape. However, there had been a tendency for him to concentrate on the physical at the expense of technical work and mental preparation. His planning for the coming year was to adhere to the same physical training, but to make time for more technical aspects that required both long-term and specific goals. There was also a need for a great deal of psychological confidence building. After the interview Peter agreed to fill in the SPSQ and to compile a Performance Profile using self-constructs. These data are presented in Tables 10.4 and 10.5, respectively:

Table 10.4 Scores from the SPSQ for Peter

Category	Score (max. score = 48)	(Deficit) = max. score less Peter's score
Imaginal skills	34	(14)
Mental preparation	31	(17)
Self-efficacy	38	(10)
Cognitive anxiety control	36	(12)
Concentration skills	33	(15)
Relaxation skill	37	(11)
Motivation	45	(3)

Table 10.5 Performance Profile as defined by Peter

Construct	Peter's definition	Current score (10)
Motivation	Drive, ability to push forward when things are not so 'hot'. Sticking power.	10
Patience	Not thinking it is going to happen overnight. Coping with failure, taking it in your stride.	3
Self-confidence	Inner belief in own ability; strong enough inside to dismiss mishaps.	6
Level-headed	See results in perspective. Don't get distressed if session or race performance is not good. Realize that highs and lows are inevitable.	7
Ability to analyze	Look at things; draw judgements about courses Training analysis; also look at your own life.	7
Ability to dismiss failure	Within sport and life. If I am paddling badly I feel it is the end of the world.	5
Concentration	Be able to focus thoughts, attention to specific issues/acts that tie in training and racing.	8

The questionnaire responses tended to confirm problems identified at interview, showing a lack of positive imagery, little effective mental preparation, low self-confidence, poor concentration skills and limited relaxation skills. It was agreed that we would concentrate on building up self-confidence and concentration, the long-term goal being to allow Peter to go into races mentally tough and in a state of mind that did not allow any distractions before and during the race. Because Peter was very organized, it was decided to set out the intervention in a format that gave both targets and explanations. An extract is presented in Table 10.6.

Table 10.6 Intervention: Target themes, explanations and strategies for Peter

Target themes and explanations	Strategies
Self-confidence programme	
(a) Build confidence in technical excellence.	Use identified targets for goal setting; measure and evaluate (Weinberg and Gould, 1995). Don't compare with others if your session is about getting into form.
(b) Reject thoughts of failure.	Use a thought-stopping technique (Meyers and Schleser 1980).
(c) Prevent confidence from draining away as competition draws nearer.	High quality workouts. Flowing gates on moving water. Remember how good your physical preparation has been. Remind yourself of your technical goal achievement. Identify your best performance (Feltz 1984) and replay until you get this competition's course plan.

Table 10.6 Intervention: Target themes, explanations and strategies for Peter (cont.)

Target themes and explanations	Strategies
(d) At competition site keep all thoughts positive (Rotella 1985). Don't let thoughts of disgrace arise. Dismiss fear of failure.	Use imaginal training (Singer 1988; White and Hardy, 1998). Do the moves in a relaxed state. Any doubts: *thought stop.* Use relaxation/centring to bring you back to positive thoughts.
(e) In training talk yourself (Silva 1982) into doing well. Do not worry about other competitors; rather, use them to help you with your analysis. Identify only with their single technical moves.	Observe and analyze the move; don't identify with the paddler. Decide whether you should copy. Evaluate your *own* performance, not yours against his. Improve on yours. Give yourself a score out of ten each time.
(f) Have a system (Syer and Connolly 1996), both in training and in competitions, where you familiarize yourself with the site.	Be alone: walk around; notice controls, water; close your eyes; listen to noises; take in smells. Draw a map of the site and walk round it in your mind. Put on a 'Walkman' with the sort of music you may hear at the competition.
(g) Relaxation before a competition to overcome feelings of being too tense	Use relaxation tapes (Hardy and Fazey 1990) to develop appropriate strategy. Experiment to decide which is best, then develop competence in this system to the point where it requires only a short period to use effectively; use before full runs. Use centring on the start line.
(h) Feeling in your comfort zone is important before the big race begins.	See the race as a problem with many really enjoyable challenges (Bunker, Williams and Zinsser 1993). You will feel comfortable when you realize you can control yourself and the situation; let nothing eat into you.

At his own request, Peter was directed to appropriate texts in order to train his mental skills (Loehr 1986; Albinson and Bull 1988; Orlick 1990; Syer and Connolly 1998). As the author was seeing him almost daily it was agreed that monitoring should be on as an informal basis as he felt appropriate. The informal reviews did not reveal anything untoward and Peter felt both his technical and mental skills were progressing well. The coach also noted a much more positive application of techniques in solving the problems that were presented on the slalom course. Peter insisted that his technical improvements would have happened anyway, but he felt more confident with his knowledge about mental training techniques. The real test would be in the first few international races and then at Olympic selection.

Peter's placings at internationals were 5, 7, 11, 18, 1, and, through the selection races, he qualified for the Olympic Games. The results of the races and selection were reasonably satisfactory, but there remained a lack of consistency. During our evaluation of his mental training Peter commented, 'I am more knowledgeable, and it has probably helped me in training, which overall contributes to my international performance. But it has not eliminated the problem (lack of confidence) when I am faced with the big race, and the next big one is the Olympics'. This was somewhat alarming to the author, who had thought that mentally Peter was in good control and all was well. As there were less than two weeks to go to the Olympics it was decided to explore this issue further. Peter explained that at major events he still experienced a loss of confidence and an increase in negative self-talk, at times leading to doubting his own technical decisions and losing concentration during his performance. As there was limited time in which to attempt to help Peter with his problem, it was decided to use his existing understanding of mental skills. I attempted to make it more robust by adopting a more direct gestalt approach (Ferrucci 1990; Clarkson 1992) and the outline details of this are presented in Table 10.7.

Table 10.7 Outline of the detail and purpose of the gestalt intervention

Intervention	Purpose
'What?' and 'How?' questions	Explore Peter's experience of the situation and help increase his awareness of 'What's so'. Avoid the use of 'Why?' questions in order not to increase his somatic and emotional experience.
Visualization	Ask him to recall in detail an example of the situation. Identify more closely his complete response to the situation: cognitive, somatic, emotional, behavioural.
Chair work	Help him to explore the origin and underlying positive intent of the doubting self-talk, through role-play to express the 'gifts and needs' of each underlying sub-personality. Peter wanted to feel confident and focused, but tended to hide from the discomfort of problem areas and technical weaknesses. His 'critic' wanted him to do well and was prepared to face the hard facts.
Re-framing	Rather than ignoring the doubts or getting stressed, he could recognize them as part of his desire to perform well and acknowledge the consequences of poor performances.
Visualization	Affective integration of previous work and imagined application of new responses on race day. Included metaphor of checking under the boat for any fears or doubts that would otherwise be ignored.

The Olympic race was Peter's worst result of that year. This was mainly due to the design of the slalom course, which included a particular gate (known as the lottery) that required competitors to risk a penalty in a situation largely out of their control. Peter did risk everything and in so doing made a serious error. However, he acknowledged that he was happy taking the risk, and that the final gestalt intervention had been most helpful. The reality was that probably this should have been the type of intervention applied from the outset. However, it may have been that it was necessary to have had in place a number of basic psychological skills before the more advanced gestalt techniques were used.

Discussion

Although all case studies are unique, it became clear that some issues and themes are common to all, including the two reported in this chapter. It is evident that both these slalom canoeists had various problems to deal with, supporting the view of Hardy, Jones and Gould (1996) that the elite athlete is likely to be faced with adversity on a fairly regular basis. Such performers need to be able to cope with a wide range of potential and actual problems.

Self-confidence was seen to be of critical importance for both paddlers. Even while the athletes' CSAI-2 scores were indicating high confidence and low anxiety, they revealed mental problems that were clearly reducing their self-confidence and affecting their preparation and performance. The nature and extent of these problems became clearer during the relatively long timescale of the case study and in the context of the variety of investigative methods used. The flexibility inherent in a case study approach enabled the author to respond to clues and to also focus attention on particular problems as they became evident, rather than being constrained by a pre-structured experimental design.

The effects of interventions were monitored using both observation and interviews, and feedback allowed for adjustments to be made. In attempting to evaluate the effectiveness of the interventions, a distinction needs to be drawn between success in enhancing an athlete's self-awareness and success in improving performance. Over the period of time in question it was difficult to be sure how much improvement in mental skills had emanated from the intervention programme and how much stemmed from improvements in other aspects of the athlete's training. Also there are often observable individual differences in the ways that enhanced self-awareness affects concentration, either positively or negatively, and subsequent performance.

The studies reported here have highlighted the need for a greater understanding of how athletes' mental states affect their behaviour. This would concur with the notion that much is known about the structure of processing systems, but little about their function, especially in ecologically valid settings (Smyth *et al.* 1994). It is proposed that a case study approach can be used to explore causal links in real-life situations that may be too complex for survey or experimental strategies to evaluate effectively.

References

Abernethy, B. (1994) 'Introduction: Special issue on expert–novice differences in sport', *International Journal of Sport Psychology* 25:241–248.

Abernethy, B., Neal, R. J. and Koning, P. (1994) 'Visual-perceptual and cognitive differences between expert, intermediate and novice snooker players', *Applied Cognitive Psychology* 8:185–211.

Albinson, J. G. and Bull, S. J. (1988) *The Mental Game Plan*, Ontario: Spodym.

Anshel, M. H. (1994) *Sport Psychology: From Theory to Practice*, Scottsdale, AZ: Gorsuch Scarisbrick.

Beck, A. T., Rush, A. J., Shaw, B. F. and Emery, G. (1979) *Cognitive Therapy of Depression*, New York: Guilford Press.

Bromley, D. B. (1986) *The Case Study Method in Psychology and Related Disciplines*, Chichester: Wiley.

Bryan, A. J. (1987) 'Single-subject designs for evaluation of sport psychology interventions', *The Sport Psychologist* 1:283–292.

Bunker, L., Williams, J. M. and Zinsser, N. (1993) 'Cognitive techniques for improving performance and self-confidence'. In J. M. Williams (ed.), *Applied Sport Psychology: Personal Growth to Peak Performance*, pp. 225–242, Mountain View, CA: Mayfield.

Butler, R. J. and Hardy, L. (1992) 'The performance profile: Theory and application', *Sport Psychologist* 6:253–264.

Carter, K. (1993) 'The place of story in the study of teaching and teacher education', *Educational Researcher* 22:5–12.

Clandimin, D. J. and Connelly, F. M. (1994) 'Personal experience methods'. In N. K. Denzin and Y. S. Lincoln (eds.), *Handbook of Qualitative Research*, London: Sage.

Clarkson, P. (1992) *Gestalt Counselling in Action*, London: Sage.

Coles, R. (1989) *The Call of Stories: Teaching and the Moral Imagination*, Boston: Houghton Mifflin.

Cox, R. (1990) *Sport Psychology: Concepts and Applications*, Iowa: Brown.

Feltz, D.L. (1984) 'Self-efficacy as a cognitive mediator of athletic performance'. In W. F. Straub and J. M. Williams (eds.), *Cognitive Sport Psychology*, pp. 191–198, New York: Mouvement Publications.

Ferrucci, P. (1990) *What We May Be, The Vision and Techniques of Psychosynthesis*, London: Mondala.

Glasser, B. G. and Strauss, A. L. (1967) *The Discovery of Grounded Theory: Strategies for Qualitative Research*, Chicago: Aldine.

Hardy, L. and Fazey, J. A. (1990) *Mental Training*, Leeds: National Coaching Foundation.

Hardy, L., Jones, G. and Gould, D. (1996) *Understanding Psychological Preparation for Sport: Theory and Practice of Elite Performers*, Chichester: Wiley.

Herriott, R. E. and Firestone, W. A. (1983) 'Multisite qualitative policy research: Optimizing description and generalisability', *Educational Researcher* 12(2):14–19.

Hersen, M. and Barlow, D. (1976) *Single Case Experimental Designs: Strategies for Studying Behavior Change*, New York: Pergamon.

Kazdin, A. E. (1982) *Single-case Research Designs*, New York: Oxford University Press.

Kelly, G. A. (1955) *The Psychology of Personal Constructs*, New York: Norton.

Lederer, W. J. and Jackson, D. D. (1968) *The Mirages of Marriage*, New York: Norton.

Lincoln, Y. S. and Guba, E. G. (1985) *Naturalistic Inquiry*, Beverly Hills, CA: Sage.

Loehr, J. E. (1986) *Mental Toughness Training for Sports*, New York: Plume.

Lofland, J. and Lofland, L. H. (1984) *Analysing Social Settings: A Guide to Qualitative Observational Research*, Belmont, CA.: Wadsworth.

Mackewn, J. (1997) *Developing Gestalt Counselling*, London: Sage.

Macleod, J. G. (1973) *Clinical Examination*, London: Churchill Livingstone.

Mahoney, M. J., Gabriel, T. J. and Perkins, T. S. (1987) 'Psychological skills and exceptional athletic performance', *Sport Psychologist* 1:181–199.

Mantle, H. (1997) *The Examination of Selected Physiological and Psychological Parameters in the Preparation of Elite Slalom Canoeists for an Olympic Competition*, Unpublished Ph.D. dissertation, University of Wales.

Martens, R., Burton, D., Vealey, R. S., Bump, L. A. and Smith, D. E. (1990) 'Development and validation of the Competitive State Anxiety Inventory-2'. In R. Martens, R. S. Vealey and D. Burton (eds.), *Competitive Anxiety in Sport*, Champaign, IL: Human Kinetics.

Meyers, A. W. and Schleser, R. A. (1980) 'A cognitive behavioural intervention for improving basketball performance', *Journal of Sport Psychology* 2:69–73.

Miles, M. B. and Huberman, A. M. (1984) *Qualitative Data Analysis: A Source Book of New Methods*, Beverly Hills, CA: Sage.

Nelson, D. and Hardy, L. (1990) 'The development of an empirically validated tool for measuring psychological skill in sport', *Journal of Sports Sciences* 8:71.

Orlick, T. (1990) *Psyching for Sport*, Champaign, IL: Leisure Press.

Orlick, T. and Partington, J. (1988) 'Mental links to excellence', *The Sport Psychologist* 2:105–130.

Rotella, R. J. (1985) 'Strategies for controlling anxiety and arousal', In L. K. Bunker, R. J. Rotella, and A. Reilly, (eds), *Sport Psychology*, Michigan: McNaughton and Gunn.

Russell, S. J. and Salmela, J. H. (1992) 'Quantifying expert athlete knowledge', *Journal of Applied Sport Psychology* 4:10–26.

Silva, J. M. (1982) 'Performance enhancement in sport environments through cognitive intervention', *Behaviour Modification* 6:433–463.

Singer, R. N. (1988) 'Strategies and metastrategies in learning and performing self-paced athletic skills', *Sport Psychologist* 2:49–68.

Smith, J. K. (1989) *The Nature of Social and Educational Enquiry*, Norwood, NJ: Ablex.

Smyth, M. M., Collins, A. F., Morris, P. E. and Levy, P. (1994) *Cognition in Action*, second edition, Hove: Lawrence Erlbaum.

Stake, R. E. (1994) 'Case studies'. In N. K. Denzin and Y. S. Lincoln (eds.), *Handbook of Qualitative Research*, London: Sage.

Steckler, A., McLeroy, K. R., Goodman, R. M., Bird, S. T. and McCormick, L. (1992) 'Toward integrating qualitative and quantitative methods: An introduction', *Health Education Quarterly* 19:1–8.

Stern, R. and Drummond, L. (1991) *The Practice of Behavioural and Cognitive Psychotherapy*, Cambridge University Press.

Syer, J. (1986) *Team Spirit, The Elusive Experience*, London: Heinemann.

Syer, J. and Connolly, C. (1998) *Sporting Body Sporting Mind*, second edition, London: Cambridge University Press.

Thomas, K. T. and Thomas, J. R. (1994) 'Developing Expertise in Sport: The Relation of Knowledge and Performance, *International Journal of Sport Psychology* 25:295–312.

Treacher, A. (1985) 'Working with marital partners: Systems approaches'. In W. Dryden (ed.), *Marital Therapy in Britain*, Vol. 1, London: Harper and Row.

Trower, P., Casey, A. and Dryden, C. (1988) *Cognitive-Behavioural Counselling in Action*, London: Mondale.

Weinberg, R. S. and Gould, D. (1995) *Foundations of Sport and Exercise Psychology*, Champaign, IL: Human Kinetics.

White, A. and Hardy, L. (1998) 'An in-depth analysis of the uses of imagery by high-level slalom canoeists and artistic gymnasts', *Journal of Sports Science* 12, 4:387–403.

Yin, R. K. (1994) *Case Study: Research Design and Methods*, London: Sage.

part (four)

Injury, counselling and social support

chapter eleven

The psychological rehabilitation of a severely injured rugby player

RICHARD COX

This is an account of the process, procedures and programme adopted to help a rugby player back into the game after severe injury. The account is unusual insofar as it gives the perspective of both parties involved in the process. This is because the young man in question, 21-year-old David Hoff (not his real name), was willing to record his perceptions of what I had asked him to do without being prompted in any way. His account has been edited from a grammatical perspective, but what appears in the text is precisely what he wanted to say.

The sport psychologist's account

David called me on the telephone to book an appointment during the week beginning Monday 3rd March, 1997. We agreed to meet after work the following Friday when he told me that he desperately wanted to play rugby again, but was extremely fearful of what might happen if he did. This was because he had been deeply traumatized by a severe injury while playing in a match almost exactly one year earlier.

He had taken the ball into a tackle and set up a ruck by going to ground with his back to the opposition. While lying on the ground he was kicked hard in the back, close to the base of his spine. When he tried to stand up his legs gave way and he found he had lost all feeling down the left side of his body, from hip to toe. An ambulance was called and David was admitted to the local infirmary an hour later. Naturally, at this stage he feared the worst – permanent paralysis of some kind – and it wasn't until he received the diagnosis of 'severe spinal shock' that his spirits lifted. Even so, it was another three weeks before he could wiggle his toes and a further two weeks before he was discharged from hospital on crutches. Two weeks later he graduated from crutches to a pair of walking sticks, but it was not until three months after the incident that he could walk unaided.

David told me that he was an all-rounder at sport and felt he was equally proficient at rugby, football and golf. However, his first love was rugby and before the injury he had been a stand-off half of some note, having played representative rugby at junior level. He was missing the 'buzz' of training and playing the game, as well as the social side of things, which, although still available to him, was not to his liking. He felt people were pitying him and occasionally avoiding him because he was no longer playing. As a consequence, he had stopped going to the club except to watch an occasional game but this had only served to make matters worse because he now felt cut off from those who were important to him.

I asked him to give me an estimate of how fit he felt he was, with ten-tenths being supremely fit; his response was six-tenths. His current level of fitness was mainly attributable to playing five-a-side football once a week and to being a volunteer stage-hand, moving large pieces of scenery around every night for a local drama production. However, his day-to-day job was sedentary, working in an office as an insurance sales-man, and it was an occupation, he stated with considerable feeling, in which he was not happy. The next question I asked was about his goals for the future. He replied that his first goal was to start the next pre-season club training that was scheduled for 20th June, a little over three months away.

PROGRAMME BACKGROUND

At this point I felt obliged, from a professional point of view, to explain the nature of and theoretical justification for the programme of work in which I was about to invite David to take part. I showed him a pamphlet produced by the British Association of Sport and Exercise Sciences (BASES) which described the type of service a client can expect from accredited personnel (biomechanists, exercise physiologists, and sport and exercise psychologists). In particular, I drew his attention to the sentence that stated: 'Following discussions with the client which identify what they hope to gain from the intervention, the assessment proposed for use on them will be explained, along with its theoretical rationale' (BASES 1996, p. 3).

I proceeded by explaining to David that the philosophy of the science of human behaviour I espoused was 'radical behaviourism', which had given rise to what is known as Reinforcement Theory which, in turn, had generated a number of techniques for helping clients like himself. I continued by identifying the remaining four major theoretical stances that a psychologist might adopt – humanistic, psychoanalytical, cognitive and psychobiological – and the reasons why I had chosen the stance that I had. I explained that if he had gone to a psychologist who had adopted a different position then he would be treated somewhat differently from the way I intended to work with him. However, I took this no further as to have done so would almost certainly have confused him. Thus, having tried to clarify this complicated issue I asked him if he was happy to proceed and he replied that he was.

To a behavioural psychologist, everything that a person does, thinks, feels and says is a form of behaviour. More importantly, individuals see Man as an entity rather than as a mind within a body. Thus, David's cognitive behaviour (thinking) could be studied through what he said (verbal behaviour) and did, and his emotional behaviour through how and when he said and did things. A behavioural psychologist believes that all forms of human behaviour above the level of reflex are products of the interaction between a person and their environment and are therefore motivated by external stimuli of various kinds. They are also influenced to a lesser degree by one's genetic endowment. Behavioural psychologists also believe that almost all types of problems can be defined in terms of behaviour and either solved, or at least reduced, in effect by techniques that are known collectively as 'behaviour modification' (Martin and Pears 1992).

The most important characteristic of behaviour modification is its strong emphasis on defining problems in terms of behaviour that can be measured in some way and how it uses changes in the behavioural measure of those problems as the best indicator of the extent to which the problems are being solved. Behaviour modification involves rearranging an individual's environment to help them to function better or more fully. A number of procedures and techniques have emerged from laboratory research in experimental psychology (Skinner 1938) and can be described in precise detail. Consequently, behaviour modification emphasizes that a particular intervention is responsible for a particular change in behaviour.

This is a very simplified account of the behaviourist's concern, which typically is a highly contentious view of human behaviour among psychologists and philosophers alike (Skinner 1971; 1974; 1984). The debates to which behaviourism has given rise have been ongoing for almost a century and show no sign of being settled. However, many regard this as a healthy situation for it means that a definitive account of why Man behaves in the ways that he does will be sought after for some time to come and will generate much research in the process.

In trying to help a client such as David, behavioural psychologists must start by asking themselves three important questions. First, what is the client's history of reinforcement and punishment in relation to the problem in question? Secondly, what stimuli, pertinent to the problem, are operating on the client at the time? Thirdly, what is the client's current state of deprivation of those stimuli he is wanting to experience without the problem stimuli interfering in some way?

In David's case, these three questions were relatively easy to answer from the outset. First, he had enjoyed a great deal of positive reinforcement from being successful in his chosen sport over a long period of time, having started playing rugby at secondary school and representing his school at all age levels. Furthermore, he had enjoyed three successful years of rugby since leaving school, with only the expected minor injuries that are the inevitable consequence of playing a contact sport. However, his most recent experience of playing rugby had provided an extreme form of punishment through injury and temporary paralysis of one side of his lower body. In turn, this had led him to experience negative reinforcement, which leads to avoidance behaviour of the stimuli giving rise to it every time he even thought about playing rugby again, simply because he feared a similar type of injury. Secondly, the stimuli operating on him that were pertinent to his particular problem were mixed insofar as he wanted to play again in order to enjoy the positive reinforcement he had experienced prior to the injury, but was afraid to do so for fear of the possible punishment he might incur. Thirdly, he was sufficiently deprived of the positively reinforcing consequences of playing rugby to want to overcome his problem. This is always an excellent starting point for any therapist, regardless of their chosen theoretical stance and level of experience.

Despite his obvious desire to get back into the game, I decided that the programme of work I would suggest to him should be based on the behavioural principle of 'successive approximation' (Leslie 1996). Briefly, this means that a programme must start only one step ahead of where the client sees himself at the time and then build up in small stages, each designed to ensure as much positive reinforcement as possible. At the opposite end of the continuum to this principle is a technique known as 'flooding', sometimes identified as 'implosion'. In colloquial terms, this means 'throwing someone in at the deep end and expecting them to swim'. For David, this would have meant him doing nothing connected with rugby during the following 13 weeks and then asking him to go straight into full contact training and playing on 20th June. There are certain people with particular types of problem who, through the technique of 'flooding', can be helped to overcome anxieties, fears and phobias in a single session. However, by definition, this is a high-risk technique and I was not prepared to take such a risk in David's case, simply because of the amount of trauma he had suffered from the incident.

David had come to see me with his heart set on returning to full club training 13 weeks hence, which is a limited amount of time in which to recover fully from traumatic injury. Consequently, I put it to him that there were at least three fronts on which he must advance simultaneously if he was to achieve his goal; these were physical (fitness), motor (skill) and psychological, optimal progress in the latter being dependent largely upon success in the other two.

Physically, he wasn't fit enough to embark upon a typical pre-season training programme. He had a basic level of fitness that allowed him to get through his weekly five-a-side football session, but he needed much more if he was to sustain the rigours of three tough rugby training sessions each week. In terms of his rugby skills, he had been out of the game for over a year and his sharpness would have deteriorated considerably during that time. This meant that if he had tried to play rugby again in his present state, the probability of being caught in possession and taking physical punishment was high. For obvious reasons, this was a probability that had to be reduced if he was to gain maximum positive reinforcement from the programme and, ultimately, to enjoy playing rugby again. Psychologically, his confidence and self-esteem were very low but, as I explained to him, these aspects were likely to improve once he began to see improvements in his level of physical fitness and basic rugby skills.

In order to develop a greater all-round level of fitness, I devised a circuit training programme of six exercises that he was asked to complete twice each week at home.

The six exercises were press-ups, sit-ups, burpees, star-jumps, step-ups and running up and down the stairs two steps at a time. The number of repetitions in each set was calculated in accordance with his previous experience of this type of work and in conjunction with his perceived current level of fitness. He was to complete three sets of of each exercise, with no more than 30 seconds' rest between each, before moving on to the next exercise. I also asked him to do two, steady state runs each week, each of approximately five miles, and to swim continuously for at least 20 minutes once a week. Moreover, he was not to do the same type of exercise two days in succession, which is in accordance with the principle of Cross Training described by Slaymaker (1989; 1996) and Bompa (1993).

Thus, together with his five-a-side football once a week, he was being invited to undertake some form of physical training on six days each week. However, I explained to him that one session a day and lasting no more than a maximum of 40 minutes, except possibly for his five-a-side football, was not excessive for a young man who had been used to being supremely fit and that this would be necessary if he were to regain a high level of fitness relatively quickly. He agreed to this programme of work and to keeping a written record of what he did each day and how he felt about it. The reason for this was the diary would most likely provide a rich source of positive reinforcement as he progressed through the programme. I also asked him to plan (on his rest day) exactly what his next week's activity would look like and to see me again in four weeks' time.

A 12-STAGE APPROACH

In accordance with the principle of 'successive approximation' I drew up the following programme of gradated work which I thought David would be able to cope with over the following 13 weeks. However, it should be noted that I did not reveal the programme to David, except in discrete stages during discussion, because I felt that to see it in advance would have overwhelmed him and perhaps even prevented him from starting. The 12 stages were as follows:

1. Circuit training, running (around the perimeter of a local park) and swimming to be added to his five-a-side football but none of it to take place at his rugby club.

2. Continue with (1) above, except that the two weekly running sessions should now involve a partner (he had identified a close friend from the rugby club who was willing to train with him), a rugby ball and various skills with it, such as passing, grubber kicking (10 metres), sprinting to retrieve it and making a pass immediately, and kicking it into the air and catching it. Thus, the running would move from steady state to a type of 'fartlek' (speed play), which is more demanding.

3. As for (2) above but in full rugby gear except for boots.

4. As for (3) above, but around the perimeter of one of the pitches at his rugby club and wearing rugby boots.

5. As for (4) above, but at the ground where the original incident took place.

6. As for (5) above, but now adding tackle bag practice.

7. Taking part in the first, pre-season training session at his rugby club.

8. Playing at either full-back or centre-three-quarter for (preferably) the third team.

9. As for (8) above, but for the second team.

10. Playing at stand-off for either the third or second team (his choice).

11. Playing at either stand-off or one of the other back positions (his choice) for the first team.

12. Being first choice for stand-off in the first team.

The time constraints placed on this programme by David's personal goals, up to and including Stage 7, were considerable insofar as it is normal practice with this technique to move on to the next stage only when the client has successfully completed the previous one(s). At times I felt that things were being rushed somewhat and I was particularly concerned for him when it came to Stage 5, where he was able to complete his training programme on the very ground where the incident had happened some 14 months earlier. Given the fact that he had not been near the ground in question since the incident, visiting it was obviously going to cause some of the memories of that incident to recur through association with the same visual stimuli. Thus, during David's fourth visit to me I deliberately spent a great deal of time getting him to highlight his achievements to date and offering praise and reassurance at every opportunity. When I was convinced that he was feeling fully confident about everything he had achieved up to that time, I introduced the prospect of Stage 5 as a challenge that he would have to meet sooner rather than later, but one for which I felt he was now ready. However, the most important question I had to ask was did *he* feel ready for it? He assured me that he did and duly planned his visit to that ground for an evening of the following week. He told me later that he had experienced some anxiety in being there, but controlled it by focusing his mind and energy on completing the training programme to the best of his ability. He also focused on trying to do it better than his training partner, as I had asked him to, as we believed this would help to prevent him from thinking about the incident.

Completing Stage 5 was a major achievement for David, although some might argue that it was introduced into the programme too early, particularly as it caused him to experience some rather painful memories. However, getting the successive approximations exactly right for one human subject in a non-laboratory setting, such that no negative reinforcement is experienced at any stage, is extremely difficult, if not impossible. In David's case the programme worked, as he reveals later in this chapter, principally because he was highly motivated and cut no corner in his efforts to succeed. He was actively seeking positive reinforcement at every opportunity and focused almost exclusively on the likely outcomes of the behaviours that we had discussed and planned. As a consequence, and with a modicum of good fortune, as injuries can be incurred all too readily in any physical training programme, he reached Stage 7 without any major setback and presented himself well prepared for pre-season training on 20th June of that year.

Although David was personally successful, a typical problem with this approach is the client's impatience. If the successive approximations have been designed appropriately, then little difficulty is experienced in achieving success. As a consequence, the subject may be led by his own rate of success to conclude that the programme is too easy and is likely to become impatient to move on to the next stage. A form of this can be witnessed almost every day of the year in fitness classes and gymnasia throughout the country when, for whatever reason, people take on new exercise regimes without seeking advice beforehand and end up doing too much during their first visit. Admittedly, those managing health clubs and gymnasia now usually recommend a fitness test for newcomers and will give advice on what and how much to do on a first visit. However, accepting such advice is seldom compulsory and some are encouraged to try a programme that is too demanding. Not surprisingly, they suffer the next day when they can hardly move from stiffness and soreness. As a result, some will decide that exercise is not for them.

David was impatient, but he is also intelligent and through our discussions he was able to appreciate the need for what might, at times, have seemed to be slow progress. He was also young and reasonably fit to start with and had experienced what it was like to undertake hard training at the start of a season. Thus, he experienced little difficulty keeping to the programme we had agreed on and suffered no real setback in his progress towards his first goal.

Once that particular playing season had started I only saw David twice more in the following 12 months when, at different times, he was presented with the opportunity to move on to Stages 8, 9 and 10. He negotiated each stage successfully, and it was in February 2000 that he finally achieved his ultimate goal of playing at stand-off half for the first team. Thus, his full rehabilitation had taken almost three years, 'from zero to hero', as we liked to describe it, which is not atypical in cases of this kind. The most important outcome for me, however, was not that David was playing rugby again, satisfying though that was, but that he was now a young man full of enthusiasm for life in general. He smiled readily and his new-found confidence could be seen in his face, his gait and his general demeanour. This, in turn, contributed to greater success in both his working and social life, as well as to his rugby. The difference in him, compared to the traumatized individual who presented himself in March 1997, was plain for all to see and it is what makes this type of work so rewarding.

The client's account

BEFORE

My reason for seeking help from a psychologist was to help me to recover from a very serious rugby injury, so that I could play again. It all began on a bright Saturday morning in February 1996, the day of a Scottish rugby international. It was, and still is, traditional for rugby clubs to play 'friendly' games on the morning before an international match, as league fixtures are never scheduled for these occasions. We were due to play our main local rivals who, in recent years, had slipped down several divisions of the league but who, nevertheless, always managed to raise their game against us.

Shortly before I incurred the injury I had played several games for Edinburgh District Under-18 team at stand-off and had been really enjoying my rugby. However, this feeling was not to last much longer. The game was one to forget for our team. We had fielded a team of mixed ability players with approximately equal numbers from our first, second and third teams. By half time we were 20 points down but, in the second half, had pulled back to be within three points when the incident occurred. All I remember of it was that I took the ball into a ruck situation, went to ground in a tackle, set the ball back for our scrum-half and then felt a hard kick at the bottom of my back. As the ruck cleared I tried to stand up, but couldn't, and collapsed to the ground in great pain. The next thing I remember is lying with a brace strapped to my left leg and an ambulance parked beside me. From there I was taken to the local infirmary where I was examined and diagnosed as having severe muscular damage to the base of my spine, which resulted in my having no feeling down my left leg for more than three weeks. In total, I was in hospital for over five weeks and off work for more than three months. Being partially paralysed and in a wheelchair is by far the most frightening thing that has ever happened to me and, hopefully, ever will. Thankfully, the support I received from my friends and, more importantly, my family was enormous and without their help and love I doubt whether I would have ever regained the quality of life I had enjoyed previously.

After leaving hospital on crutches I continued to receive physiotherapy three times a week to help restore the movement and flexibility I had before the incident. I say 'incident' rather than 'accident', because I still believe that what happened was deliberate foul play. The physiotherapy was successful and helped me to return to work after three months, though it was another three months or so before I could bounce on the spot and do some light jogging.

Slowly, but surely, my life was returning to something approaching normality; I was able to go out with the boys again, to get stuck into my work and to enjoy the everyday things I had previously taken for granted. However, there was something important missing from my life, namely rugby. I had been to our club ground to watch a few games and to listen to the banter and had also watched the guys in training, but it just wasn't the same. I wanted to be involved again, much to the disapproval of my friends and family who all thought I was mad. But it was such an important part of my life, the team-work, keeping fit, winning and, most importantly, the social side. It just wasn't the same, watching as opposed to playing.

So, in early January 1997, I returned to very light training and, after a few weeks, I felt ready to get involved in some team exercises. However, as much as I tried, I just wasn't able to put any real effort into it and there were several occasions when I knew that tack-ling was going to be practised and, looking back on it now, I made excuses not to go training those nights. I tried to justify to myself that the reasons I wasn't going to train-ing were valid. This went on for some time and still I didn't feel ready to play games because I hadn't been involved in tackling practice and so felt trapped. I discussed this with my father who had incurred a serious rugby injury himself and had had to retire at age 21 as a result. Thus, he had a good understanding of what I was going through. However, there were some things I didn't say to him simply because he is my father; I think he realized this and so, between us, we came up with the idea of getting help from a psychologist. After speaking to doctors in the National Health Service and being told that I could join a very long queue to see somebody, I spoke to officials at my rugby club and they suggested I contact the Scottish Rugby Union to see if they could help. They told me that they employed the services of Doctor Cox for this type of support and gave me his address and telephone number. At our first meeting I told him what had happened and what I was trying to achieve and he agreed to try and help me.

DURING

Not knowing what to expect, I was pleasantly surprised when I met Doctor Cox as I wasn't invited to lie down on a couch and talk about my childhood experiences. In fact, none of the stereotyped impressions I, and possibly others, had about psychologists was borne out during that first meeting and I was able to relax very quickly.

Our first meeting was by far the most important for me. I spent a lot of time explain-ing in detail what I had been through, what I was trying to achieve and how much I hoped he could help me, and his reaction was exactly what I had hoped for. He started talking about working together, planning out where I thought I was and where I wanted to be at some point in the future, but also that he would be there as a support if required. He also said something that I subsequently held in mind for the whole time I was visit-ing him. This was that he could only advise and guide me as to what to do to achieve my goal but that, at the end of the day, it was I who would make it work or not. Taking full, personal responsibility for everything I was to be asked to do became a major focus for my mind, whether I was actually with Doctor Cox or trying out his suggestions alone.

He explained to me that it would be necessary to go back to basics and build up in small stages until my confidence was restored. He also asked me to stop going to the club in the meantime. One of the first things he did was to draw a representation of a ladder, with the bottom rung representing where I thought I was at that point in time and the top rung being where I wanted to be, which was to be playing first-team rugby again but without the emotional hang-ups I had developed as a result of the injury. We also looked closely at everything else that was going on in my life at that time to see if anything could be affecting my attitude to playing rugby again. What emerged very quickly from this was the fact that I was not happy at work and this, he felt, was not helping me to commit myself to rugby. The reason for this, he explained, was that it added yet another emotional down-turn to those already heaped upon me by the trauma caused by the injury. It made me realize that when I returned from yet another bad day at work, the last thing I wanted was to go to a hard training session. This might appear to be a simple deduction but, until it was pointed out to me, the association between the two was not apparent to me and perhaps would never have become so. As a consequence, I began to look for another job which was something I probably should have done earlier, but I lacked the drive to do so.

Doctor Cox explained to me that moving up to the second rung of the ladder would involve completing a number of exercises that would begin with getting hold of a rugby ball and literally playing with it in and around the house. I was asked to hold it, to throw it from one hand to the other and back again as quickly as possible; to 'grubber-kick' it on the lawn outside onto a wall and collect the rebound; and to walk across the lawn parallel to the wall and pass the ball against the wall and catch it on the rebound. It was also suggested that I should pass the ball to someone, either my father or a friend, who was willing to catch it and pass it back to me, both standing still and moving around the lawn; even to take the ball to bed with me and hold it before I went to sleep! All of these activities, I was told, would start the process of helping to remove my fear of playing rugby again. I was also recommended to develop my physical fitness to a much higher level and Doctor Cox set a circuit training programme which I was to complete twice a week at home. This involved multiple repetitions of six exercises, three times each, and recording the time taken from start to finish. I was also asked to fit in steady state running of approximately five miles, twice each week, to build up my stamina and to swim for a minimum 20 minutes each week. I went away from that first session feeling much more confident than I had done when I arrived because I knew that I would be able to do these exercises, even though the amount of time I would have to spend doing them was considerable.

Some four weeks later I went to see Doctor Cox for a second time and we spent the first half hour or so going over in detail what I felt I had achieved during those four weeks and how I had reacted to the demands I had agreed to. I was feeling good and considerably fitter than I had done since before the injury. Thus I felt as though I had made progress and I was eager to progress further. So what would moving another rung up the ladder look like?

For the two steady state running sessions, I had been running with a friend around the perimeter of a local park. Now my training partner and I were asked to take the rugby ball with us whenever we ran and to pass it to each other. We were to pass it from different distances, at different heights and at different speeds. We also had to change sides every 10 passes so that we weren't always passing in the same direction. On the second lap of the park we were asked to take turns at grubber-kicking the ball directly in front of us as we ran and the other had to accelerate before picking it up and passing it immediately back to the one who had kicked it. Three passes later the roles were to be reversed and at no time was the distance of the grubber-kick to exceed 10 metres. Finally, we were to progress to kicking the ball in the air and to catch it as we were running and we were asked to integrate these activities into 35/40 minutes of continuous running, which I realized would no longer be steady state and would be much harder work.

In accepting the programme recommended to me and achieving the targets I had agreed to, I began to realize that I was taking greater control over my life and the idea of setting short-term and even day-to-day goals for myself was no longer the threat I had thought it to be at the outset. I began to enjoy thinking through my days in advance and planning precisely what it was I wanted to achieve on any given day. Thus, when I went to see Doctor Cox for the third time, also some four weeks after the previous visit, I was feeling much better about myself and was impatient to move on to the next part of the programme.

The next stage involved completing the programme in full rugby kit and I began to feel more like a rugby player, as opposed to someone who was simply training with a rugby ball. I was also asked to persuade my training partner to go with me to our club training ground when it was empty and to repeat everything on a rugby pitch that we had been doing around the local park. This was a particularly good move for me as it made me feel even more like a rugby player, and a successful one at that, because everything I was asked to do was relatively easy.

Returning to the scene of the incident

Two weeks later, when I saw Doctor Cox again, I was asked if I felt ready to climb the next rung in the ladder, which was to be something of an 'acid test' for me. He explained that, sooner or later, I would need to visit the ground where the incident took place and complete a training session with my training partner, just as we had been doing up to that point, on the same pitch where I had been injured. Doctor Cox thought I was ready for this and I saw no real problem in it. So we arranged to go there at a time when we knew the pitch would be free and when we were unlikely to be questioned by anyone in authority.

When we arrived, wearing our rugby gear, we changed our footwear (now we were wearing rugby boots) and jogged around the touchlines of that pitch. It was a weird feeling initially, being at the place where it all happened, and I was glad my training partner was with me. However, I soon relaxed and later in the session when I finally ventured to stand over the actual spot where I had been injured I thought only of how good I was feeling, that I was healthy and in no physical pain. When I left that scene I knew that I would play rugby again without the emotional block I had developed and my confidence soared as a result.

Climbing the next rung of the ladder involved my training partner and me going to our club training ground, taking out a couple of tackle bags and hitting them with each shoulder in turn, over and over again. We started from close in at walking pace and generally built up the speed and force with which we were hitting the bags. We even got to the stage where we would time each other from a set point, sprint 10 metres into the first tackle bag, get to our feet as quickly as possible, sprint another 10 metres into the next tackle bag, get to our feet again and back to the starting point. I found this to be an excellent way of building up my confidence in the part of the game that puts a lot of people off rugby.

After we had done this exercise on five different occasions I became aware that both my stamina and upper body strength were improving and, again, I felt a surge of confidence. Over the whole time I was working with Doctor Cox I felt this was quite possibly the best exercise I was asked to do in terms of developing explosive power and confidence at the same time and it made me want to play rugby again more than ever. It led naturally to attempting the next rung of the ladder – to be involved in the club's first organized, pre-season training session, which was only a week away. When we assembled on that first evening, 20th June, 1997, I was feeling good because I knew I had done a great deal of work during the club's closed season and as a consequence would be much-fitter than many others. Because of the tackling exercise I also felt confident about getting involved in contact situations, which took place even during the first session.

Pre-season training seemed to come and go very quickly and it was no time at all before the selectors were asking if I wanted to play in a lower level game as an easy reintroduction. This was obviously the next big step for me and I felt nervous from the moment the suggestion was made, never mind playing in the game. I met with Doctor Cox again and he suggested that there were at least two rungs of the ladder left to climb if I wanted to. He suggested that I should accept the invitation to play but not in the position I was playing when I was injured. He recommended playing at full-back, which is a 'sweeper' type of role and has totally different demands from those placed on a stand-off half. I had played at full-back on two previous occasions so it wasn't a totally new position to me. It hadn't entered my mind that I could try playing elsewhere, but I liked the suggestion and so did the selectors when I put it to them.

Even though that first game back was a minor friendly game I had never been so nervous in my life as I was in the build-up to the game. However, I kept reminding myself of what Doctor Cox had said to me right from our first meeting together, which was that it was up to me, and me alone, whether or not I wanted to play again. After not sleeping well the night before, the game flew by, thankfully without any mishap and I felt pleased and reassured after it was all over.

I played again in this position and at this lower level for another four matches and I now felt that I was back into the routine of playing regularly. However, because of the high standards I had set for myself previously, I was becoming more and more frustrated with feeling less involved and less influential than I had been at stand-off in the first team. When I consulted Doctor Cox about this he pointed out what should have been obvious to me but I had been too blinkered to see it. This was that, after being out of the game for almost a whole year, there was no way I could just step back into it at the same level. While I was still feeling frustrated, I realized that he was right and that I would have to work my way up to that level, as the sharpness of my skills would almost certainly have deteriorated during my time away from the game. I felt a lot better in myself because of this and became more determined to work hard in order to regain my position in the first team.

I continued to play at full-back for the third team until Christmas time and in the nine games we played during that period I scored an average of a try a game. Not surprisingly, this helped me to regain even more confidence and desire for the game and this extended run in the third team also helped me to regain my perspective on playing rugby and I became less impatient as a result. However, in the first week of 1998 the regular stand-off half for the second team went on holiday for three weeks and so I had the chance to climb another rung of the ladder. The second team, like the first team, also played in a league and so I knew that the standard of rugby would be much higher and harder than anything I had met since the injury. Nevertheless, I took the chance with enthusiasm and held the position until the end of the season. The team improved its position in the league by several places after I joined it and I thoroughly enjoyed everything about it, including the banter in the dressing room and the nights out with the boys that I had missed so much. When the 15-a-side season came to an end I was asked to play in a number of seven-a-side tournaments for the first team and this further heightened my keenness to play at the top level again.

During the summer of 1998 I trained regularly and in a similar way to that which Doctor Cox had asked me to do the previous year. As a consequence of this and my early season form I became first choice for the stand-off half position for the second team. I had also changed my job during the summer, which was something Doctor Cox and I had identified as likely to improve matters for me in my life outside rugby. The new job, selling telecommunications services to the business world, was a breath of fresh air and I loved every minute of it. Thus, I was happy with my life in every way for the first time in over two years. However, the challenge of the next rung of the ladder was not far away and it came in February 1999 when I was asked to play for the first 15, but on the wing rather than at stand-off half. Again, in the build-up to that match I experienced a lot of anxious moments, but I had learned to interpret my feelings as a form of positive preparation and so I looked forward to the match rather than dreading it. It passed off well and I even scored a try, so at least I felt that I had showed what I could do. That was my only appearance in the first team that season but I didn't mind. The fact that I had played at that level again and the challenge of my new job were more than enough to keep me happy.

Playing at stand-off half for the first team – the final rung of the ladder – didn't happen until February 2000. For the first half of the 1999–2000 season I had been playing quite happily for the second team. I had been working hard in my job and had been promoted, but this had meant less time to devote to rugby. Thus, I didn't really expect to be chosen for the first team and it came as something of a shock when it finally happened. Moreover, the team was pushing for promotion so I knew I would be under scrutiny from selectors and fellow players alike. However, I was able to focus on that first match properly and profitably and retained the position for the remainder of the season.

An added bonus was the team winning promotion and so, after three years of hard work and heartache, I had finally achieved the goal I had set myself at the beginning. More importantly, I had regained my confidence and self-respect, both of which I had lost in 1996, as well as the belief that I could ever regain them.

AFTER

My experience of sport psychology has been the most rewarding of my life so far and I don't doubt that it will prove to be so for a long time to come. It took me from rock bottom and has helped to make me a positive, confident and optimistic person. The steps we took together seemed simple and straightforward but they were ideal for me. I didn't know what to expect when I first went to see Doctor Cox and I was pleasantly surprised. The time spent with him has made me learn to be positive and, I'd like to think, a more rounded personality. Above all, he taught me that you can only achieve something like this if you really want it yourself and are willing to work hard in the process.

As a final thought, I think it is worth recording that writing this account has been beneficial for me. It has reminded me how low I really was when I first sought help, how far I have come since then and how much I have changed in the process. I would recommend anyone who has gone through a traumatic experience similar to mine to seek help in a similar way.

(📖 References)

BASES (1996) *Scientific Support Services Provided by BASES – Accredited Sport and Exercise Scientists.* Pamphlet published by The British Association of Sport and Exercise Sciences, Leeds.

Bompa, T. (1993) *Power Training for Sports,* Ontario: Coaching Association of Canada.

Leslie, J. C. (1996) *Principles of Behavioural Analysis,* Amsterdam: Harwood Academic Publishers.

Martin, G. L. and Pears, J. J. (1992) *Behaviour Modification: What It Is and How to Do It,* Englewood Cliffs, NJ: Prentice-Hall International Editions.

Skinner, B. F. (1938) *The Behaviour of Organisms,* New York: Appleton-Century-Crofts.

Skinner, B. F. (1971) *Beyond Freedom and Dignity,* New York: Alfred K. Knopf.

Skinner, B. F. (1974) *About Behaviourism,* New York: Alfred K. Knopf.

Skinner, B. F. (1984) *The Behavioural and Brain Sciences,* December, Vol. 7, No. 4. (This edition was dedicated to a debate about Skinner's work.)

Slaymaker, R. (1989) *Serious Training for Serious Athletes,* Champaign, IL: Human Kinetics Publishers Inc.

Slaymaker, R. (1996) *Serious Training for Endurance Athletes,* Champaign, IL: Human Kinetics Publishers, Inc.

chapter twelve

Football for facilitating therapeutic intervention among a group of refugees

RACHEL TRIBE

The issue to be discussed in this chapter is the possible role of sport as a therapeutic intervention in enhancing psychological and physical health and well-being. It will be discussed in relation to a real clinical example where a discrete group of refugees who had been tortured were facilitated to form a football team by the author; similar principles might be applied with other groups of people. Psychological theories about the importance of social support, group dynamics and clinical theory, the Cartesian split and team building each played an important role, as did the dedication and motivation of the team captain, or team leader. The author is primarily a clinician and not a sport psychologist, and therefore the emphasis is more on the possible role of sport as a therapeutic solution rather than on sport per se.

Refugees come from every continent in the world, arriving in Britain from more than 41 countries (British Home Office 2000). People seek asylum because of political repression, war or civil conflict. Amnesty International (1999) has stated that people were reportedly tortured or ill-treated by state authorities in 125 countries, despite international legislation and conventions against torture and ill-treatment. One London-based organization working with survivors of torture has on record that in 1999 they assisted 3114 clients from 89 countries, while similar organizations in other countries saw comparable numbers.

The development of the football team

While working as a psychologist at an organization for refugees and survivors of torture based in a London hospital, a young refugee, John, was brought to see me by a fellow countryman, David, a service-user himself (though neither are their real names). David was convinced that John was going to commit suicide and he wanted me to 'do something to stop him'. John was unable to speak any English, although he was fluent in a number of other languages. David had met John on a street in south London and they had recognized each other as being from the same part of Africa. David was extremely worried about John, and also about the effect that John's distress was having upon himself, as it reactivated his own distress. John initially had strong suicidal ideation; he would appear to lose all muscle tone, frequently slipping off his chair on to the floor wailing. He showed many of the symptoms of post-traumatic stress disorder with depressive features.

After a number of meetings together it transpired that John had been accused of supporting a group of rebels/freedom fighters in his country of origin, as a result of which he had been tortured and forced to undergo hard labour. He had feared for his life, but had eventually managed to escape from his country and flee to Britain, leaving his wife and two small children behind, and he was desperately worried for them. John's view of the world as a safe and predictable place had been entirely shattered and he had lost all faith in his future or in his ability to impact upon it. Tribe (1998a) has written about the existential significance of the loss of a future that many refugees experience and which may be worse than the many other losses experienced – for example their country, language, culture and their position within it. John saw himself as a shattered and hopeless man with no will to attempt any purposeful interaction with his environment. He described himself as 'having no strength, as being broken both in body and mind'.

During this period John spoke constantly of feeling he had been irretrievably violated, of having no control, and of his body and mind being damaged beyond repair by his experiences. A number of medical investigations and tests were carried out during this period, as the violence and hard labour had physically affected him. Survivors of torture and organized violence frequently report feeling that their bodies have been irreparably ruined (Schlapobersky 1990), even when medical examinations are unable to find concrete evidence of this.

THE CARTESIAN SPLIT

The relationship between psychological and physical health is frequently not linear, but recursive, and may be positioned differently by each individual as well as by different social groups. The Cartesian body–mind split may be reflective of Western thinking rather than a reality for many refugees who are survivors of organized violence and torture. The relationship between the two may have become further entwined, as torturers are frequently only too aware of the potential interrelationship and often use one to impact negatively upon the other.

For survivors of organized violence and torture, the body and their perception of their own physicality may have particular resonance. Their experiences may have changed the way they feel about their physical being, having lost a previous image of control and choice over what happens to it. They may have been left with feelings of immense rage, grief, guilt and shame, alongside other emotions. Personal circum-stances, or fear of political repression, may have meant that these emotions have had to be sublimated (Tribe 1998b).

PRINCIPAL PSYCHOLOGICAL THEORIES UNDERLYING THE ISSUES IDENTIFIED

The reverse or antithesis of part of this relationship between body and mind might be that there could be a positive and health enhancing relationship between good physical healthcare, or activity, and psychological health or feelings of well-being. In reviewing the literature on physical and psychological health, Biddle (1995) suggested that 'Despite methodological problems, the literature is clear in showing the potential for physical activity to make a positive impact on mental health. This seems to hold for diverse psychological outcomes, all ages and both genders, although the evidence for different age groups is not extensive.'

Calfas and Taylor (1994), Leith (1994) and Mutrie (1997) have also written on this theme, and the potential benefits on psychological well-being of undertaking physical activity through sporting activity is becoming increasingly recognized, although it has proved difficult to isolate specific characteristics associated with exercise from the actual exercise itself (Fox 1994; Ojanen 1994). The exact process that explains the psychological benefits of exercise is still being investigated and research methodologies improved, while tentative hypotheses have been proposed and tested. Consequently, the relationship between exercise and mental health has become an increasingly popular research area, with a four-fold increase in publications in two of the major journals between1985–89 and 1990–94, while the Health Education Authority has recently spon-sored a three-year campaign to promote regular exercise as a way of improving the quality of life. Also, achievement in sport can be self-confirming, as can the need to feel valued and have control over one's environment (Biddle 1994). In addition, taking part in sport may contribute to positive feelings of self-identity and achievement (Twin 1979: Mitchell and Dryer 1985; Plante 1993). While the basic need to feel competent forms a major component of Deci's (1975) theory of motivation to participate in sport, as does the role of reinforcement through winning. John certainly felt that he lacked a positive identity and felt impotent in relation to his situation and environment during his early months in London. One of our joint tasks was to enable him to regain a positive sense of self and a belief in a future.

John and I continued to meet for counselling over the following year and slowly he began to believe that his life was not finished; he began to be able to see a reason for continuing to live and to see evidence of his ability to impact upon his environment. He was able to reconnect with his past in a way that made it possible to see a future for himself and also to consider what had effected his recovery. Horowitz (1986), Blackwell (1989) Omer and Alon (1994) and have each emphasized the notion of life's perceived continuity. A traumatic event, series of events or a continuous threat may lead to these schemata being shattered and a range of negative psychological, somatic and physiolog-ical symptoms being displayed. In an attempt to help people reconstitute their sense of well-being and continuity, there may be a need to process and integrate experiences into their perception of the world in a way that makes sense to them. If there are political or community issues involved, they may make assimilation either cognitively difficult or extremely easy. This is likely to have particular resonance for a displaced refugee whose sense of continuity is likely to be seriously disjointed.

John's life had always focused on his family and groups he had been a member of and with whom he had shared social and sporting activities. He found the anonymity and individualism of London extremely unwelcoming and confusing. In addition, the idea of seeking therapeutic help or a talking treatment from a stranger was initially extremely alien; medical help for physical ailments was far more acceptable. Bracken and Petty (1998) and Richman (1998) and have written about the overgeneralizing of a Western discourse on trauma and subsequent psychological interventions. Refugees and survivors of organized violence may be suspicious of trusting others, or talking about their experiences. This may be because the open articulation of dissent, or opposition, was what led to them being forced to flee their country and become refugees to be tortured in the first place.

John began to reconnect with his external world, he found a better place to live, started to learn English at college and began to make friends. He discovered that other asylum-seekers and refugees had experienced similar atrocities and also felt lost and powerless in a hostile and unfamiliar culture. John was unable to make contact with his family for some time as they had gone into hiding in Africa after he fled the country. He eventually managed to contact them, however, which was a source of much rejoicing and solace for him. He slowly began to make more sense of his life and the circumstances that had led to his arriving in the United Kingdom. Alongside obtaining psychological help, practical issues were also being sorted out and plans made for his family to join him. He had always been a philosophical man and a devout Christian. He began to think about what had helped him regain his equilibrium as he wished to be able to help other refugees and survivors of torture and organized violence. Hobfoll *et al.* (1991) have claimed that supporting others may benefit both the recipient and the giver, while the growth in a range of self-help health groups in the United Kingdom indicates anecdotal support for this.

John was a sociable individual and he wanted to continue being a community-oriented person in London and to help people who had been through similar experi-ences to his. He felt strongly that newly arrived refugees who did not speak English were those most in need of help. This, plus his concern for his own and others' physical and emotional welfare, led to us reflecting many months later about what had been most helpful to him on first arriving as a refugee in London and what (in terms of things not available) might have helped. We continued to focus on this issue for some time, as John felt it was important to him and he wished to be able to offer to others something that he would have wished for himself. After much consideration and reflection, John decided that one tangible thing that would have helped him gain his physical and psychological strength would have been an opportunity to become involved in some kind of team sports activity with those who had similar experiences to him (i.e. other refugees and survivors of torture).

He believed that playing team sports with peers, which he had enjoyed before and which he believed was good for his health and recovery, would be beneficial and enjoyable. Finding a sport that was as inclusive as possible took time, but football was decided upon as a sport that is played in the majority of countries of the world. It would also not have required participants to wait to develop sophisticated language skills. Hargreaves (1982) stated, 'Historically the political relevance of the body has been given scant attention in our society which is dominated by verbal language.' She argued that this is a cultural artefact from Western society, which sees the mind and the body as separate entities.

The positioning of sport as therapy

Foucault (1979) stated 'The body is directly involved in a political field; power relations have an immediate hold on it; they invest it, train it, torture it, force it to carry out tasks, to perform ceremonies and to emit signs' (pp. 25–26).

John believed that football would be a way of beginning to reclaim control over his physical self and subsequently his emotional self as well. It was felt important that this was within a supportive environment, where a common experience of surviving organized violence and torture was shared, but was not necessarily the major focus.

In addition to the atrocities that the players had been subjected to in their countries of origin, refugees in the United Kingdom are frequently seen as unwelcome and powerless. Many of my refugee clients have reported feeling that they must not draw attention to themselves and should remain 'invisible'. However, on the football pitch they would meet other teams as equals and would be able to regain their physical strength, feelings of belonging, competence and self-esteem.

FUNDAMENTAL HUMAN MOTIVES WITHIN THE CONTEXT OF SPORT

Work by Gauron (1985), among others, has been instrumental in developing classification systems for what are claimed to be motives that may be associated with sport. The principal motives associated with sport are considered to be affiliation, the need for friendship, the need to excel, intrinsic pleasure, achievement/need for success, autonomy and health, and this football team were observed to share those motives or needs. Also evident, however, were motives that included social support and a normalizing of existence, as well as the need to retain physical health and competence, to obtain a place for social interaction with peers and, for many of the players, a sense of continuity with their former life.

Of the issues considered to be important in establishing a sports team as an alternative medium of therapeutic intervention, some we were aware of at the time, some we recognized after the team had become established and others with the benefit of hindsight. Interventions from group therapy, sport psychology and team building were also relevant, as were those associated with the disruption and reconstitution of family, network and community, following organized violence and torture.

SPORT AS AN ALTERNATIVE THERAPEUTIC MEDIUM

Eventually an open meeting was held at an organization working with refugees and survivors of torture to discuss the possibility of starting a football team; posters were put up advertising the meeting in a variety of languages. A first match was held with eight nations represented and with no common language between any of the players. Soon afterwards we were fortunate in securing seed funding and obtaining the services of an experienced coach who had connections with a major London team. This was not an easy task, for although therapists have sometimes included art and other creative therapies in their work, sport has often been identified solely with play, which has meant that it has frequently been seen as being unworthy of serious attention. Faulkner and Biddle (1999) have commented upon the exclusion of exercise from the majority of treatments within mental health, despite an increasing literature suggesting its efficacy. They suggest the body–mind duality perspective, with a perception that exercise and sport do not fit into the traditional treatment paradigm. An absence of understanding of their benefits and their very simplicity have all militated against them being employed as a treatment by clinical psychologists.

It was extremely difficult to gain acceptance from colleagues of our perception that the football team would offer therapeutic or health enhancing benefits, which was our objective for the exercise. Easy and continuous wins on the football field appeared to enhance our case, although it is necessary to point out that we were assisted considerably in our success by two former international players. Significant funding was obtained from a grant-making body, German television made a programme about the team and a film-maker from Channel 4 expressed an interest in making a television film and offered welcome support and encouragement. Each of these factors confirmed our belief that a football team could perform a therapeutic role. The team began to develop a feeling of individual and team efficacy, enthusiasm, mastery, achievement and competence. Other teams' officials in the league began to show respect and admiration for the team. The players began to see that they could achieve a degree of mastery in sport and they gradually came to believe that the new-found confidence and success might transfer to other areas of their lives.

We entered a local league, which we won easily at the end of the season. Unfortunately, no psychometric measures were completed by the players, largely because the team was viewed as a therapeutic intervention and was located within an organization that did not have a research ethic and viewed research as largely getting in the way of clinical practice. In addition, refugees are frequently apprehensive about information being collected about them, since it may have been the outcome of what they wrote or said that led to them being forced to flee their countries anyway. Thus, the therapeutic ethic might have been compromised. The belief that the football team was therapeutically effective is based on narrative accounts provided by the players as the team developed and by examples of positive changes in their lives. For example, 57 per cent of the team enrolled on college courses and 19 per cent of the team obtained jobs and reported that being part of the football team had impacted positively upon their lives.

SOCIAL SUPPORT

The team rapidly developed a strong sense of community and common purpose, as well as providing a source of support, friendship and information exchange. The importance of social support as a mediating variable in enabling people who have experienced trauma to cope with, or hasten recovery from, serious emotional distress has been documented over the past two decades (Figley 1986; Solomon 1989; Stiles 1987; Chester 1992; Joseph 1999; Yule 1999). These were specific accounts of women who had survived torture and reinforced claims that establishing support groups is a promising procedure for empowering women to identify their strengths, especially when based within a country of exile where conventional sources of support are often unavailable. This finding has been replicated by Tribe and Shackman (1989), while the importance of joining with other refugees for support has also been emphasized by Chester (1992) and Light (1992).

The way that social support has been defined and operationalized in the literature on trauma remains problematic, since defining whether social support is actually received, or merely perceived, remains a methodological issue. It may be argued that one of the ways in which a clinician can assist a patient is by helping them to develop a suitable social support network for themselves. Refugees are frequently bereft of their support network, with its members having remained in their country of origin. The loss may be exacerbated by inadequate language skills and cultural connections with which to reconstitute, or develop, a support network in the United Kingdom. Gorst-Unsworth and Goldenberg (1998) studied London-based Iraqi asylum-seekers and found that an absence of social support was more closely associated with depression than was a history of torture.

Schlaporbersky (1990), writing about torture survivors, described survival as a creative act and emphasized the importance of appearing resilient in the face of adversity, noting that this may not only be a strategy for coping, but a creative challenge. It was argued that a relationship network and prior experience of mastery and self-confidence through challenge and adaptation are important determinants in the nature of the response to massive trauma. Succeeding at a task, which could include sport and exercise either individually or a part of a team, and mastery over the body, may provide a healing role. Certainly it appeared to provide this function for the refugees' football team.

THE ACCEPTABLE FACE OF SPORT AS THERAPY

It is interesting to note that many of the players who came regularly for training, matches and as supporters, became very involved in the life of the team, but did not avail themselves of the other therapeutic activities offered by the agency. The traditional verbal therapeutic dyad may not always be appropriate, or accessible, to many refugees and survivors of organized violence. It is interesting to speculate why the football team was successful both on the field and in benefiting participants through its use as a vehicle for therapeutic intervention. While there are no psychometric data to reinforce this observation, there are narrative accounts, case notes and changes in life patterns, such as starting college or obtaining a job, to substantiate the benefits of the football team as a therapeutic intervention for those who played in it.

The team's operational function

The team's development is discussed generally in terms of Tuckman's (1965) model of group functioning, which contains four stages, namely forming, norming, storming, and performing. The team passed through the first two stages in a fairly straightforward manner; forming a team, holding regular training sessions and establishing group norms and a team culture. The third phase, storming, proved more problematic, as the team was not always able to provide a containing space and, at times, feelings of immense rage, anger and despair were expressed during a game; so much so that on two occasions we were threatened with expulsion from the league. These feelings were associated with players' feelings about their experiences as survivors of organized violence. They were further exacerbated by language barriers and a variety of difficulties associated with being an asylum-seeker in London. It is well known that much aggression in sport results from frustration that may be attributed to the blocking of individual motives and aspirations. For example, Birch and Veroff (1966) and Alderman (1975) have referred to the motive-state of aggression as resentment. They suggested that by being constantly subjected to aggression in situations where a person has no control or form of defence, they grow resentful. This may manifest itself through aggressive behaviour on the field, or elsewhere. Survivors of organized violence or torture have frequently been repeatedly subjected to aggression, for example with the right to free speech being removed. Perhaps Freud's concept of displacement may have relevance here. Displacement occurs when the frustrating individual, or object, is too powerful, remote or dangerous to retaliate against. This would certainly be the case with organized violence, or torture, by the state.

The team ultimately felt ready to move to the fourth stage, namely performing, not only meeting with team-mates for a game, but also holding regular group meetings with a psychologist. Feelings associated with being a survivor of organized violence and an asylum-seeker could be addressed in a structured and more formal way in that situation.

Summary

The success of the football team can probably best be measured by its success as a vehicle that continued to be used regularly by survivors of organized violence and by others as supporters. It was evident that many used the team as a stepping-stone towards their recovery into a new and very different life in the United Kingdom. More specifically, it appeared to assist players in regaining positive feelings of physical and psychological well-being within a safe and culturally familiar environment, to develop feelings of both competence and mastery and to become part of a new community, or team, in every sense.

It is pleasing to report that John's personal circumstances improved greatly and he went on to obtain a prestigious academic qualification. He now runs a charitable organization, is active in local politics and is a valued member of his church community. He describes himself as content and views his future with optimism and hope.

Note

The author would like to acknowledge the contributions of Pedro Rodriguez for his assistance with the team in its infancy, Gary for helping to organize training facilities and for his knowledge of the game, and Michael Robbins, film-maker, for being a constant supporter of the team and its players.

References

Alderman, R. B. (1975) *Psychological Behaviour in Sport,* Philadelphia: W.B. Saunders.

Amnesty International (2000) Press and Information Office.

Biddle, S. J. H. (1994) 'Motivation and participation in exercise and sport'. In S. Serpa, J. Alves, and V. Pataco (eds.), *International Perspectives on Sport and Exercise Psychology*, Morgantown, WV: Fitness Information Technology.

Biddle, S. J. H. (1995) 'Exercise and psychosocial health', *Research Quarterly for Exercise and Sport* 66:292–297.

Birch, D. and Veroff, J. (1966) *Motivations: A Study of Action,* Belmont, CA: California Press.

Blackwell, R. D. (1989) *The Disruption and Reconstitution of Family, Network and Community Systems Following Torture, Organized Violence and Exile.* Paper presented at the Second International Conference of Centres, Institutions and Individuals Concerned with the Care of Victims of Organised Violence, Costa Rica.

Bracken, P. and Petty, C. (eds.) (1998) *Rethinking the Trauma of War,* London: Free Association Books.

British Home Office (2000) Press and information office.

Calfas, K. J. and Taylor, W. C. (1994) 'Effects of physical activity on psychological variables in adolescents', *Paediatric Exercise Science* 6:406–423.

Chester, B. (1992) 'Refugee women and their mental health', *Women and Therapy* 13(1–2): 209–220.

Deci, E. L. (1975) *Intrinsic Motivation,* New York: Plenum Press.

Faulkner, G. and Biddle, S. (1999) *Exercise as Therapy*. Paper presented at the BPS Annual Conference, Winchester, England, April.

Figley, C. R. (1986) *Trauma and It's Wake* (Vol. 2), New York: Brumer Mazell.

Foucault, M. (1979) *Discipline and Punish: The Birth of a Prison*, New York: Random House.

Fox, K. (1994) *Exercising for the Mind*. Paper presented at the Annual Conference for the British Association for the Advancement of Science, Loughborough University, England.

Gauron, E. (1985) *Mental Training for Peak Performance*, Lansing, New York: Sport Science Associates.

Gorst-Unsworth, C. and Goldenberg, E. (1998) 'Psychological sequalae of torture and organized violence suffered by refugees from Iraq', *British Journal of Psychiatry* 172:90–94.

Hargreaves, J. (1982) 'Theorising sport: An introduction'. In J. Hargreaves (ed.), *Sport, Culture and Ideology*, pp. 1–30, London: Routledge and Kegan Paul.

Hobfoll, S. E., Speilberger, C. D., Folkman, S., Lepper-Green, B., Saranson, I. and Van der Volk, A. (1991) 'War-related stress: Addressing the stress of war and other traumatic events', *American Psychologist* 46:848–855.

Horowitz, M. J. (1986) *Stress Response Syndromes*, Northvale, NJ: Aronson.

Joseph, S. (1999) 'Social Support and mental health fostering trauma.' In W. Yule (ed.), *Post-Traumatic Stress Disorders: Concepts and Therapy*, Chichester: Wiley.

Leith, L. M. (1994) *Foundations of Exercise and Mental Health*, Morgantown, WV: Fitness Information Technology.

Light, D. (1992) 'Healing their wounds: Guatemalan refugee women as political activists', *Women and Therapy* 13:281–296.

Mitchell, S. and Dryer, K. (1985) *Winning Women: Challenging the Norms in Australian Sport*, Ringwood: Penguin.

Mutrie, N. (1997) 'The therapeutic effects of exercise on the self'. In K. R. Fox (ed.), *The Physical Self from Motivation to Well-being*, pp. 287–314, Champaign, IL: Human Kinetics.

Ojanen, M. (1994) 'Can the true effects of exercise on psychological variables be separated from placebo effects?', *International Journal of Sport Psychology* 25:63–80.

Omer, H. and Alon, N. (1994) 'The continuity principle: A unified approach to treatment and management in disaster and trauma', *American Journal of Community Psychology* 8:273–287.

Plante, T. G. (1993) 'Aerobic exercises in prevention and treatment of psychopathology'. In P. Seraganian (ed.), *Exercise Psychology*, pp. 358–379, London: Wiley-Interscience.

Richman, R. (1998) 'Looking before and after: Refugees and asylum-seekers in the West'. In P. J. Bracken and C. Petty (eds.), *Rethinking the Trauma of War*, pp. 170–186, London: Free Association Books.

Schlapobersky, J. (1990) 'Torture as the perversion of a healing relationship'. In J. Gruschow, and K. Hannibal, K. (eds.), *Health Services for the Treatment of Torture and Trauma Survivors*, pp. 51–72, Washington DC: American Association for the Advancement of Science.

Soloman, Z. (1989) 'A three-year prospective study of post-traumatic stress disorder in Israeli combat veterans', *Journal of Traumatic Stress* 2: 59–73.

Stiles, W. B. (1987) 'I have to talk to somebody': A fever model of disclosure'. In V. J. Derlega and J. H. Berg (eds.), *Self-Disclosure: Theory, Research and Therapy*, pp. 257–282, New York: Plenum Press.

Tribe, R. (1998a) 'What can psychological theory and the counselling psychologist offer in situations of civil conflict and war overseas', *Counselling Psychology Quarterly* 11(1): 109–115.

Tribe, R. (1998b) 'If two is company is three a crowd/group'. A review of a support and clinical supervision group for interpreters working with refugees in Britain', *Group Work Journal* 10(3): 196–214.

Tribe, R. and Shackman, J. (1989) 'A way forward: A group for refugee women', *Group Work Journal* 2:159–166.

Twin, S. L. (1979) *Out of the Bleachers*, New York: Feminist Press.

Tuckman, B. W. (1965) 'Developmental sequence in small groups', *Psychological Bulletin* 63:384–399.

Yule, W. (ed.). (1999) *Post-Traumatic Stress Disorders: Concepts and Therapy*, Chichester: Wiley.

chapter thirteen

Coping with retirement from professional sport

DAVID LAVALLEE, JIM GOLBY AND RUTH LAVALLEE

Retirement is one of the most significant experiences in professional sport (Murphy 1995; Lavallee and Andersen 2000). Although one of the inevitabilities in high-performance sport is that eventually every competitor will have to terminate their career at the elite level, some individuals have been found to experience psychological adjustment difficulties when faced with retirement. Based on a review of 14 studies that examined retiring athletes across a wide range of sports, Lavallee *et al.* (2000) found that 20 per cent of the individuals studied required considerable psychological adjustment upon career termination. Furthermore, in an archival investigation examining verbatim quotes from British newspapers of professional athletes immediately following their retirement, more than 40 per cent of rugby players were found to experience a distressful reaction to career termination (Lavallee 2000).

The purpose of this chapter is to examine the topic of retirement from professional sport, with a particular focus on professional rugby. In view of the fact that few publications exist on the psychological processes associated with retirement from rugby per se (e.g. Butlin 1980), theoretical perspectives related to sport career termination in general are initially described. A review of the growing body of research conducted on retirement from professional sport is then presented. The chapter concludes with an overview of an intervention developed for professional rugby players.

Theoretical perspectives

A number of theoretical models have been outlined in the sport psychology literature in order to explain the process of retirement from professional sport. These models, which have predominantly been derived from mainstream psychological literature, have been developed and revised following research conducted in the area. Some of the earliest models to be associated with sport retirement were theories related to retirement from work (e.g. McPherson 1980; Lerch 1981; Rosenberg 1981). These models were applied from the literature related to gerontology and the social psychology of ageing and suggested that retirement from sport is a system-induced mechanism that forces individuals to terminate their career involuntarily (Greendorfer and Blinde 1985; Curtis and Ennis 1988). Despite the intuitive appeal of this analogy, theorists questioned the applicability of these models with retiring athletes, who would inevitably continue into a post-sporting career. As Murphy (1995) has also suggested, it is difficult to compare retirement from work with sport retirement, which biologically and chronologically occurs at a much younger age. Contemporary sport psychologists have, therefore, agreed that models related to retirement from work are unable to capture adequately the nature and dynamics of the process of sports career termination (Taylor and Ogilvie 1998).

The series of stages associated with grief and loss (Kübler-Ross 1969) has also been employed to explain the psychological experiences associated with retirement from sport. These stages, as applied to sports career termination, have been proposed to include the following: denial and isolation, in which the individual initially refuses to acknowledge their inevitable retirement; anger, in which the retiring athlete becomes disturbed at the overall situation; bargaining, in which they try to negotiate for a lengthened career in sport; depression, in which the former player experiences a distressful reaction to retirement; and acceptance, in which the individual eventually comes to accept their career termination. Although a number of authors have utilized stage theories to describe the process of sport retirement (e.g. Lerch 1984; Rosenberg 1984), their clinical utility has been questioned because they were developed with non-sport populations (Crook and Robertson 1991). A number of theorists have also suggested that stage models are merely a generalizable disposition of what happens to the majority of retiring athletes (Gordon 1995; Taylor and Ogilvie 1998).

The most frequently employed theoretical framework that has been used to examine the process of sport retirement has been Schlossberg's (1981) developmental model of transition. Whereas stage models view retirement from sport as a singular event, Schlossberg's model characterizes retirement from sport as a transition (Petitpas, Brewer and Van Raalte 1996). Sinclair and Orlick (1994) have suggested that the model has relevance in terms of the characteristics of the retiring athlete, the perception of the particular career transition, and the characteristics of the pre-transition and post-transition environments. Support for this perspective has been documented in Parker's (1994) investigation of retired football players, as well as Baillie's (1993) study of former elite amateur and professional athletes. Schlossberg's model incorporates a wider range of influence than social gerontological and thanatological models and allows for the possibility of both positive and negative adjustment (Crook and Robertson 1991; Parker 1994).

Overall, the theoretical models applied to retirement from sport have been instrumental in stimulating research in the area. However, each of the models that has been proposed in the literature possesses limitations that indicate the need for further theoretical development of the area. For example, sport retirement theories have not presented information about how to individualize approaches, because they have formulated generalizations across a wide range of sports and individual athletes (Grove, Lavallee and Gordon 1997). Stage models and models related to retirement from work do not indicate which factors influence the quality of adaptation to sport retirement. Moreover, those transition models that have been applied to sport do not provide an adequate framework within which interventions can be employed (Taylor and Ogilvie 1994). For these reasons, contemporary sport psychologists have employed conceptual models of retirement from sport to guide both practice and research (Taylor and Ogilvie 1994; Gordon 1995). These models examine the entire course of the career transition process and focus upon how the quality of adjustment is influenced by the reasons for retirement, developmental factors related to the transition process and coping resources that affect responses to retirement. A review of the debate regarding the prevalence of psychological difficulties experienced upon retirement from sport is presented, followed by an examination of research conducted in specific areas.

The research

Research into the psychology of retirement from competitive sport has grown markedly in recent years. In 1980, McPherson reported that an extensive literature search generated 20 references on the topic. In 1998, more than 270 references were identified on sports retirement (Lavallee, Sinclair and Wylleman 1998; Lavallee, Wylleman and Sinclair 1998). A number of the earlier studies suggested that sports career termination is an inevitable source of psychological distress (Bookbinder 1955; Hallden 1965; Mihovilovic 1968). That research focused on professional male athletes and emphasized the dysfunctional issues that athletes are occasionally confronted with after retirement. As empirical data began to accumulate, several researchers challenged the widespread assumption that sports retirement is inherently stressful. For example, Gorbett (1985) advanced a developmental perspective by suggesting that former athletes are not universally overwhelmed by retirement-induced stress. In an important series of studies it was found that approximately 90 per cent of the athletes surveyed looked forward to life after competitive sport (Blinde and Greendorfer 1985; Greendorfer and Blinde 1985; Kleiber *et al.* 1987; Kleiber and Brock 1992).

During this period other researchers demonstrated that retirement has the potential to be a major source of life adjustment. Svoboda and Vanek (1982), for example, reported that 83 per cent of a sample of former Olympic athletes experienced psychological stress following retirement from sport. In addition, Werthner and Orlick (1986) interviewed a sample of Canada's most successful amateur athletes and found that 78.6 per cent felt some degree of difficulty in making the transition. In a survey of former ice-hockey players, Curtis and Ennis (1988) reported that 63 per cent experienced feelings of loss after disengaging from organized sport. McInally, Cavin-Stice and Knoth (1992) also indicated that 88 per cent of retired professional football players in the United States found the overall career transition process to be extremely problematic.

Notwithstanding evidence of adjustment difficulties, 67 per cent of the McInally, Cavin-Stice and Knoth (1992) sample reported that they would still seek a professional sport career for their sons, while 85.6 per cent of the Curtis and Ennis (1988) sample would prefer their sons to be as heavily involved in competitive ice-hockey as they were themselves.

Despite the extensive empirical literature that has emerged in this area, there still exists considerable debate about how athletes adapt to retirement. A number of factors have been shown to influence the overall quality of adjustment to career termination. As previously mentioned, these factors include the reasons for retirement, developmental experiences and coping resources (Gordon 1995; Taylor and Ogilvie 1998). First, researchers have found retirement from sport to be a function of a variety of involuntary and voluntary reasons (Lavallee, Grove and Gordon 1997; Fortunato and Marchant 1999). Although it has been suggested that the causes are influenced by the structure of sport, studies have demonstrated that the most common are career-ending injuries, chronological age, deselection and personal choice.

An unexpected and sudden retirement from sport can take place as a result of an injury. Empirical research supports the notion that terminating a sports careers is difficult when caused by injury because it is something for which individuals are seldom prepared (Werthner and Orlick 1986). In addition, Kleiber and Brock's (1992) study of competitive athletes who suffered career-ending injuries indicates that an injury need not be severe to force athletes out of continued participation in competitive sport. As Ogilvie and Taylor (1993) have suggested, elite athletes perform at such a high level that even small reductions in their physical capabilities may be sufficient to make them no longer competitive at the highest level.

Research by Mihovilovic (1968) with former Yugoslavian athletes has shown that retirement from sport can also be a function of chronological age. In his study of former professional soccer players, decline in performance accompanying the ageing process was identified as one of the major causes for retirement. Taylor and Ogilvie (1998) maintained that age is one of the most significant reasons for retirement, because psychological motivation, social status and physical capabilities can all complicate an individual's ability to continue competing at an elite level.

Associated with the physiological processes of ageing is the structural factor of an athlete failing to progress to the next highest level of elite competition, namely deselection. Lavallee's (2000) study, which showed that 29 per cent of professional rugby players retired because they were deselected from their teams, demonstrated that this involuntary reason is a particularly important contributor to sports career termination.

The final notable reason for retirement from sport is that of voluntary choice. Research by Wylleman et al. (1993) has demonstrated that many individuals freely elect to terminate their sporting career for a combination of personal and psychological reasons. Some athletes may decide to end their careers because of financial complications, ethnic or gender-related issues, or an overall lack of life satisfaction, whereas others may want to spend more time with their families and friends (Baillie 1993). A voluntary decision to retire from sport is perhaps the most attractive reason, not least because it eases the career transition process (Taylor and Ogilvie 1998).

With regard to developmental factors associated with transition, researchers have shown that athletic identity – that is the degree to which an individual identifies with the role of athlete (Brewer, Van Raalte and Linder 1993) – can have a significant effect on the quality of adjustment. Chamalidis (1997), for example, has demonstrated that those who ascribe great importance to their involvement in elite sport are more at risk of experiencing retirement-related difficulties than those who place less value on the athletic component of their self-identity. In addition, other researchers have shown how individuals who strongly commit themselves to the athlete role may be less likely to explore other career, education and lifestyle options (Murphy, Petipas and Brewer 1996; Lavallee, Gordon and Grove 1997; Lavallee *et al.* 1998).

Sport psychologists have also examined the ways in which coping resources influence the overall quality of adjustment to retirement from sport (Crook and Robertson 1991; Gordon 1995). A number of early studies reported that many high-performance athletes turn to alcohol as a way of coping with their career transition (e.g. Hallden 1965; Mihovilovic 1968), while Canadian researchers found that having a new focus after retirement predicts better adjustment (Werthner and Orlick 1986; Baillie 1993; Sinclair and Orlick 1993). In an individual's attempt to manage the career transition process, not surprisingly those high in coping resources tend to experience less stress than athletes possessing few coping skills (Pearson and Petitpas 1990; Murphy 1995).

A study by Reynolds (1981) with former professional football players in the United States was perhaps the first to outline the general importance of social support as a significant coping resource among retired sports performers. In recent years, other career transition researchers have documented the importance of social support from friends, family, team-mates and coaches (Alfermann and Gross 1997). However, Kane's (1991) study of former professional male American athletes in the midst of a career transition demonstrated that social support networks can also suffer following retirement.

Despite the fact that retirement from sport is one of few certainties in a professional athlete's career, a recurring theme of research is the athlete's resistance to plan a post-sporting career prior to their retirement. Haerle's (1975) study, for example, demonstrated that 75 per cent of professional athletes surveyed did not engage in pre-retirement planning as a coping resource during their sporting career. Also, Blann and Zaichkowsky (1989) reported that only 37 per cent of professional ice-hockey players and 25 per cent of professional baseball players had devised a post-sport career plan before ending their careers. Although this career indecision among retired athletes has been illustrated in other studies (McInally, Cavin-Stice and Knoth 1992; Wylleman *et al.* 1993), it has become clear that since sport requires a considerable commitment of time and energy, it is argued that professional athletes have little time for planning while playing.

Retirement from professional rugby

The game of professional rugby presents an interesting perspective from which to examine and exemplify some of these important issues. Recent and rapid changes in both the structure and the regulations governing the playing of the game continue to have an impact. Additionally, the proliferation of paid players means a commensurate increase in the number of retiring players facing psychological problems. In order to understand these potential problems, it is important to place the game of rugby in a brief historical context. This will help in comprehending both the general and specific nature of difficulties faced by players.

Many of the sports we currently enjoy trace their formal origins from the Victorian age. Indeed, the Victorians were great originators and codifiers of sporting pastimes. Although rugby has a clear lineage predating this period, it was during this epoch that the formalities and regulations of the game were laid down. The original game existed in an amateur form until a split in 1895, which occurred over the issue of payment for 'broken time' or the right to the reimbursement of time or money lost from work due to playing commitments. The dispute led to the separate development of amateur (Rugby Union) and professional (Rugby League) versions of the game, as well as rules modifications that were more suited to professionalism.

In recent years, two major developments have increased the number of full-time professional players in rugby. First, the advent of a 'Super League' in Rugby League and, secondly, in August 1995 as a consequence of pressure to maximize its commercial value, to develop the profile of the sport and keep its top stars in their game, Rugby Union legislators declared the game 'open'. Thus, players deemed to possess sufficient skill could be paid and, if good enough, become full-time professional players.

Rugby Union is played in more than 100 countries and membership of the International Rugby Board encompasses 91 National Unions and one Regional Association. In 2000, Rugby League Headquarters indicated there are in the region of 1500 registered Rugby League players and the figures provided by the English Rugby Partnership shows in the order of 2500 registered professionals.

Thus, both codes have recently experienced rapid and significant changes in their structure. The changes have generated uncertainty about the direction that rugby will take and there have been a number of casualties induced by various power struggles that include clubs folding or merging and high-profile individuals walking away from the game altogether. However, it is likely that rugby will continue to flourish in the immediate future and that commercial interests will continue to impose increasing demands on players, administrators and support staff. There is also no doubt that the greatest demands will be placed on those players who choose to make a full-time career in the game.

As an example of the demands made on a typical top-level professional rugby union player, it is worth noting that players can expect to play, on average, about 13 international matches a year. When league and cup matches are added to this schedule, an impression of the physical and mental strains placed on the player can be gained. As well as an increase in the number of big games played by top players, there has been a further discernible shift in the physical components of the game at a high level. Rugby has become a 'hitting', as opposed to a 'contact' sport, and both media and players now focus on 'the big hit' as an important feature of the game. The potentially harmful effects of these shifts on players are axiomatic.

While the physical demands placed on professional Rugby League players were always greater than those of their amateur Rugby Union counterparts, there has been a narrowing of this gap since Rugby Union became a professional game. Recent research (Treasure, Carpenter and Power 2000) has demonstrated a clear shift in attitudes to the game, whereby professional players have moved away from amateur and score higher on the purposes of playing rugby being related to aggression, financial remuneration and fitness, but score lower on sportsmanship. Additionally, both codes have seen a significant increase in the physical preparation required to enable players to compete at the level of intensity currently encountered in the game. Both codes of the game now support full-time professionals as well as numerous part-time paid players.

In recent years, several career-transition programmes have been developed to help competitive athletes across the world prepare for retirement from competition. For example, the Olympic Athlete Career Center in Canada and the Athlete Career and Education Programme in Australia and the United Kingdom have been designed to assist athletes in their preparation for retirement (Anderson and Morris 2000). Also, the Olympic Job Opportunities Programme has been launched in the United States, Australia and South Africa to assist Olympic athletes who are committed to developing a professional career alongside the achievement of their sport-related goals (Wylleman, Lavallee and Alfermann 1999). In terms of professional sport, the National Football League in the United States offers career transition and continuing education services to its athletes, and the United States National Basketball Players Association has developed a career and education programme for its professional players. In the United Kingdom, however, few sports retirement programmes are available for professional athletes and none specifically for professional rugby players. For this reason, a sport psychology intervention was developed for a sample of professional Rugby League and Rugby Union players who retired in 1997.

The intervention involved the development of the British Athlete Lifestyle Assessment Needs in Career and Education (BALANCE) Scale in order to identify the rugby players at risk of experiencing difficulties during their career transition (Lavallee and Wylleman 1999). Based on existing research in the area and conceptual models of adjustment to career transition (Gordon 1995; Taylor and Ogilvie 1998), an initial pool of 13 moderators of career transition adjustment was proposed for the screening tool. They were: perception of control over the cause for retirement (Fortunato and Marchant 1999); identity as an athlete (Chamalidis 1997); social support (Alfermann and Gross 1997); previous experience with transitions (Swain 1991); continued involvement in sport-related activities following retirement from competition (Curtis and Ennis 1988); degree of occupational planning (Grove, Lavallee and Gordon 1997); identity foreclosure (Murphy, Petitpas and Brewer 1996); socio-economic status (Kleiber *et al.* 1987); transferable skills (Gordon 1995); achievement of sport-related goals (Sinclair and Orlick 1993); mentoring (Perna, Zaichkowsky and Bocknek 1996); provision of career transition support services (Wylleman *et al.* 1993); and having a new focus after retirement (Baillie 1993).

Following a content validation analysis conducted by three experts familiar with the literature on sports career transitions, social support and mentoring were merged into one variable. The 12 remaining variables were converted into questionnaire items rated on seven-point Likert-type scales anchored by 'strongly agree' and 'strongly disagree', with a higher overall score reflecting an individual being more at-risk to experiencing adjustment difficulties. A preliminary version was administered to a sample of undergraduate sport and exercise science students to establish the appropriateness of the questions (Lavallee and Wylleman 1999) and modifications were made to the wording of some of the items. The resulting questionnaire employed in the intervention is as follows:

1. I personally decided to end my sporting career.

2. At the time I ended my sporting career, I saw myself only as an athlete. (*Scored in reverse.*)

3. I lost my social support network when I ended my sporting career. (*Scored in reverse.*)

4. I have had previous experience with transitions in other areas of my life.

5. I have continued my involvement in sport-related activities since my career termination.

6. I planned for a career outside of sport prior to my career termination.

7. During my sporting career I neglected other areas of my life in order to concentrate on my sport. (*Scored in reverse.*)

8. My socio-economic status improved following my career termination.

9. I have been able to transfer skills I learned in sport to other areas of my life.

10. I achieved all of my sporting goals during my career.

11. I utilized the services of a sports career transition programme prior to my retirement.

12. I was able to develop a new focus upon ending my sporting career.

A total of 71 professional rugby league and rugby union players who had retired from their clubs in England, Scotland and Wales in 1997 completed the BALANCE Scale. They had played rugby from a mean age of 12.37 years, reached professional standard at 20.40

years, competed at a professional level for 3.90 years and retired at the mean age of 26.51 years. Results from the BALANCE Scale revealed a mean score of 53.44 (S.D. = 12.75) for the former players and, based on these data, a series of group workshops was formulated and designed for the professional rugby players.

These workshops, which were driven by the players' needs and facilitated by sport psychologists, were offered to assist the players in coping with life demands following their retirement. The sessions featured a combination of methods of delivery that included practical exercises and group discussions and focused on topics such as personality and interests, coping strategies and lifestyle management. Owing to the potential impact that retirement from sport can have on significant others, a support group was organized for parents and spouses of the players. Because several of the players were experiencing difficulties in the identification and management of a chosen career, career-planning and development workshops were offered by a counselling psychologist. Workshops provided players with an introduction to career planning, values and interest exploration, career awareness and the identification of transferable skills from rugby to the work environment.

Conclusion

As professional rugby continues to develop, there will be a commensurate increase in the number of players forced to retire from the game. Whereas some will retire early due to loss of form, others will terminate their career as a result of small reductions in physical capacity, whether attributable to the ageing process or to minor injuries (Lavallee 2000). Players will also continue to face critical career events. Injury, weekly team selection, contractual issues and forced retirement are all part of the game (Butlin 1980), with these events occurring much earlier in the life of a rugby player than hitherto. Rugby-induced injuries can also generate negative effects in respect of psychological and emotional problems, which may have a significant implication for choice of a post-sport career.

A further outcome of the spread of professionalism in rugby is the increasing demands placed upon promising young players to commence their professional careers in their teens. This trend mirrors association football, where clubs recruit potentially skilful young players at a young age. There is a very high attrition rate from such recruiting schemes, and even those players who emerge successfully from the system and enjoy full careers may have had little opportunity to develop the links required to ensure a smooth transition to life after rugby.

Prior to professionalism, successful players were frequently able to manage the conflicting demands of full-time education, a career and top-level rugby. Today, this is no longer the case. Due to the lack of a formal structure to help players when they retire from the game, it is likely that an increasing number of them will terminate their careers with only minimal experience of other forms of employment and with relatively few transferable skills. It is for this reason that we feel further attention needs to be directed at the development of career-transition programmes for rugby players.

Career-transition programmes should be multidimensional and include enhancement, support, and counselling components (Petitpas, Brewer and Van Raalte 1996). They also need to be able to assist and guide players via multiformats, such as 'one-on-one' or group sessions, written information and skills enhancement programmes, so that they can maximize their potential in different spheres of daily life (Wylleman, Lavallee and Alfermann 1999). As Petitpas and Champagne (2000) have suggested, the structural aspects of career transition programmes (e.g. group size, programme format and scheduling, and required or voluntary participation) always need to be considered when developing interventions, as well as acknowledging the idiosyncrasies of a specific sport.

Career transition programmes should not, however, be focused solely on post-retirement interventions. Although Lavallee *et al.* (2000) have identified that as many as 20 per cent of athletes require considerable psychological adjustment following their retirement, Gorely *et al.* (in press) found that individuals often do not consider their career termination to be an issue until its proximity draws near. Programmes for rugby players, therefore, should focus upon functional adjustments during the pre-retirement phase, while the emphasis in the post-retirement period should be on the provision of support to facilitate psychological adjustment.

References

Alfermann, D. and Gross, A. (1997) 'Coping with career termination: It all depends on freedom of choice'. In R. Lidor and M. Bar-Eli (eds.), *Proceedings of the Ninth World Congress on Sport Psychology*, pp. 65–67, Netanya, Israel: International Society of Sports Psychology.

Anderson, D. and Morris, T. (2000) 'Athlete lifestyle programs'. In D. Lavallee and P. Wylleman (eds.), *Career Transitions in Sport: International Perspectives*, pp. 59–80, Morgantown, WV: Fitness Information Technology.

Baillie, P. H. F. (1993) 'Understanding retirement from sports: Therapeutic ideas for helping athletes in transition', *The Counseling Psychologist* 21:399–410.

Blann, F. W. and Zaichkowsky, L. (1989) *National Hockey League and Major League Baseball Players' Post-sport Career Transition Surveys*. Final report prepared for the National Hockey League Players' Association, USA.

Blinde, E. M. and Greendorfer, S. L. (1985) 'A reconceptualization of the process of leaving the role of competitive athlete', *International Review for the Sociology of Sport* 20:87–94.

Bookbinder, H. (1955) 'Work histories of men leaving a short life span occupation', *Personnel and Guidance Journal* 34:164–167.

Brewer, B. W., Van Raalte, J. L. and Linder, D. E. (1993) 'Athletic identity: Hercules' muscles or Achilles' heel?', *International Journal of Sport Psychology* 24:237–254.

Butlin, P. A. (1980) 'Is there life after rugby?', *Rugby Post*, 4(6):15.

Chamalidis, P. (1997) 'Identity conflicts during and after retirement from top-level sports'. In R. Lidor and M. Bar-Eli (eds.), *Proceedings of the Ninth World Congress on Sport Psychology*, pp. 191–193, Netanya, Israel: International Society of Sports Psychology.

Crook, J. M. and Robertson, S. E. (1991) 'Transitions out of elite sport', *International Journal of Sport Psychology* 22:115–127.

Curtis, J. and Ennis, R. (1988) 'Negative consequences of leaving competitive sport? Comparison findings for former elite-level hockey players', *Sociology of Sport Journal* 5:87–106.

Fortunato, V. and Marchant, D. (1999) 'Forced retirement from elite football in Australia', *Journal of Personal and Interpersonal Loss* 4(3): 269–280.

Gorbett, F. J. (1985) 'Psycho-social adjustment of athletes to retirement'. In L. K. Bunker, R. J. Rotella and A. Reilly (eds.), *Sport Psychology: Psychological Considerations in Maximizing Sport Performance*, pp. 288–294, Ithaca, NY: Mouvement Publications.

Gordon, S. (1995) 'Career transitions in competitive sport'. In T. Morris and J. Summers (eds.), *Sport Psychology: Theory, Applications and Issues*, pp. 474–501, Brisbane: Jacaranda Wiley.

Gorely, T., Lavallee, D., Bruce, D., Teale, B. and Lavallee, R. M. (in press) 'A sampling of the perceptions of potential users of the Australian Athlete Career and Education Program', *Athletic Academic Journal*.

Greendorfer, S. L and Blinde, E. M. (1985) '"Retirement" from intercollegiate sport: Theoretical and empirical considerations', *Sociology of Sport Journal* 2:101–110.

Grove, J. R., Lavallee, D. and Gordon, S. (1997) 'Coping with retirement from sport: The influence of athletic identity', *Journal of Applied Sport Psychology* 9:191–203.

Haerle, R. K. (1975) 'Career patterns and career contingencies of professional baseball players: An occupational analysis'. In D. W. Ball and J. W. Loy (eds.), *Sport and Social Order*, pp. 461–519, Reading, MA: Addison-Wesley.

Hallden, O. (1965) 'The adjustment of athletes after retiring from sport'. In F. Antonelli (ed.), *Proceedings of the First International Congress of Sport Psychology*, pp. 730–733, Rome.

Kane, M. A. (1991) *The Metagonic Transition: A Study of Career Transition, Marital Stress and Identity Transformation in Former Professional Athletes.* Unpublished doctoral dissertation, Boston University, MA, USA.

Kleiber, D. A. and Brock, S. C. (1992) 'The effect of career-ending injuries on the subsequent well-being of elite college athletes', *Sociology of Sport Journal* 9:70–75.

Kleiber, D., Greendorfer, S., Blinde, E. and Sandall, D. (1987) 'Quality of exit from university sports and subsequent life satisfaction', *Journal of Sport Sociology* 4:28–36.

Kübler-Ross, E. (1969) *On Death and Dying*, NY: Macmillan.

Lavallee, D. (2000) *Retirement from Professional Sport: An Archival Investigation*, Manuscript submitted for publication.

Lavallee, D. and Andersen, M. (2000) 'Leaving sport: Easing career transitions'. In M. B. Andersen (ed.), *Doing Sport Psychology*, pp. 249–261, Champaign, IL: Human Kinetics.

Lavallee, D., Gordon, S. and Grove, J. R. (1997) 'Retirement from sport and the loss of athletic identity', *Journal of Personal and Interpersonal Loss* 2:129–147.

Lavallee, D., Grove, J. R. and Gordon, S. (1997) 'The causes of career termination from sport and their relationship to post-retirement adjustment among elite-amateur athletes in Australia', *The Australian Psychologist* 32:131–135.

Lavallee, D., Grove, J. R., Gordon, S. and Ford, I. W. (1998) 'The experience of loss in sport'. In J. H. Harvey (ed.), *Perspectives on Loss: A Sourcebook*, pp. 241–252, Philadelphia: Brunner/Mazel.

Lavallee, D., Nesti, M., Borkeles, E., Cockerill, I. and Edge, A. (2000) 'Approaches to counseling athletes in transition'. In D. Lavallee and P. Wylleman (eds.), *Career Transitions in Sport: International Perspectives*, pp. 111–130, Morgantown, WV: Fitness Information Technology.

Lavallee, D., Sinclair, D. A. and Wylleman, P. (1998) 'An annotated bibliography on career transitions in sport: Counselling-based references', *Australian Journal of Career Development* 7(2):34–42.

Lavallee, D. and Wylleman, P. (1999) 'Toward an instrument to assess the quality of adjustment to career transitions in sport: The British Athlete Lifestyle Assessment Needs in Career and Education (BALANCE) Scale'. In V. Hosek, P. Tilinger and L. Bilek (eds.), *Psychology of Sport and Exercise: Enhancing the Quality of Life*, pp. 322–324, Prague: Charles University.

Lavallee, D., Wylleman, P. and Sinclair, D. A. (1998) 'An annotated bibliography on career transitions in sport: Empirical references', *Australian Journal of Career Development* 7(3):32–44.

Lerch, S. H. (1981) 'The adjustment to retirement of professional baseball players'. In S. L. Greendorfer and A. Yiannakis (eds.), *Sociology of Sport: Diverse Perspectives*, pp. 138–148, West Point, NY: Leisure Press.

Lerch, S. H. (1984) 'Athlete retirement as social death: An overview'. In N. Theberge and P. Donnelly (eds.), *Sport and the Sociological Imagination*, pp. 259–272, Fort Worth: Texas Christian University Press.

McInally, L. J., Cavin-Stice, J. and Knoth, R. L. (1992) *Adjustment Following Retirement from Professional Football*. Paper presented at the annual convention of the American Psychological Association, Washington DC.

McPherson, B. D. (1980) 'Retirement from professional sport: The process and problems of occupational and psychological adjustment', *Sociological Symposium* 30:126–143.

Mihovilovic, M. (1968) 'The status of former sportsmen', *International Review of Sport Sociology* 3:73–93.

Murphy, S. M. (1995) 'Transitions in competitive sport: Maximizing individual potential'. In S. M. Murphy (ed.), *Sport Psychology Interventions*, pp. 331–346, Champaign, IL: Human Kinetics.

Murphy, G. M., Petitpas, A. J. and Brewer, B. W. (1996) 'Identity foreclosure, athletic identity, and career maturity in intercollegiate athletes', *The Sport Psychologist* 10:239–246.

Ogilvie, B. C. and Taylor, J. (1993) 'Career termination issues among elite athletes'. In R. N. Singer, M. Murphey and L. K. Tennant (eds.), *Handbook of Research on Sport Psychology*, pp. 761–775, Sydney: Macmillan.

Parker, K. B. (1994) '"Has-beens" and "wanna-bes": Transition experiences of former major college football players', *The Sport Psychologist* 8:287–304.

Pearson, R. E. and Petitpas, A. J. (1990) 'Transitions of athletes: Developmental and preventive perspectives', *Journal of Counseling and Development* 69:7–10.

Perna, F. M., Zaichkowsky, L. and Bocknek, G. (1996) 'The association of mentoring with psychosocial development among male athletes at termination of college career', *Journal of Applied Sport Psychology* 8:76–88.

Petitpas, A. J., Brewer, B. W. and Van Raalte, J. L. (1996) 'Transitions of the student-athlete: Theoretical, empirical, and practical perspectives'. In E. F. Etzel, A. P. Ferrante and J. W. Pinkney (eds.), *Counseling College Student-athletes: Issues and Interventions* (2nd ed.), pp. 137–156, Morgantown, WV: Fitness Information Technology.

Petitpas, A. and Champagne, D. (2000) 'Practical considerations in implementing sport career transition programs'. In D. Lavallee and P. Wylleman (eds), *Career Transitions in Sport: International Perspectives*, pp. 81–93, Morgantown, WV: Fitness Information Technology.

Reynolds, M. J. (1981) 'The effects of sports retirement on the job satisfaction of the former football player'. In S. L. Greendorfer and A. Yiannakis (eds.), *Sociology of Sport: Diverse Perspectives*, pp. 127–137, West Point, NY: Leisure Press.

Rosenberg, E. (1981) 'Gerontological theory and athletic retirement'. In S. L. Greendorfer and A. Yiannakis (eds.), *Sociology of Sport: Diverse Perspective*, pp. 119–126, West Point, NY: Leisure Press.

Rosenberg, E. (1984) 'Athletic retirement as social death: Concepts and perspectives'. In N. Theberge and P. Donnelly (eds.), *Sport and the Sociological Imagination*, pp. 245–258, Fort Worth: Texas Christian University Press.

Schlossberg, N. K. (1981) 'A model for analyzing human adaptation to transition', *The Counseling Psychologist* 9:2–18.

Sinclair, D. A. and Orlick, T. (1993) 'Positive transitions from high-performance sport', *The Sport Psychologist* 7:138–150.

Sinclair, D. A. and Orlick, T. (1994) 'The effects of transition on high performance sport'. In D. Hackfort (ed.), *Psycho-social Issues and Interventions in Elite Sports*, pp. 29–55, Frankfurt: Lang.

Svoboda, B. and Vanek, M. (1982) 'Retirement from high level competition'. In T. Orlick, J. T. Partington and J. H. Salmela (eds.), *Proceedings of the Fifth World Congress of Sport Psychology*, pp. 166–175, Ottawa: Coaching Association of Canada.

Swain, D. A. (1991) 'Withdrawal from sport and Schlossberg's model of transitions', *Sociology of Sport Journal* 8:152–160.

Taylor, J. and Ogilvie, B. C. (1994) 'A conceptual model of adaptation to retirement among athletes', *Journal of Applied Sport Psychology* 6:1–20.

Taylor, J. and Ogilvie, B. C. (1998) 'Career transition among elite athletes: is there life after sports?', In J. M. Williams (ed.), *Applied Sport Psychology: Personal Growth to Peak Performance* (3rd edn), pp. 429–444, Mountain View, CA: Mayfield.

Treasure, D. C., Carpenter, P. J. and Power, K. T. D. (2000) 'Relationship between achievement motivation, goal orientations and the perceived purposes of playing rugby union for professional and amateur players', *Journal of Sports Sciences* 18:571–577.

Werthner, P. and Orlick, T. (1986) 'Retirement experiences of successful Olympic athletes', *International Journal of Sport Psychology* 17:337–363.

Wylleman, P., De Knop, P., Menkehorst, H., Theeboom, M. and Annerel, J. (1993) 'Career termination and social integration among elite athletes'. In S. Serpa, J. Alves, V. Ferreira and A. Paula-Brito (eds.), *Proceedings: 8th World Congress of Sport Psychology*, pp. 902–906, Lisbon: International Society of Sport Psychology.

Wylleman, P., Lavallee, D. and Alfermann, D. (eds.) (1999) *Career Transitions in Competitive Sports*, Biel, Switzerland: European Federation of Sport Psychology Monograph Series.